# PRAISE FOR
# DAY MEN

"...a slick new series that suggests there's still room for another vampire comic on the market."

**—IGN**

"Stelfreeze's storytelling is crisp and efficient, but also stylish and dramatic. He makes conscious choices as to which scenes can benefit from an ornate presentation and where he needs to go sparse. His weirdly hypnotic, angular-yet-curvy style consistently informs every detail of every page, which makes the fantastical world of the comic seem real and immersive. He wants you to care as much as he does about this violent, sexy world of vampires and the men and women who work for them in the light of day."

**—COMICS ALLIANCE**

"Brian Stelfreeze is a hell of a comic book artist..."

**—IFANBOY**

"Brian Stelfreeze has a real animated bounciness to his lines, a lush inking style that reminds me a lot of the late, great Mike Weiringo. Stelfreeze has a command and control of his panel layouts that you just don't see much of these days...And you can tell when Stelfreeze just picks a moment to inject some mood—watching a vampire shoot smoke out of his nose is downright intoxicating, and watching a seductive vampire queen just exudes sexiness, even when all we can see are her lips and shoulders."

**—NEWSARAMA**

"*DAY MEN* shows that there's still life in these undead creatures yet..."
**—NERDIST**

### TOP 100 COMICS OF 2013
Comic Book Resources

### 2014 HARVEY AWARD NOMINEE
Best Inker
Brian Stelfreeze, *DAY MEN*

### 2014 HARVEY AWARD NOMINEE
Best Cover Artist
Brian Stelfreeze, *DAY MEN*

**ROSS RICHIE** CEO & Founder
**MATT GAGNON** Editor-in-Chief
**FILIP SABLIK** President of Publishing & Marketing
**STEPHEN CHRISTY** President of Development
**LANCE KREITER** VP of Licensing & Merchandising
**PHIL BARBARO** VP of Finance
**BRYCE CARLSON** Managing Editor
**MEL CAYLO** Marketing Manager
**SCOTT NEWMAN** Production Design Manager
**IRENE BRADISH** Operations Manager
**CHRISTINE DINH** Brand Communications Manager
**SIERRA HAHN** Senior Editor
**DAFNA PLEBAN** Editor
**SHANNON WATTERS** Editor
**ERIC HARBURN** Editor
**WHITNEY LEOPARD** Associate Editor
**JASMINE AMIRI** Associate Editor
**CHRIS ROSA** Associate Editor
**ALEX GALER** Assistant Editor
**CAMERON CHITTOCK** Assistant Editor
**MARY GUMPORT** Assistant Editor
**KELSEY DIETERICH** Production Designer
**JILLIAN CRAB** Production Designer
**KARA LEOPARD** Production Designer
**MICHELLE ANKLEY** Production Design Assistant
**AARON FERRARA** Operations Coordinator
**ELIZABETH LOUGHRIDGE** Accounting Coordinator
**JOSÉ MEZA** Sales Assistant
**JAMES ARRIOLA** Mailroom Assistant
**STEPHANIE HOCUTT** Marketing Assistant
**SAM KUSEK** Direct Market Representative
**HILLARY LEVI** Executive Assistant

**DAY MEN Volume Two, May 2016.** Published by BOOM! Studios, a division of Boom Entertainment, Inc. Day Men is ™ & © 2016 Matt Gagnon. Originally published in single magazine form as DAY MEN No. 5-8. ™ & © 2014, 2015 Matt Gagnon. All rights reserved. BOOM! Studios™ and the BOOM! Studios logo are trademarks of Boom Entertainment, Inc., registered in various countries and categories. All characters, events, and institutions depicted herein are fictional. Any similarity between any of the names, characters, persons, events, and/or institutions in this publication to actual names, characters, and persons, whether living or dead, events, and/or institutions is unintended and purely coincidental. BOOM! Studios does not read or accept unsolicited submissions of ideas, stories, or artwork.

A catalog record of this book is available from OCLC and from the BOOM! Studios website, www.boom-studios.com, on the Librarians Page.

BOOM! Studios, 5670 Wilshire Boulevard, Suite 450, Los Angeles, CA 90036-5679. Printed in China. First Printing.

ISBN: 978-1-60886-852-0, eISBN: 978-1-61398-523-6

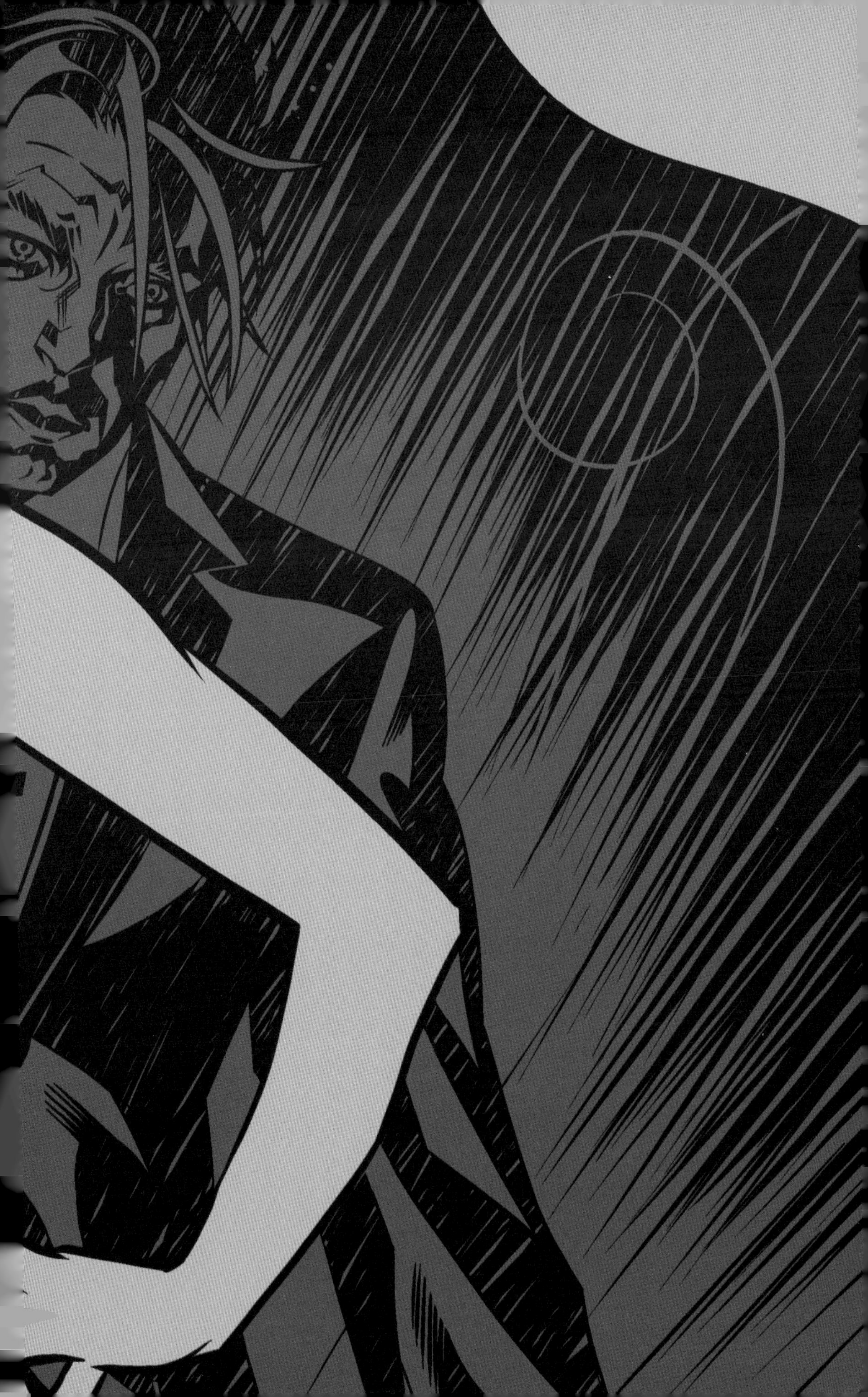

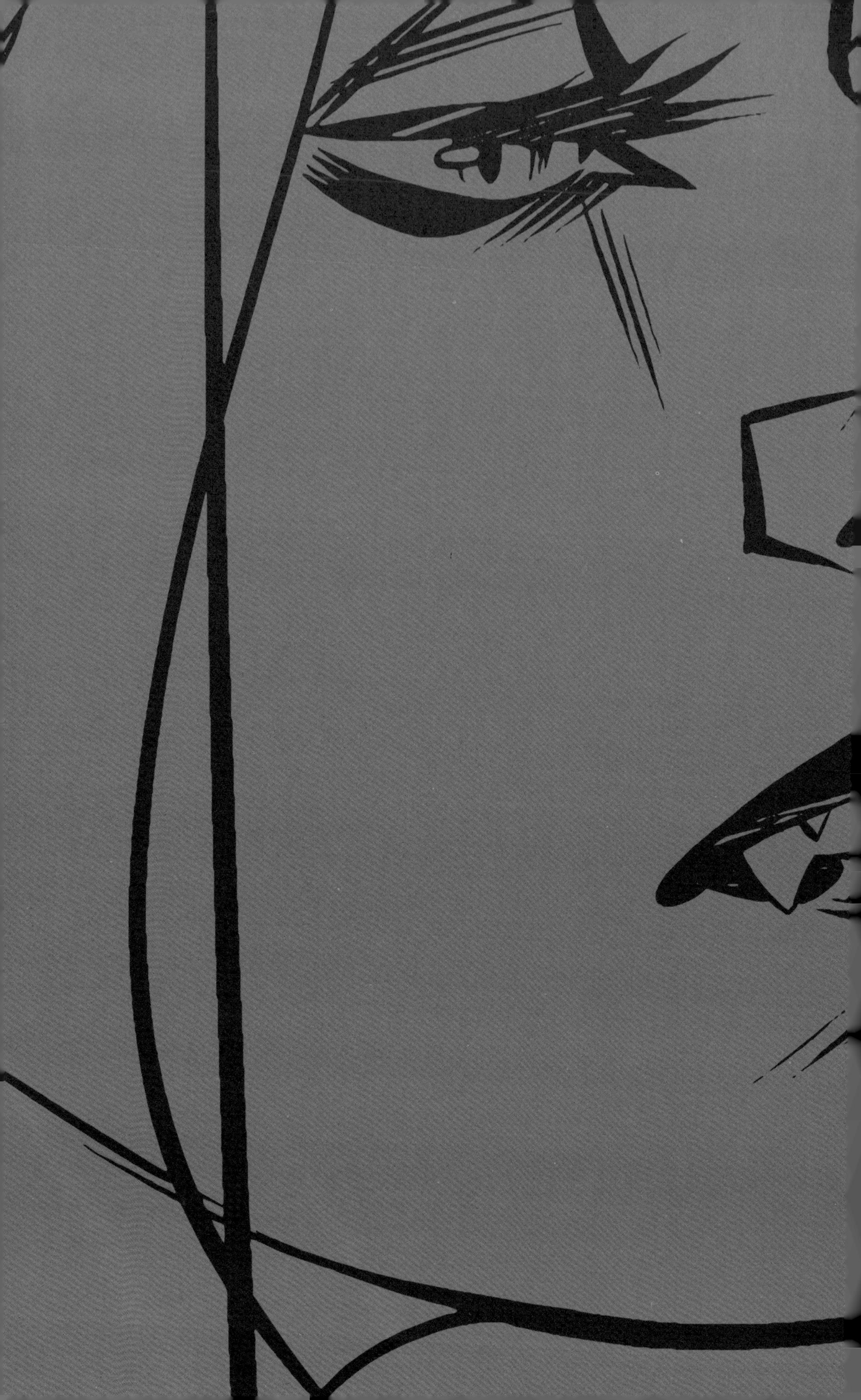

WRITTEN BY
**MATT GAGNON**
**& MICHAEL ALAN NELSON**

ILLUSTRATED BY
**BRIAN STELFREEZE**

COLORS BY
**DARRIN MOORE**

LETTERS BY
**ED DUKESHIRE**

COVER BY
**BRIAN STELFREEZE**

DESIGNER
**SCOTT NEWMAN**

EDITOR
**ERIC HARBURN**

**DAY**MEN™ CREATED BY **MATT GAGNON**

# CHAPTER FIVE

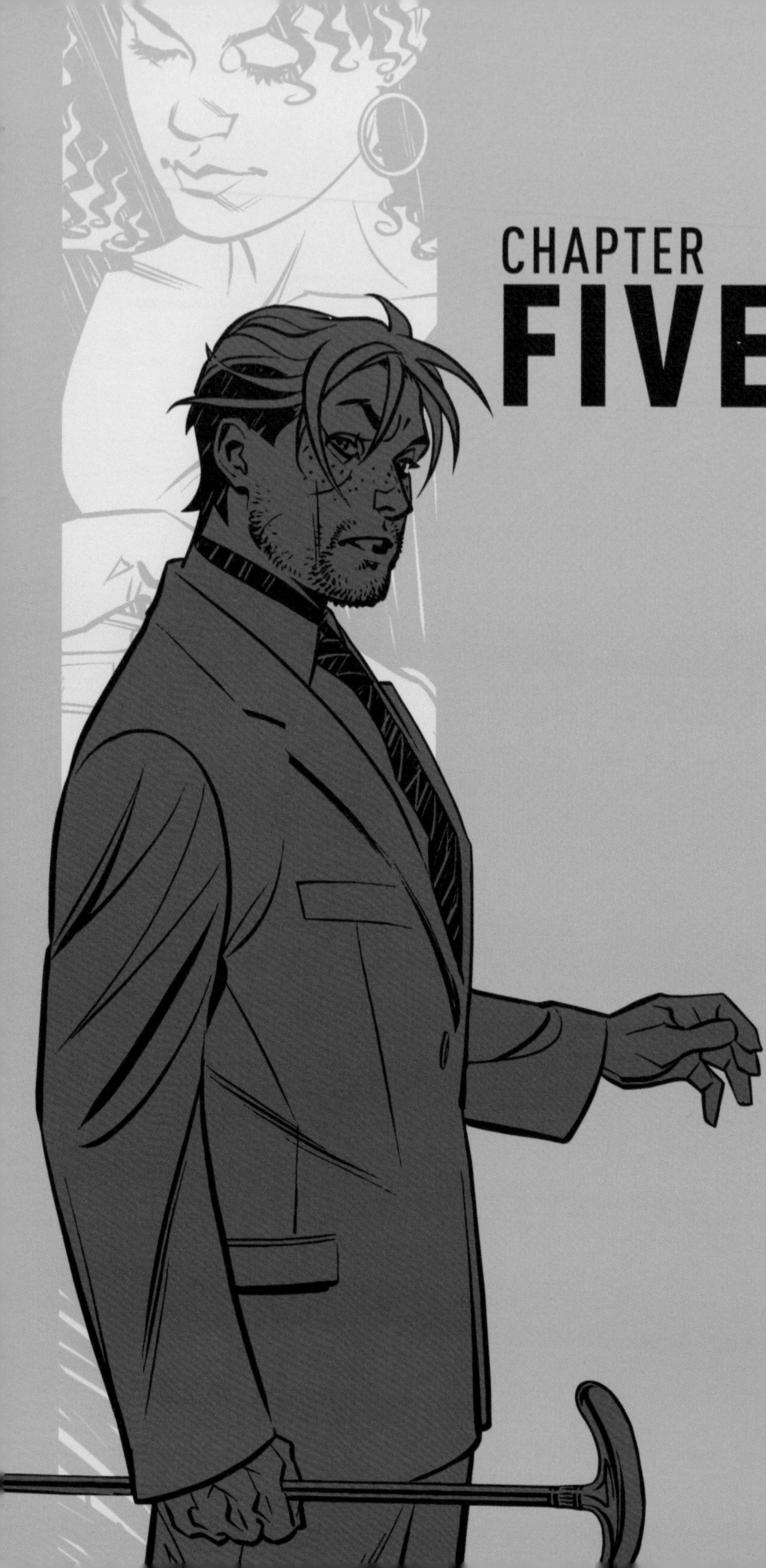

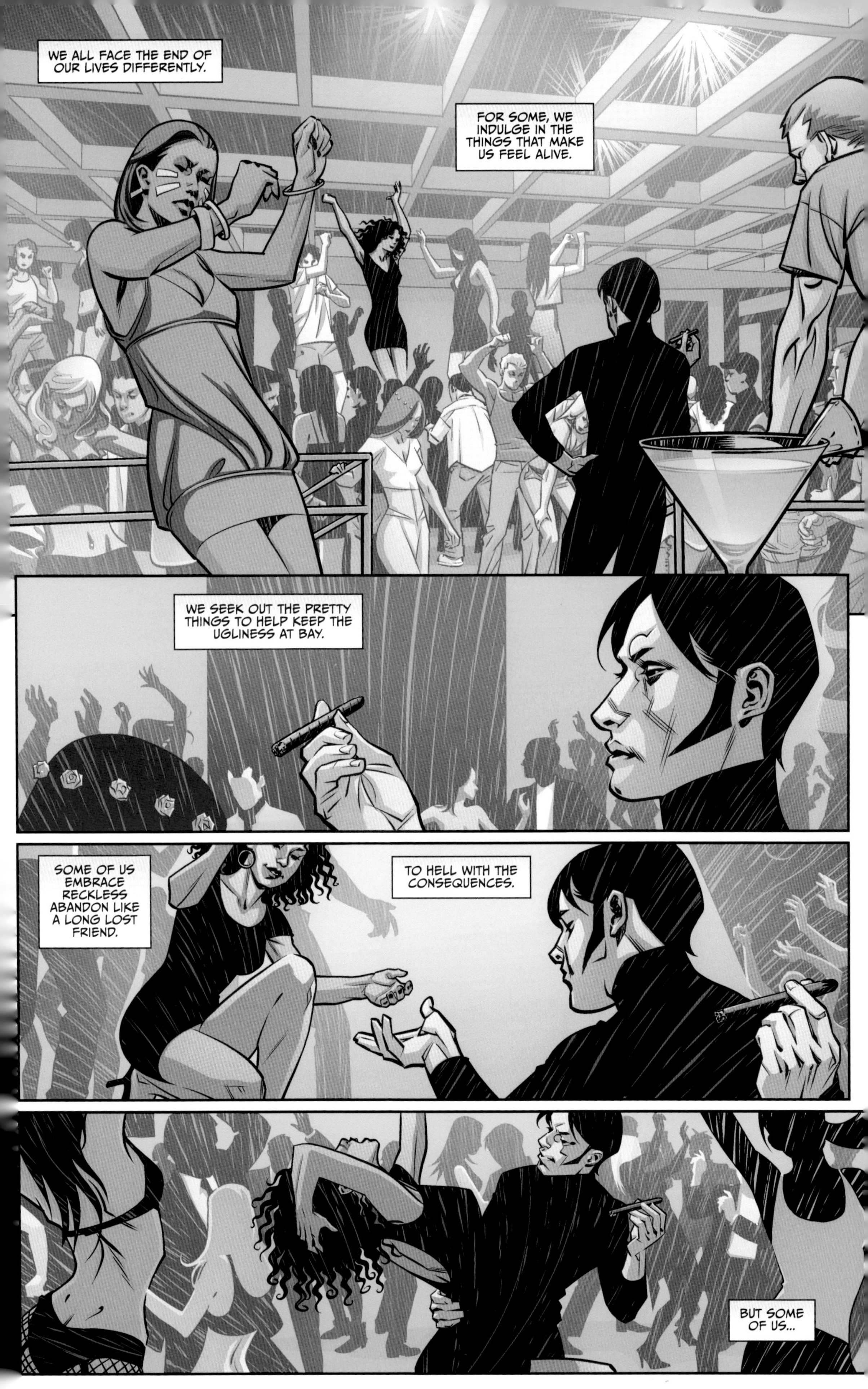
WE ALL FACE THE END OF OUR LIVES DIFFERENTLY.
FOR SOME, WE INDULGE IN THE THINGS THAT MAKE US FEEL ALIVE.
WE SEEK OUT THE PRETTY THINGS TO HELP KEEP THE UGLINESS AT BAY.
SOME OF US EMBRACE RECKLESS ABANDON LIKE A LONG LOST FRIEND.
TO HELL WITH THE CONSEQUENCES.
BUT SOME OF US...

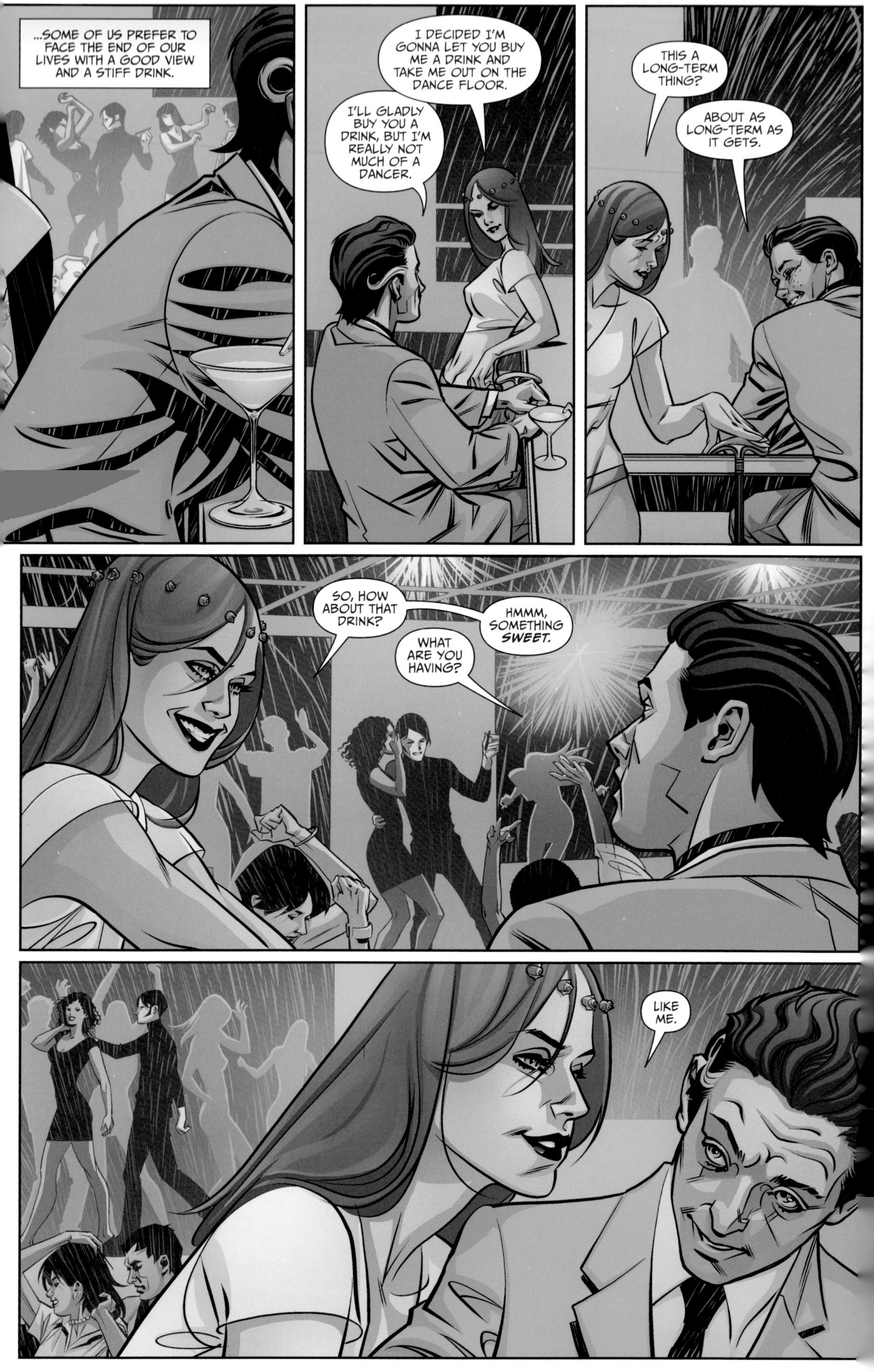
...SOME OF US PREFER TO FACE THE END OF OUR LIVES WITH A GOOD VIEW AND A STIFF DRINK.
I DECIDED I'M GONNA LET YOU BUY ME A DRINK AND TAKE ME OUT ON THE DANCE FLOOR.
I'LL GLADLY BUY YOU A DRINK, BUT I'M REALLY NOT MUCH OF A DANCER.
THIS A LONG-TERM THING?
ABOUT AS LONG-TERM AS IT GETS.
SO, HOW ABOUT THAT DRINK?
WHAT ARE YOU HAVING?
HMMM, SOMETHING SWEET.
LIKE ME.

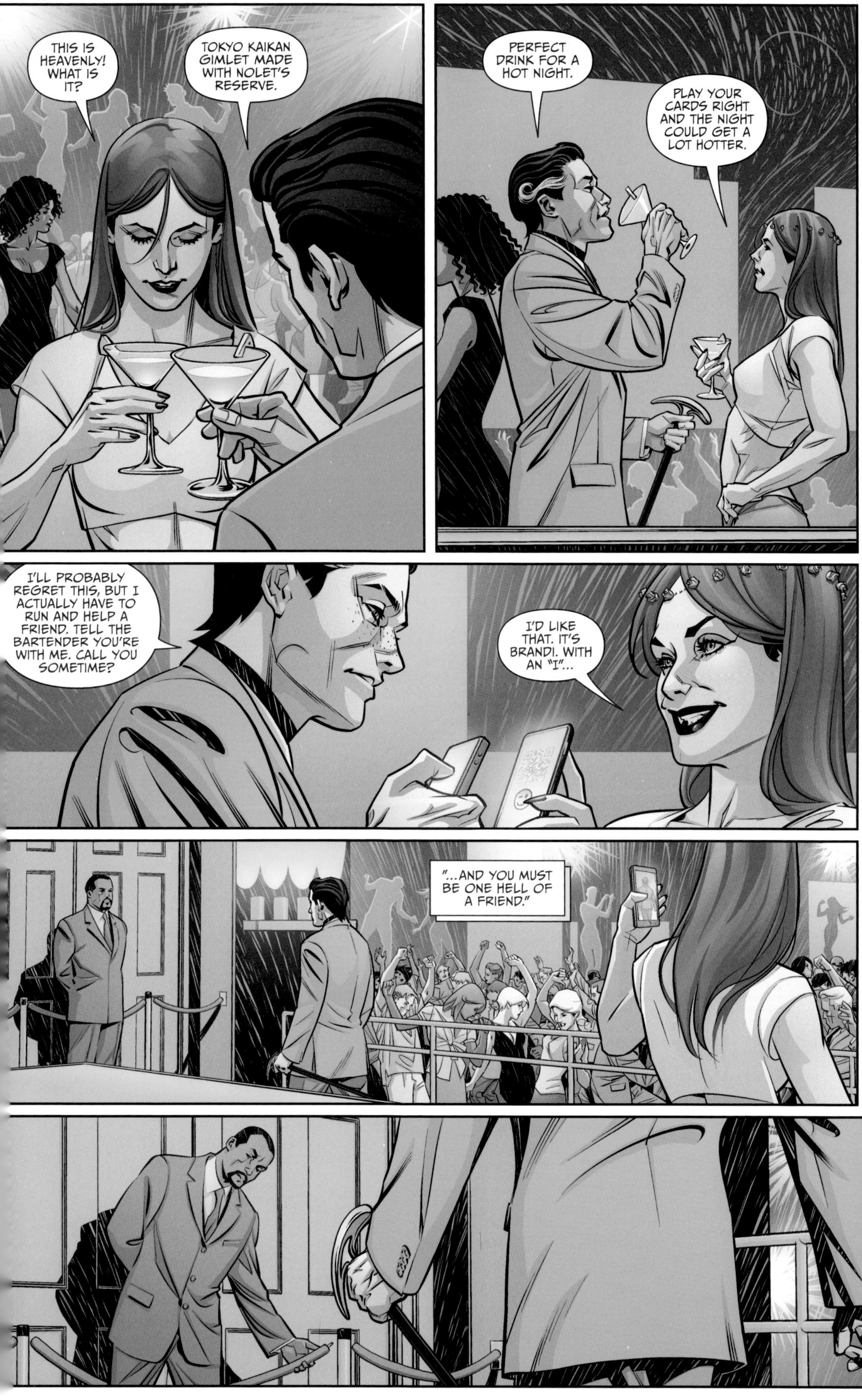
THIS IS HEAVENLY! WHAT IS IT?
TOKYO KAIKAN GIMLET MADE WITH NOLET'S RESERVE.
PERFECT DRINK FOR A HOT NIGHT.
PLAY YOUR CARDS RIGHT AND THE NIGHT COULD GET A LOT HOTTER.
I'LL PROBABLY REGRET THIS, BUT I ACTUALLY HAVE TO RUN AND HELP A FRIEND. TELL THE BARTENDER YOU'RE WITH ME. CALL YOU SOMETIME?
I'D LIKE THAT. IT'S BRANDI. WITH AN "I"...
"...AND YOU MUST BE ONE HELL OF A FRIEND."

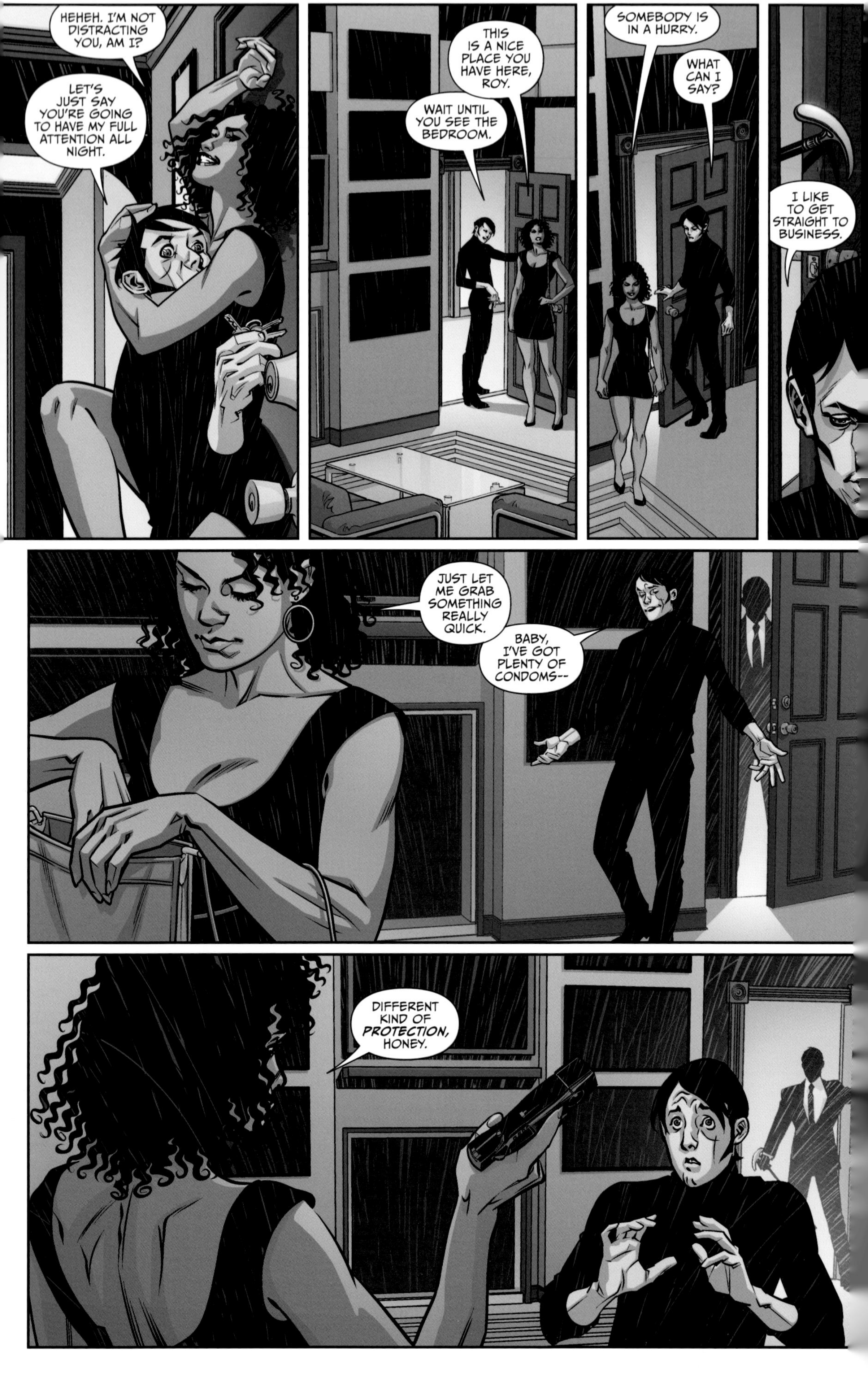
HEHEH. I'M NOT DISTRACTING YOU, AM I?
LET'S JUST SAY YOU'RE GOING TO HAVE MY FULL ATTENTION ALL NIGHT.
THIS IS A NICE PLACE YOU HAVE HERE, ROY.
WAIT UNTIL YOU SEE THE BEDROOM.
SOMEBODY IS IN A HURRY.
WHAT CAN I SAY?
I LIKE TO GET STRAIGHT TO BUSINESS.
JUST LET ME GRAB SOMETHING REALLY QUICK.
BABY, I'VE GOT PLENTY OF CONDOMS--
DIFFERENT KIND OF *PROTECTION*, HONEY.

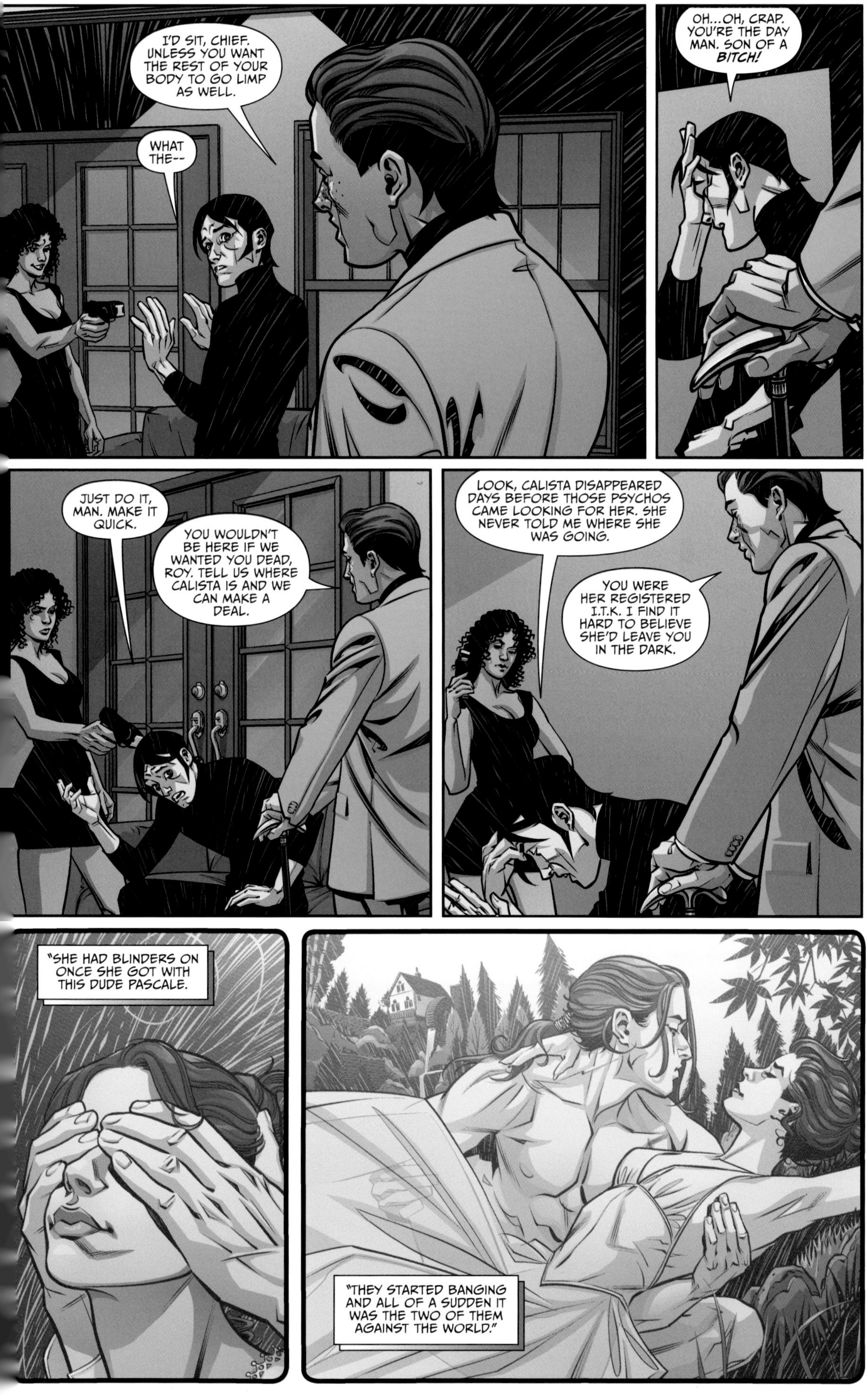
I'D SIT, CHIEF. UNLESS YOU WANT THE REST OF YOUR BODY TO GO LIMP AS WELL.
WHAT THE--
OH...OH, CRAP. YOU'RE THE DAY MAN. SON OF A *BITCH!*
JUST DO IT, MAN. MAKE IT QUICK.
YOU WOULDN'T BE HERE IF WE WANTED YOU DEAD, ROY. TELL US WHERE CALISTA IS AND WE CAN MAKE A DEAL.
LOOK, CALISTA DISAPPEARED DAYS BEFORE THOSE PSYCHOS CAME LOOKING FOR HER. SHE NEVER TOLD ME WHERE SHE WAS GOING.
YOU WERE HER REGISTERED I.T.K. I FIND IT HARD TO BELIEVE SHE'D LEAVE YOU IN THE DARK.
"SHE HAD BLINDERS ON ONCE SHE GOT WITH THIS DUDE PASCALE.
"THEY STARTED BANGING AND ALL OF A SUDDEN IT WAS THE TWO OF THEM AGAINST THE WORLD."

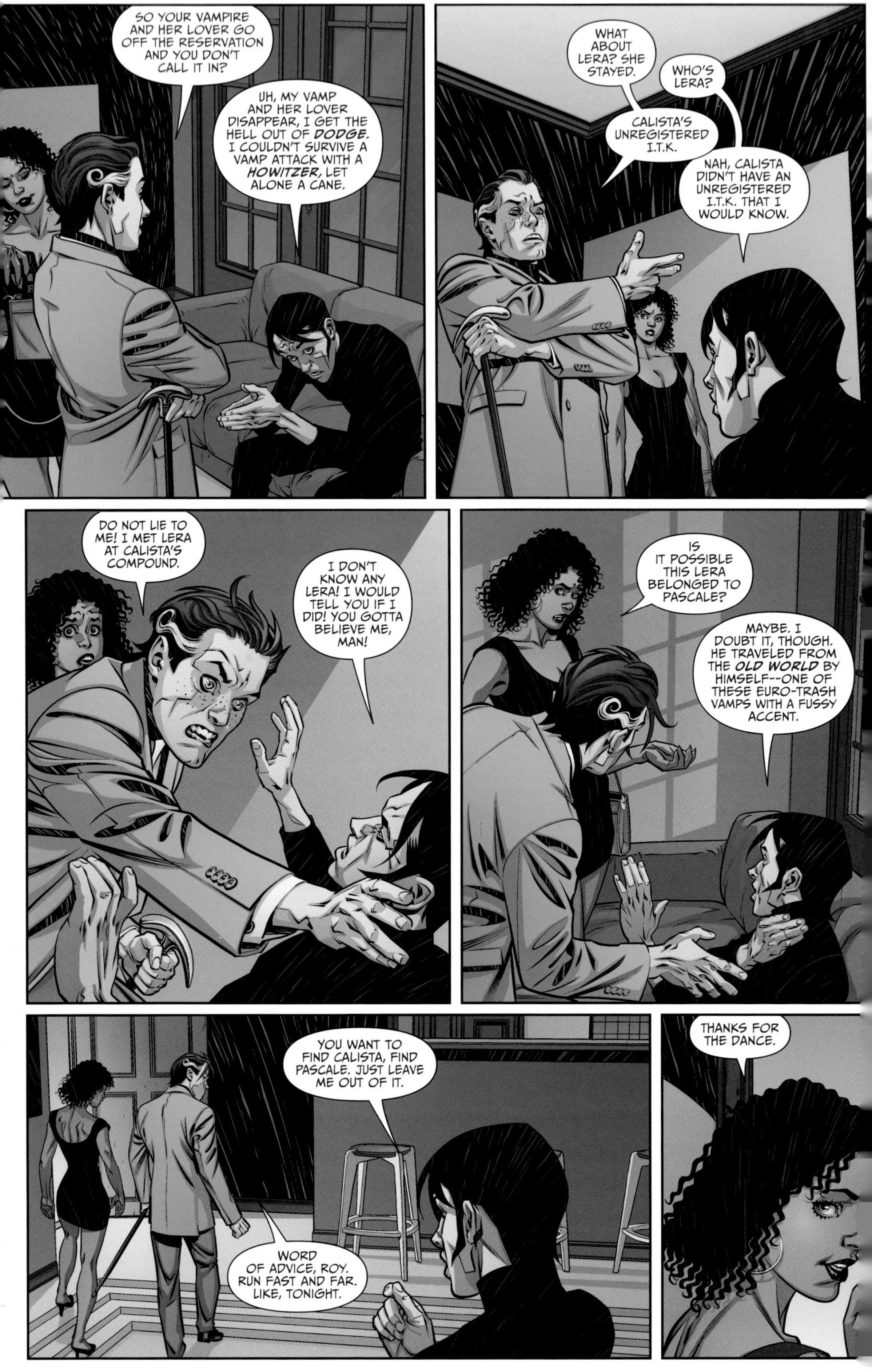
SO YOUR VAMPIRE AND HER LOVER GO OFF THE RESERVATION AND YOU DON'T CALL IT IN?
UH, MY VAMP AND HER LOVER DISAPPEAR, I GET THE HELL OUT OF DODGE. I COULDN'T SURVIVE A VAMP ATTACK WITH A HOWITZER, LET ALONE A CANE.
WHAT ABOUT LERA? SHE STAYED.
WHO'S LERA?
CALISTA'S UNREGISTERED I.T.K.
NAH, CALISTA DIDN'T HAVE AN UNREGISTERED I.T.K. THAT I WOULD KNOW.
DO NOT LIE TO ME! I MET LERA AT CALISTA'S COMPOUND.
I DON'T KNOW ANY LERA! I WOULD TELL YOU IF I DID! YOU GOTTA BELIEVE ME, MAN!
IS IT POSSIBLE THIS LERA BELONGED TO PASCALE?
MAYBE. I DOUBT IT, THOUGH. HE TRAVELED FROM THE OLD WORLD BY HIMSELF--ONE OF THESE EURO-TRASH VAMPS WITH A FUSSY ACCENT.
YOU WANT TO FIND CALISTA, FIND PASCALE. JUST LEAVE ME OUT OF IT.
WORD OF ADVICE, ROY. RUN FAST AND FAR. LIKE, TONIGHT.
THANKS FOR THE DANCE.

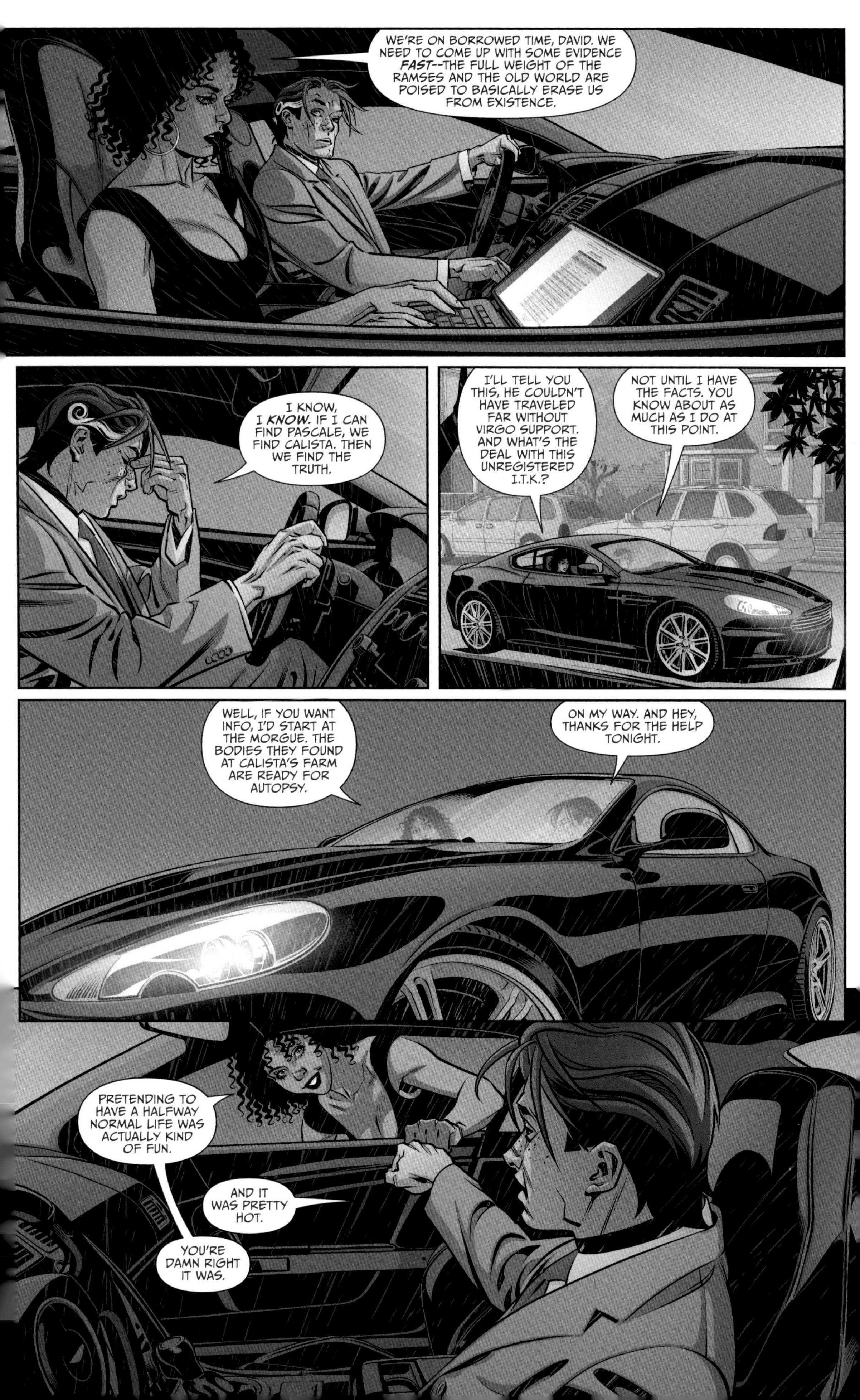
WE'RE ON BORROWED TIME, DAVID. WE NEED TO COME UP WITH SOME EVIDENCE FAST--THE FULL WEIGHT OF THE RAMSES AND THE OLD WORLD ARE POISED TO BASICALLY ERASE US FROM EXISTENCE.
I KNOW, I KNOW. IF I CAN FIND PASCALE, WE FIND CALISTA. THEN WE FIND THE TRUTH.
I'LL TELL YOU THIS, HE COULDN'T HAVE TRAVELED FAR WITHOUT VIRGO SUPPORT. AND WHAT'S THE DEAL WITH THIS UNREGISTERED I.T.K.?
NOT UNTIL I HAVE THE FACTS. YOU KNOW ABOUT AS MUCH AS I DO AT THIS POINT.
WELL, IF YOU WANT INFO, I'D START AT THE MORGUE. THE BODIES THEY FOUND AT CALISTA'S FARM ARE READY FOR AUTOPSY.
ON MY WAY. AND HEY, THANKS FOR THE HELP TONIGHT.
PRETENDING TO HAVE A HALFWAY NORMAL LIFE WAS ACTUALLY KIND OF FUN.
AND IT WAS PRETTY HOT.
YOU'RE DAMN RIGHT IT WAS.

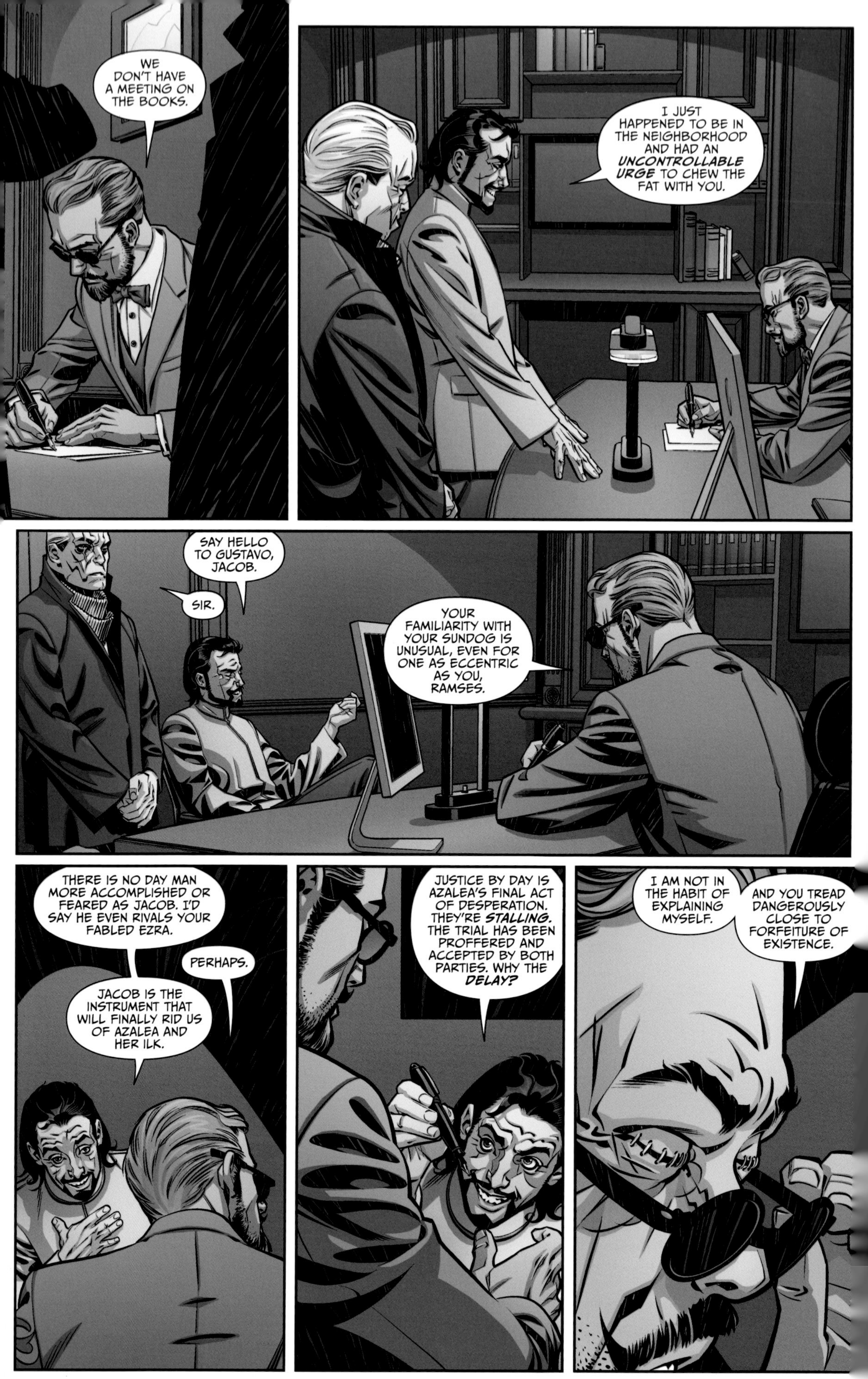
WE DON'T HAVE A MEETING ON THE BOOKS.
I JUST HAPPENED TO BE IN THE NEIGHBORHOOD AND HAD AN UNCONTROLLABLE URGE TO CHEW THE FAT WITH YOU.
SAY HELLO TO GUSTAVO, JACOB.
SIR.
YOUR FAMILIARITY WITH YOUR SUNDOG IS UNUSUAL, EVEN FOR ONE AS ECCENTRIC AS YOU, RAMSES.
THERE IS NO DAY MAN MORE ACCOMPLISHED OR FEARED AS JACOB. I'D SAY HE EVEN RIVALS YOUR FABLED EZRA.
PERHAPS.
JACOB IS THE INSTRUMENT THAT WILL FINALLY RID US OF AZALEA AND HER ILK.
JUSTICE BY DAY IS AZALEA'S FINAL ACT OF DESPERATION. THEY'RE STALLING. THE TRIAL HAS BEEN PROFFERED AND ACCEPTED BY BOTH PARTIES. WHY THE DELAY?
I AM NOT IN THE HABIT OF EXPLAINING MYSELF.
AND YOU TREAD DANGEROUSLY CLOSE TO FORFEITURE OF EXISTENCE.

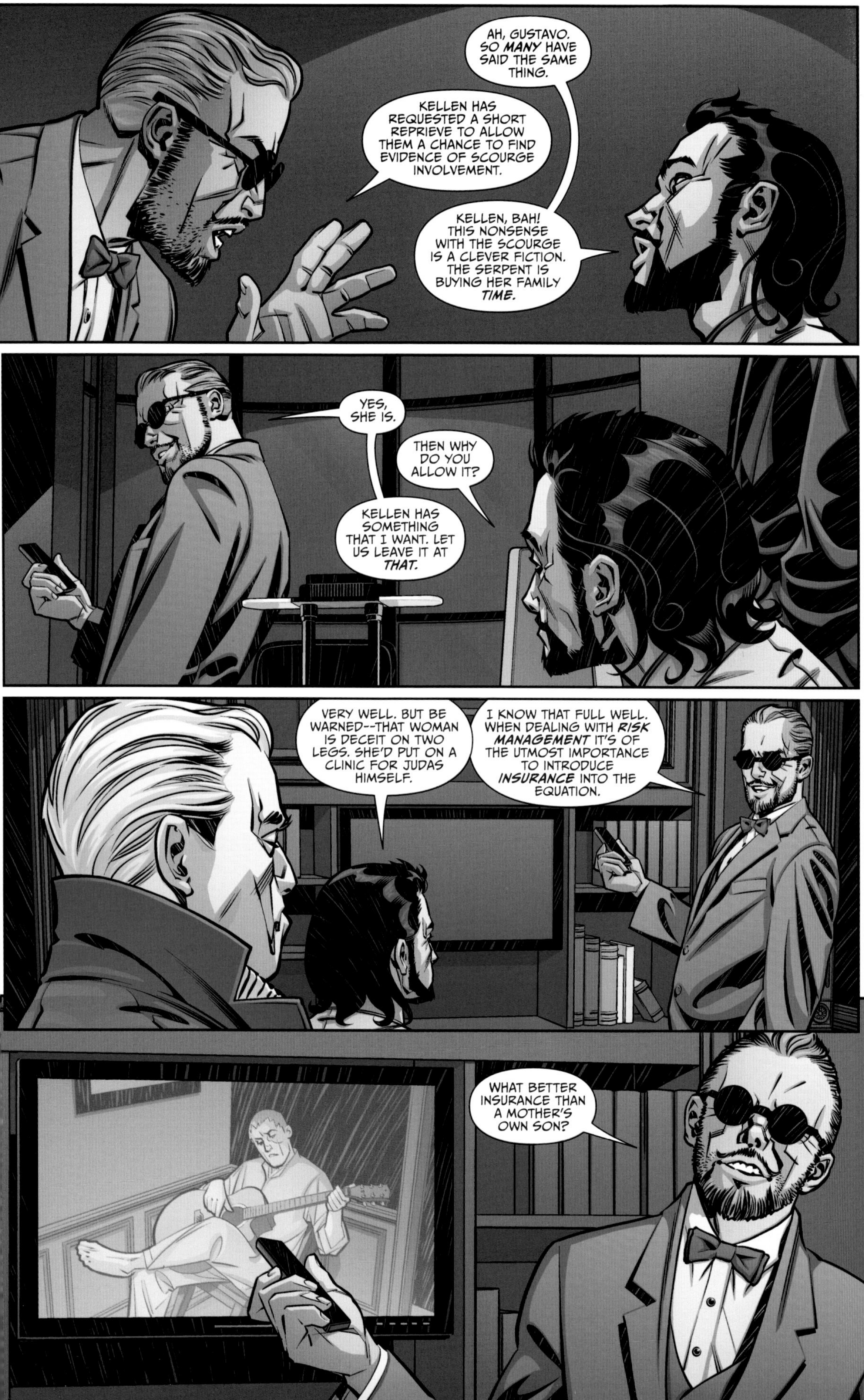

AH, GUSTAVO. SO *MANY* HAVE SAID THE SAME THING.
KELLEN HAS REQUESTED A SHORT REPRIEVE TO ALLOW THEM A CHANCE TO FIND EVIDENCE OF SCOURGE INVOLVEMENT.
KELLEN, BAH! THIS NONSENSE WITH THE SCOURGE IS A CLEVER FICTION. THE SERPENT IS BUYING HER FAMILY *TIME.*
YES, SHE IS.
THEN WHY DO YOU ALLOW IT?
KELLEN HAS SOMETHING THAT I WANT. LET US LEAVE IT AT *THAT.*
VERY WELL. BUT BE WARNED--THAT WOMAN IS DECEIT ON TWO LEGS. SHE'D PUT ON A CLINIC FOR JUDAS HIMSELF.
I KNOW THAT FULL WELL. WHEN DEALING WITH *RISK MANAGEMENT* IT'S OF THE UTMOST IMPORTANCE TO INTRODUCE *INSURANCE* INTO THE EQUATION.
WHAT BETTER INSURANCE THAN A MOTHER'S OWN SON?

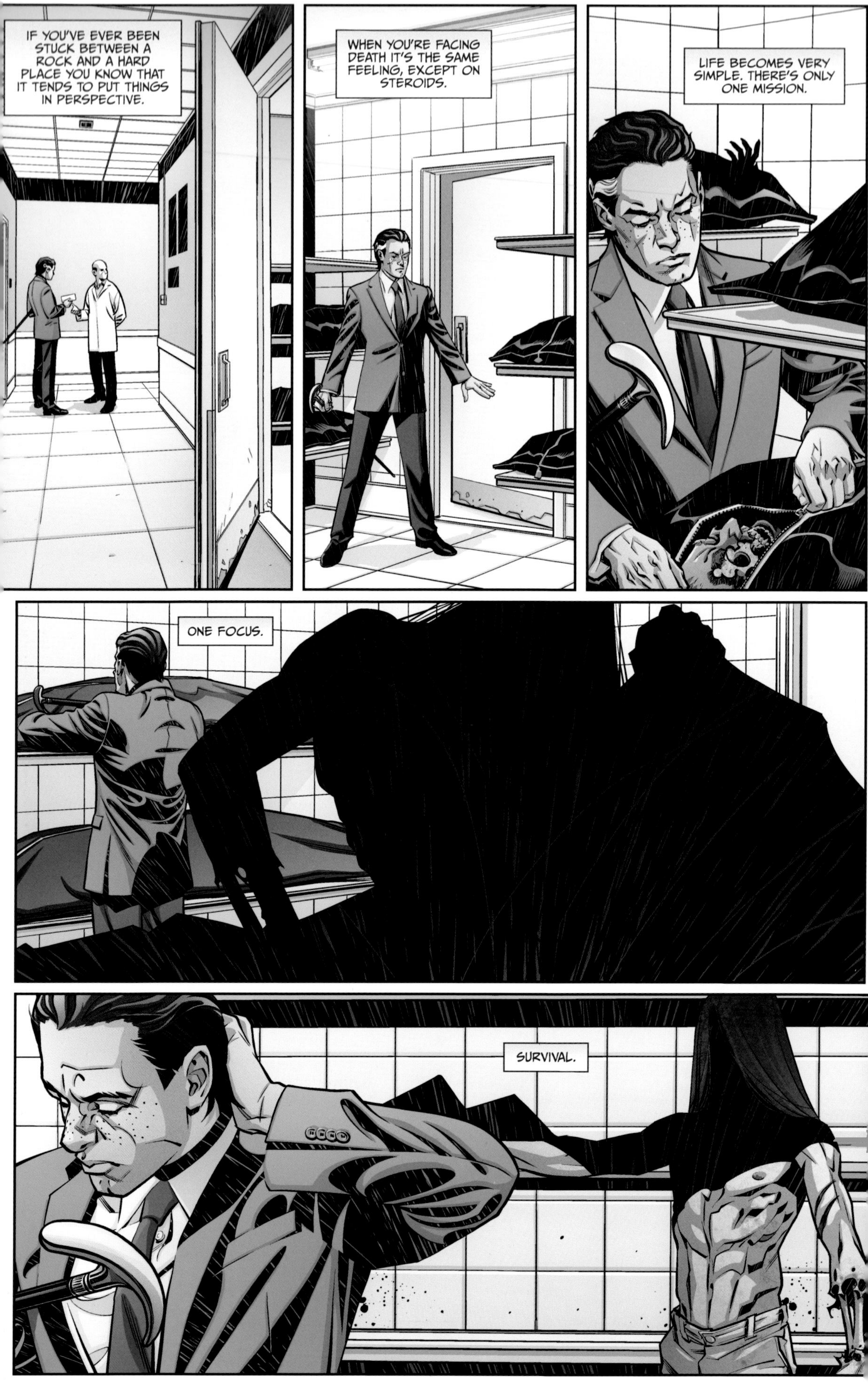
IF YOU'VE EVER BEEN STUCK BETWEEN A ROCK AND A HARD PLACE YOU KNOW THAT IT TENDS TO PUT THINGS IN PERSPECTIVE.
WHEN YOU'RE FACING DEATH IT'S THE SAME FEELING, EXCEPT ON STEROIDS.
LIFE BECOMES VERY SIMPLE. THERE'S ONLY ONE MISSION.
ONE FOCUS.
SURVIVAL.

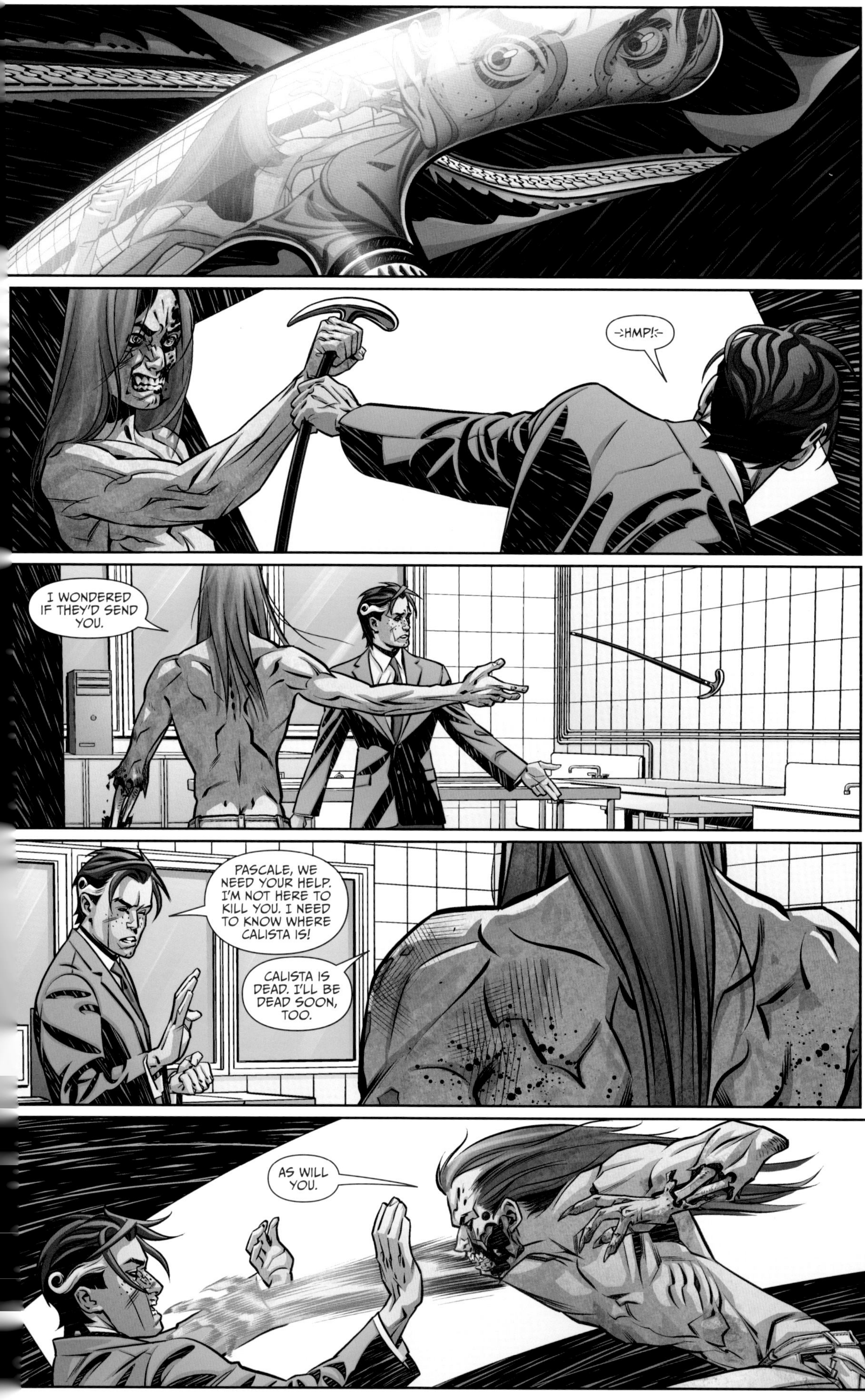

HMP!
I WONDERED IF THEY'D SEND YOU.
PASCALE, WE NEED YOUR HELP. I'M NOT HERE TO KILL YOU. I NEED TO KNOW WHERE CALISTA IS!
CALISTA IS DEAD. I'LL BE DEAD SOON, TOO.
AS WILL YOU.

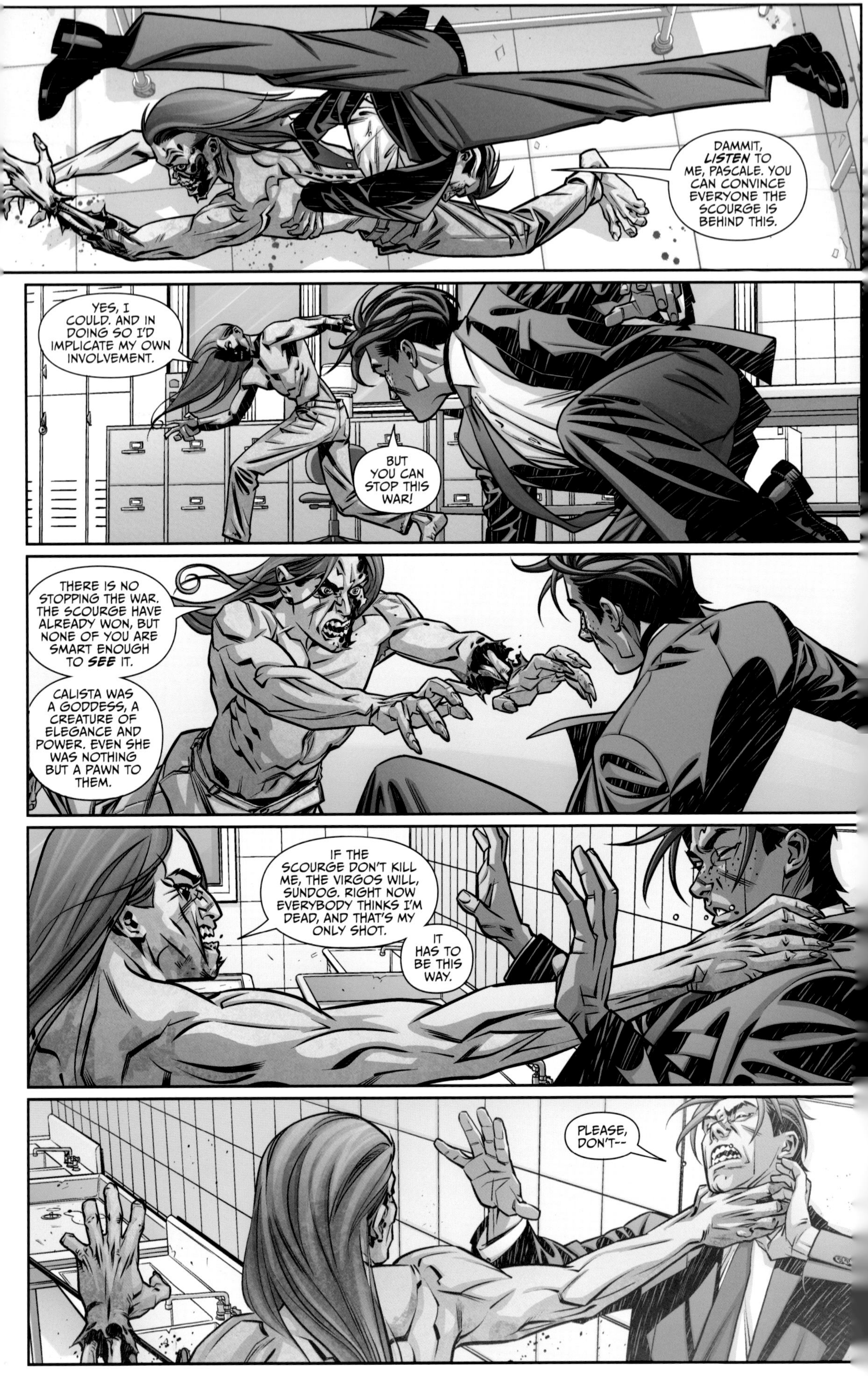
DAMMIT, LISTEN TO ME, PASCALE. YOU CAN CONVINCE EVERYONE THE SCOURGE IS BEHIND THIS.
YES, I COULD. AND IN DOING SO I'D IMPLICATE MY OWN INVOLVEMENT.
BUT YOU CAN STOP THIS WAR!
THERE IS NO STOPPING THE WAR. THE SCOURGE HAVE ALREADY WON, BUT NONE OF YOU ARE SMART ENOUGH TO SEE IT.
CALISTA WAS A GODDESS, A CREATURE OF ELEGANCE AND POWER. EVEN SHE WAS NOTHING BUT A PAWN TO THEM.
IF THE SCOURGE DON'T KILL ME, THE VIRGOS WILL, SUNDOG. RIGHT NOW EVERYBODY THINKS I'M DEAD, AND THAT'S MY ONLY SHOT.
IT HAS TO BE THIS WAY.
PLEASE, DON'T--

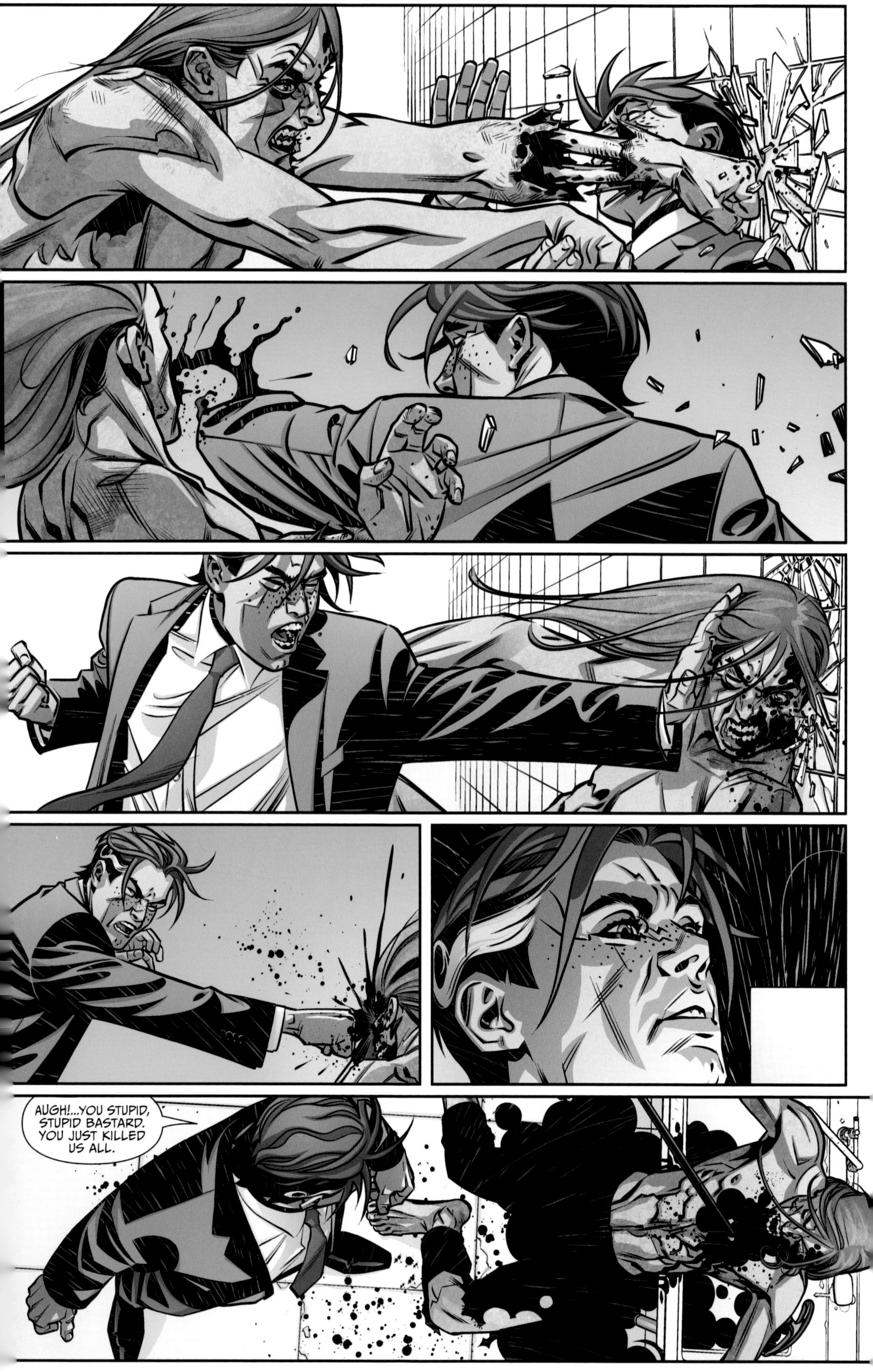
AUGH!...YOU STUPID, STUPID BASTARD. YOU JUST KILLED US ALL.

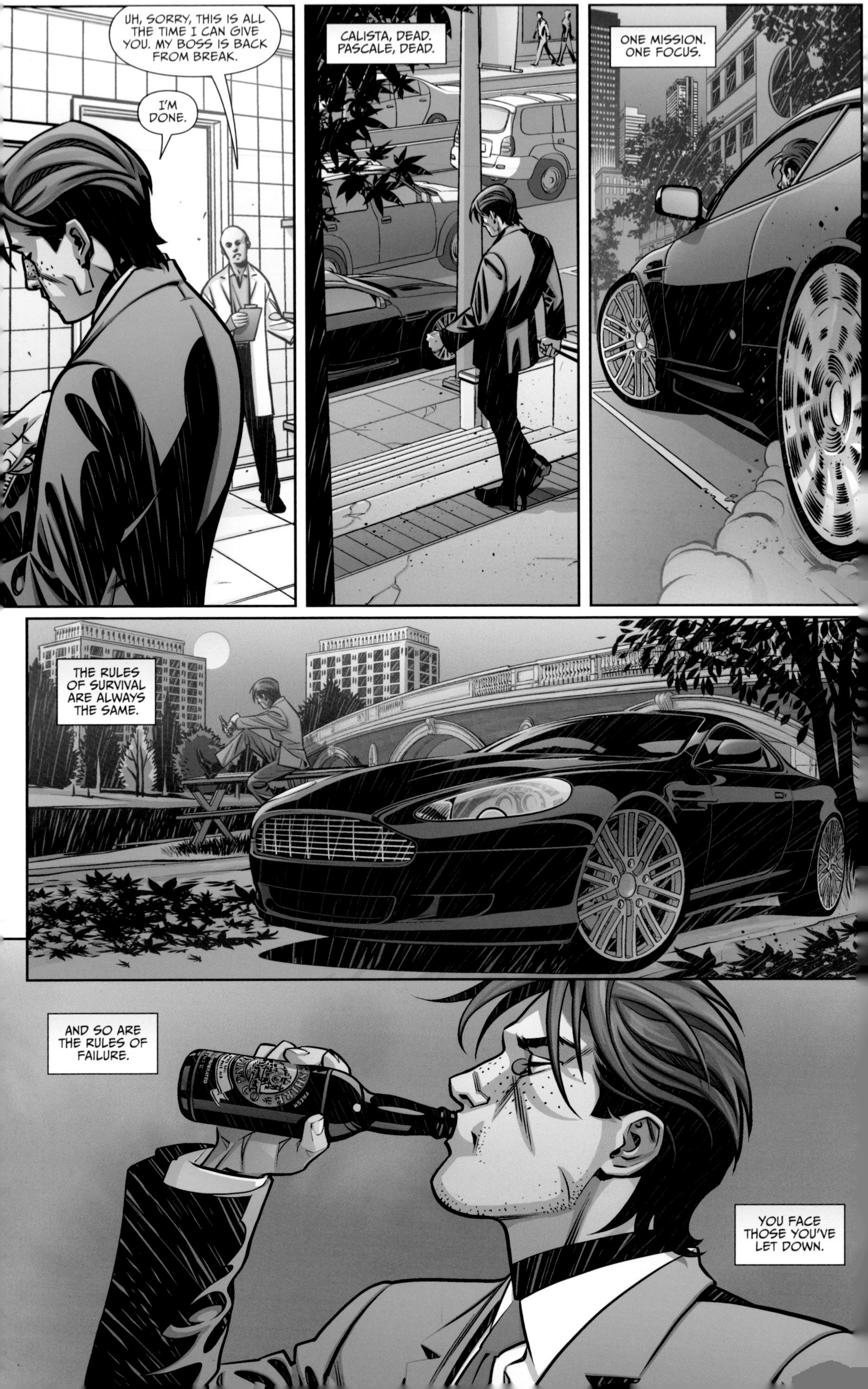
UH, SORRY, THIS IS ALL THE TIME I CAN GIVE YOU. MY BOSS IS BACK FROM BREAK.
I'M DONE.
CALISTA, DEAD. PASCALE, DEAD.
ONE MISSION. ONE FOCUS.
THE RULES OF SURVIVAL ARE ALWAYS THE SAME.
AND SO ARE THE RULES OF FAILURE.
YOU FACE THOSE YOU'VE LET DOWN.

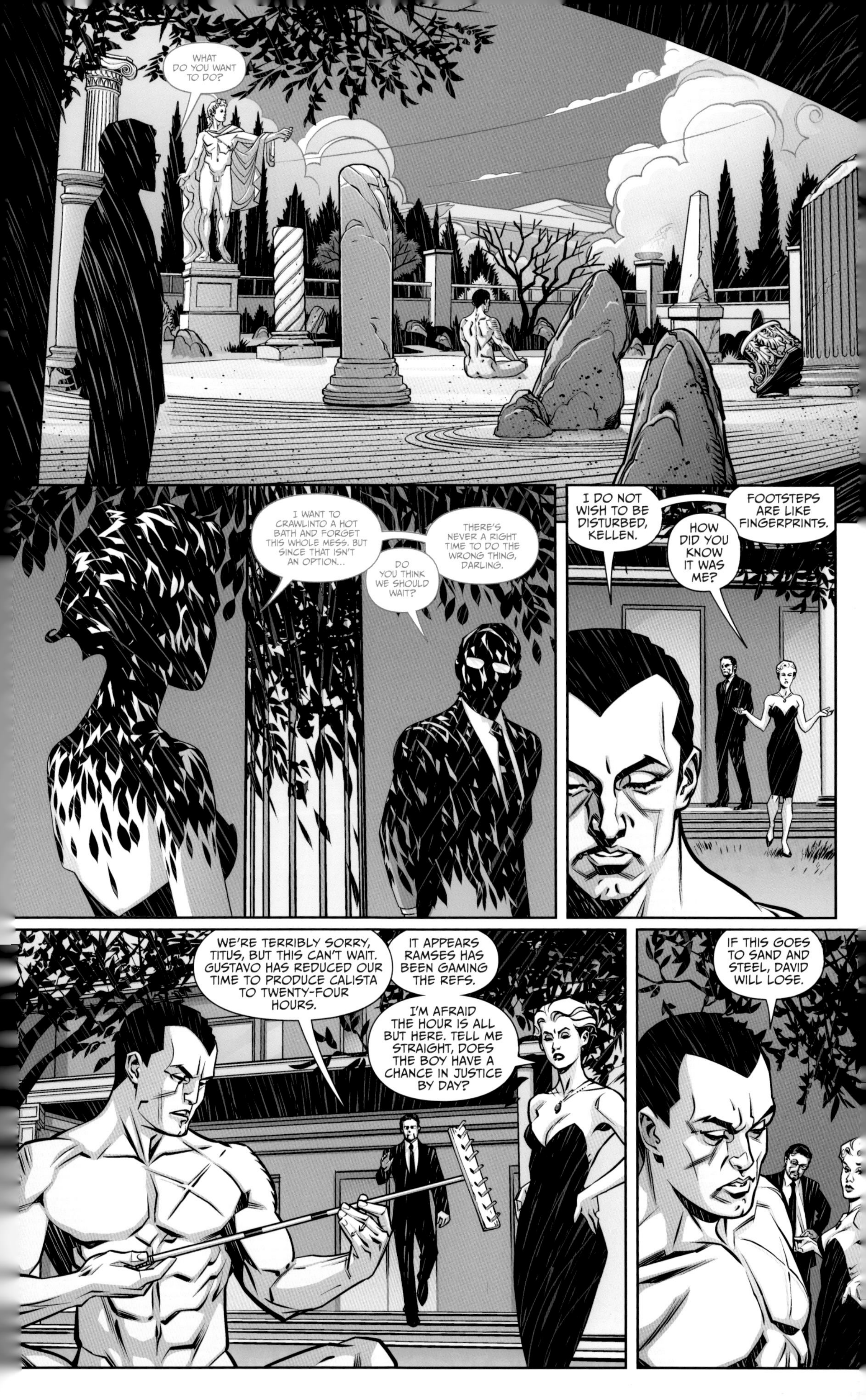
WHAT DO YOU WANT TO DO?
I WANT TO CRAWLINTO A HOT BATH AND FORGET THIS WHOLE MESS. BUT SINCE THAT ISN'T AN OPTION...
DO YOU THINK WE SHOULD WAIT?
THERE'S NEVER A RIGHT TIME TO DO THE WRONG THING, DARLING.
I DO NOT WISH TO BE DISTURBED, KELLEN.
HOW DID YOU KNOW IT WAS ME?
FOOTSTEPS ARE LIKE FINGERPRINTS.
WE'RE TERRIBLY SORRY, TITUS, BUT THIS CAN'T WAIT. GUSTAVO HAS REDUCED OUR TIME TO PRODUCE CALISTA TO TWENTY-FOUR HOURS.
IT APPEARS RAMSES HAS BEEN GAMING THE REFS.
I'M AFRAID THE HOUR IS ALL BUT HERE. TELL ME STRAIGHT, DOES THE BOY HAVE A CHANCE IN JUSTICE BY DAY?
IF THIS GOES TO SAND AND STEEL, DAVID WILL LOSE.

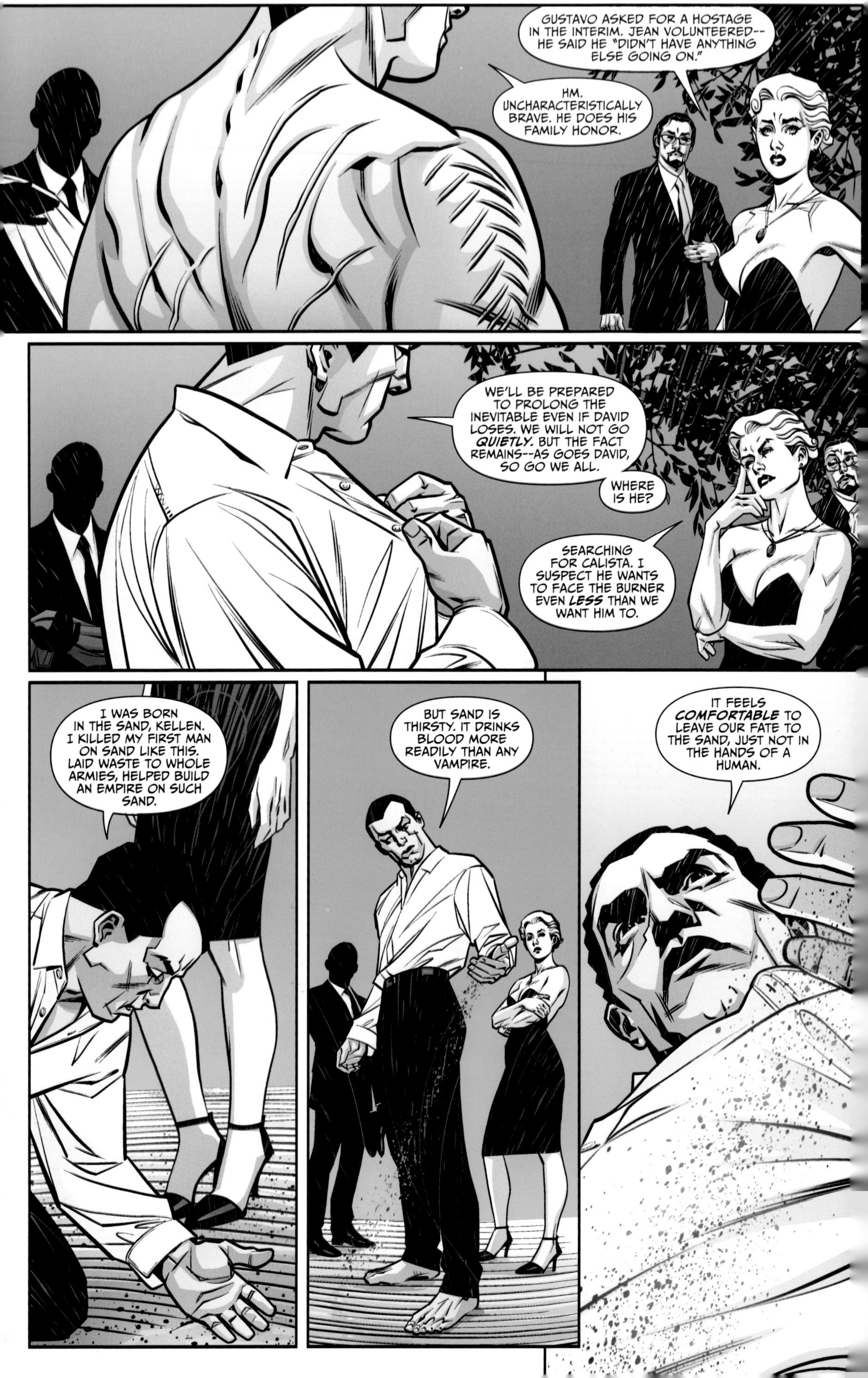
GUSTAVO ASKED FOR A HOSTAGE IN THE INTERIM. JEAN VOLUNTEERED-- HE SAID HE "DIDN'T HAVE ANYTHING ELSE GOING ON."
HM. UNCHARACTERISTICALLY BRAVE. HE DOES HIS FAMILY HONOR.
WE'LL BE PREPARED TO PROLONG THE INEVITABLE EVEN IF DAVID LOSES. WE WILL NOT GO QUIETLY. BUT THE FACT REMAINS--AS GOES DAVID, SO GO WE ALL.
WHERE IS HE?
SEARCHING FOR CALISTA. I SUSPECT HE WANTS TO FACE THE BURNER EVEN LESS THAN WE WANT HIM TO.
I WAS BORN IN THE SAND, KELLEN. I KILLED MY FIRST MAN ON SAND LIKE THIS. LAID WASTE TO WHOLE ARMIES, HELPED BUILD AN EMPIRE ON SUCH SAND.
BUT SAND IS THIRSTY. IT DRINKS BLOOD MORE READILY THAN ANY VAMPIRE.
IT FEELS COMFORTABLE TO LEAVE OUR FATE TO THE SAND, JUST NOT IN THE HANDS OF A HUMAN.

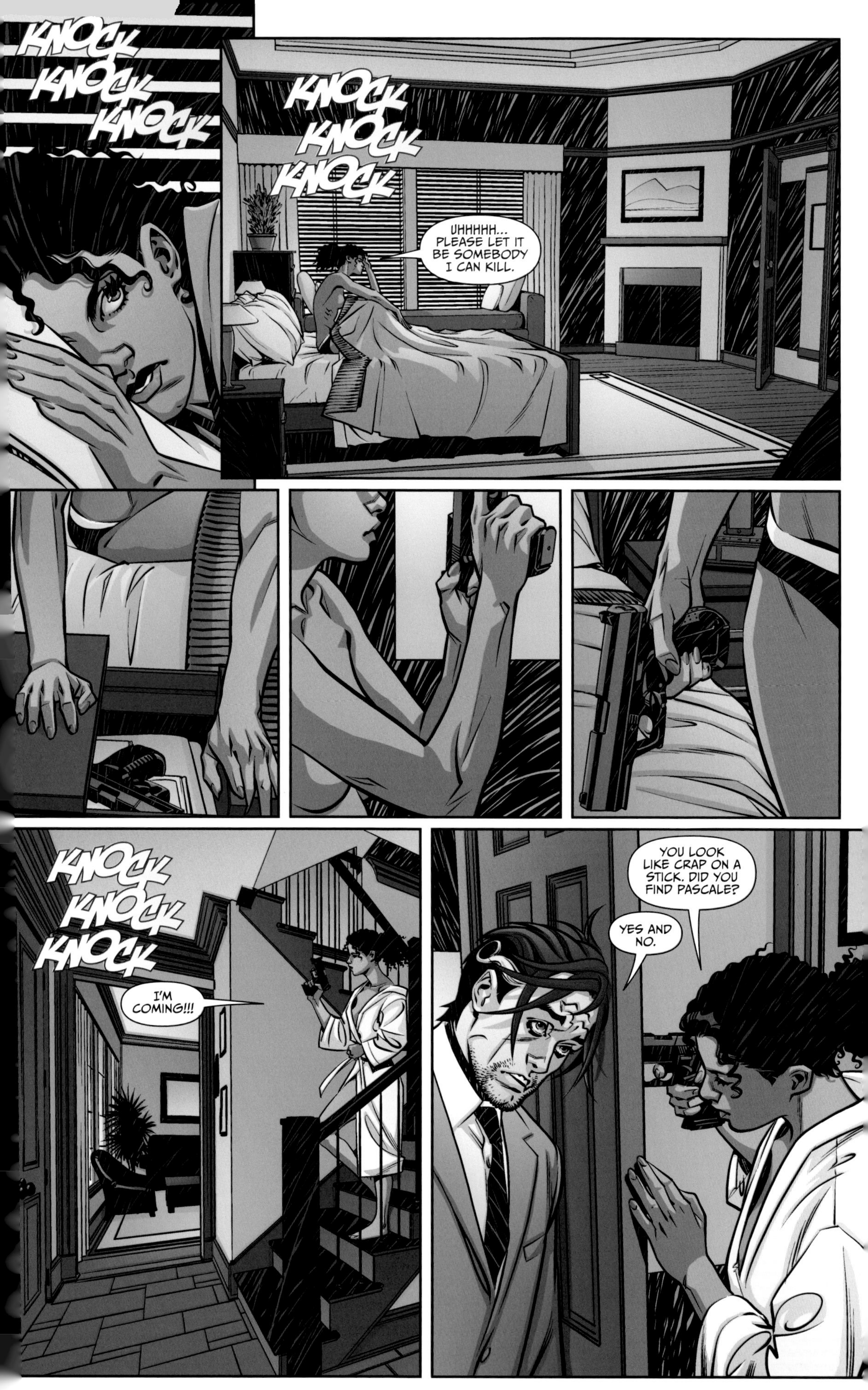

KNOCK KNOCK KNOCK
KNOCK KNOCK KNOCK
UHHHHH... PLEASE LET IT BE SOMEBODY I CAN KILL.
KNOCK KNOCK KNOCK
I'M COMING!!!
YOU LOOK LIKE CRAP ON A STICK. DID YOU FIND PASCALE?
YES AND NO.

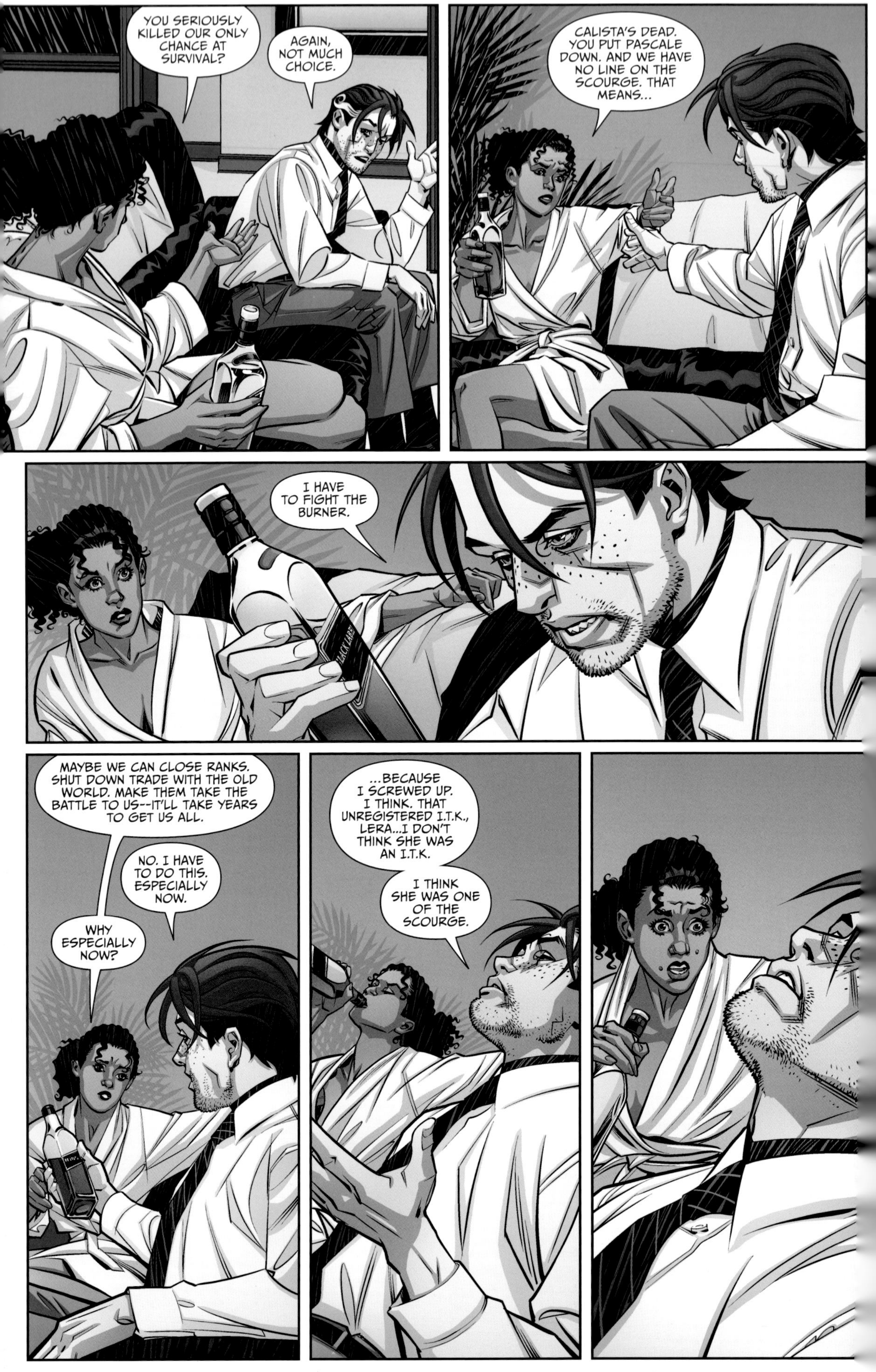
YOU SERIOUSLY KILLED OUR ONLY CHANCE AT SURVIVAL?
AGAIN, NOT MUCH CHOICE.
CALISTA'S DEAD. YOU PUT PASCALE DOWN. AND WE HAVE NO LINE ON THE SCOURGE. THAT MEANS...
I HAVE TO FIGHT THE BURNER.
BLACK LABEL
MAYBE WE CAN CLOSE RANKS. SHUT DOWN TRADE WITH THE OLD WORLD. MAKE THEM TAKE THE BATTLE TO US--IT'LL TAKE YEARS TO GET US ALL.
NO. I HAVE TO DO THIS. ESPECIALLY NOW.
WHY ESPECIALLY NOW?
...BECAUSE I SCREWED UP. I THINK. THAT UNREGISTERED I.T.K., LERA...I DON'T THINK SHE WAS AN I.T.K.
I THINK SHE WAS ONE OF THE SCOURGE.

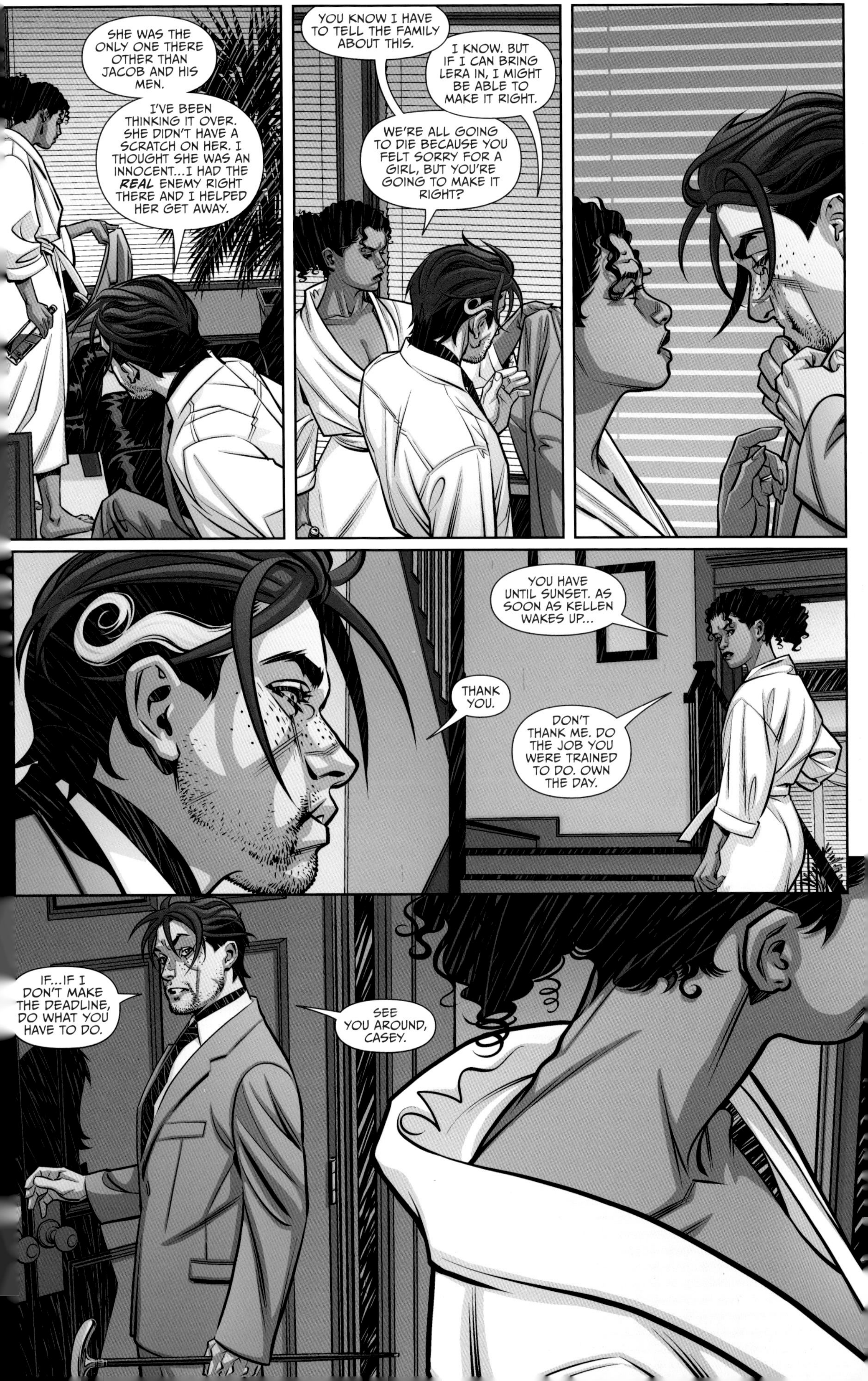
SHE WAS THE ONLY ONE THERE OTHER THAN JACOB AND HIS MEN.
I'VE BEEN THINKING IT OVER. SHE DIDN'T HAVE A SCRATCH ON HER. I THOUGHT SHE WAS AN INNOCENT...I HAD THE REAL ENEMY RIGHT THERE AND I HELPED HER GET AWAY.
YOU KNOW I HAVE TO TELL THE FAMILY ABOUT THIS.
I KNOW. BUT IF I CAN BRING LERA IN, I MIGHT BE ABLE TO MAKE IT RIGHT.
WE'RE ALL GOING TO DIE BECAUSE YOU FELT SORRY FOR A GIRL, BUT YOU'RE GOING TO MAKE IT RIGHT?
YOU HAVE UNTIL SUNSET. AS SOON AS KELLEN WAKES UP...
THANK YOU.
DON'T THANK ME. DO THE JOB YOU WERE TRAINED TO DO. OWN THE DAY.
IF...IF I DON'T MAKE THE DEADLINE, DO WHAT YOU HAVE TO DO.
SEE YOU AROUND, CASEY.

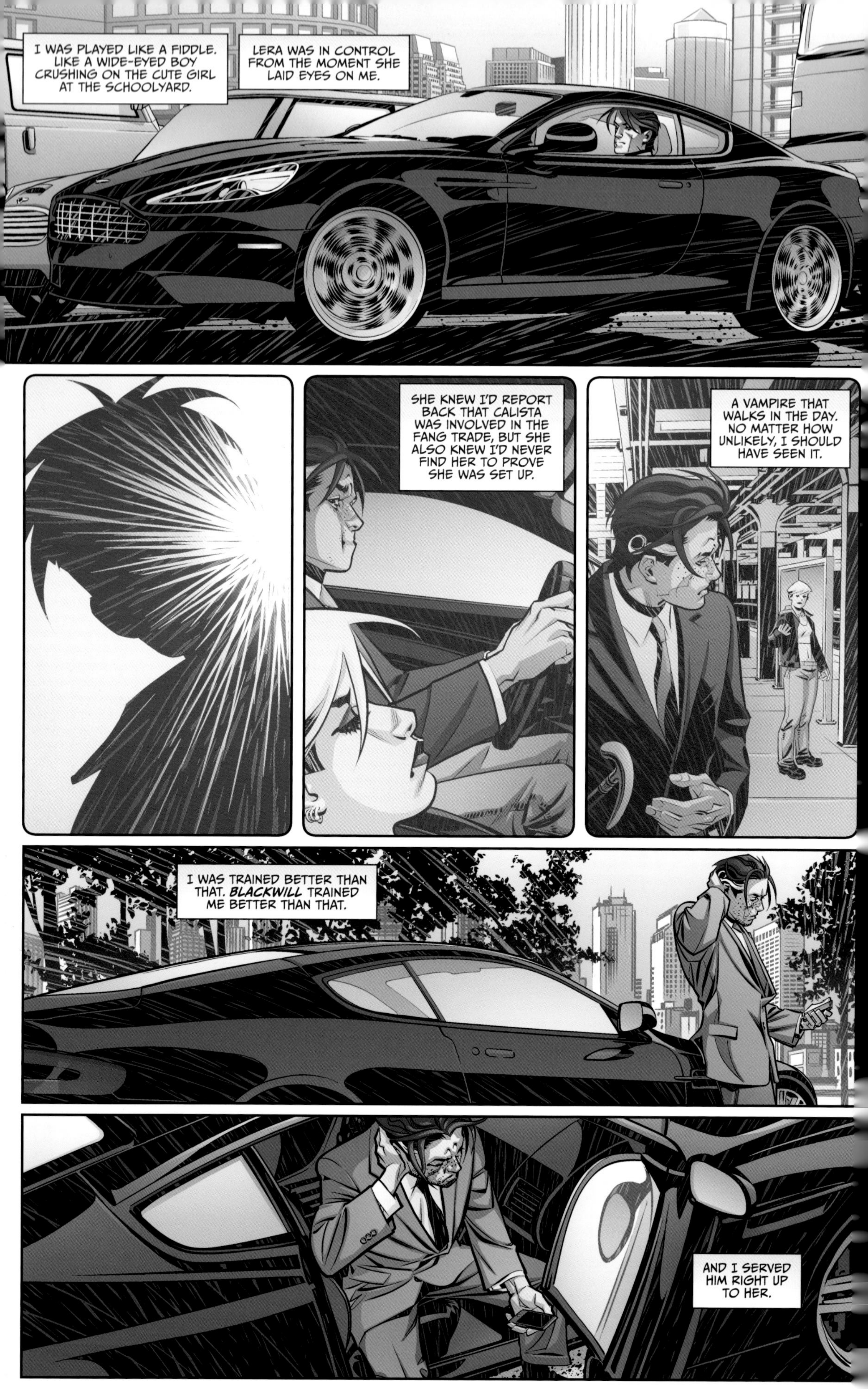
I WAS PLAYED LIKE A FIDDLE. LIKE A WIDE-EYED BOY CRUSHING ON THE CUTE GIRL AT THE SCHOOLYARD.
LERA WAS IN CONTROL FROM THE MOMENT SHE LAID EYES ON ME.
SHE KNEW I'D REPORT BACK THAT CALISTA WAS INVOLVED IN THE FANG TRADE, BUT SHE ALSO KNEW I'D NEVER FIND HER TO PROVE SHE WAS SET UP.
A VAMPIRE THAT WALKS IN THE DAY. NO MATTER HOW UNLIKELY, I SHOULD HAVE SEEN IT.
I WAS TRAINED BETTER THAN THAT. BLACKWILL TRAINED ME BETTER THAN THAT.
AND I SERVED HIM RIGHT UP TO HER.

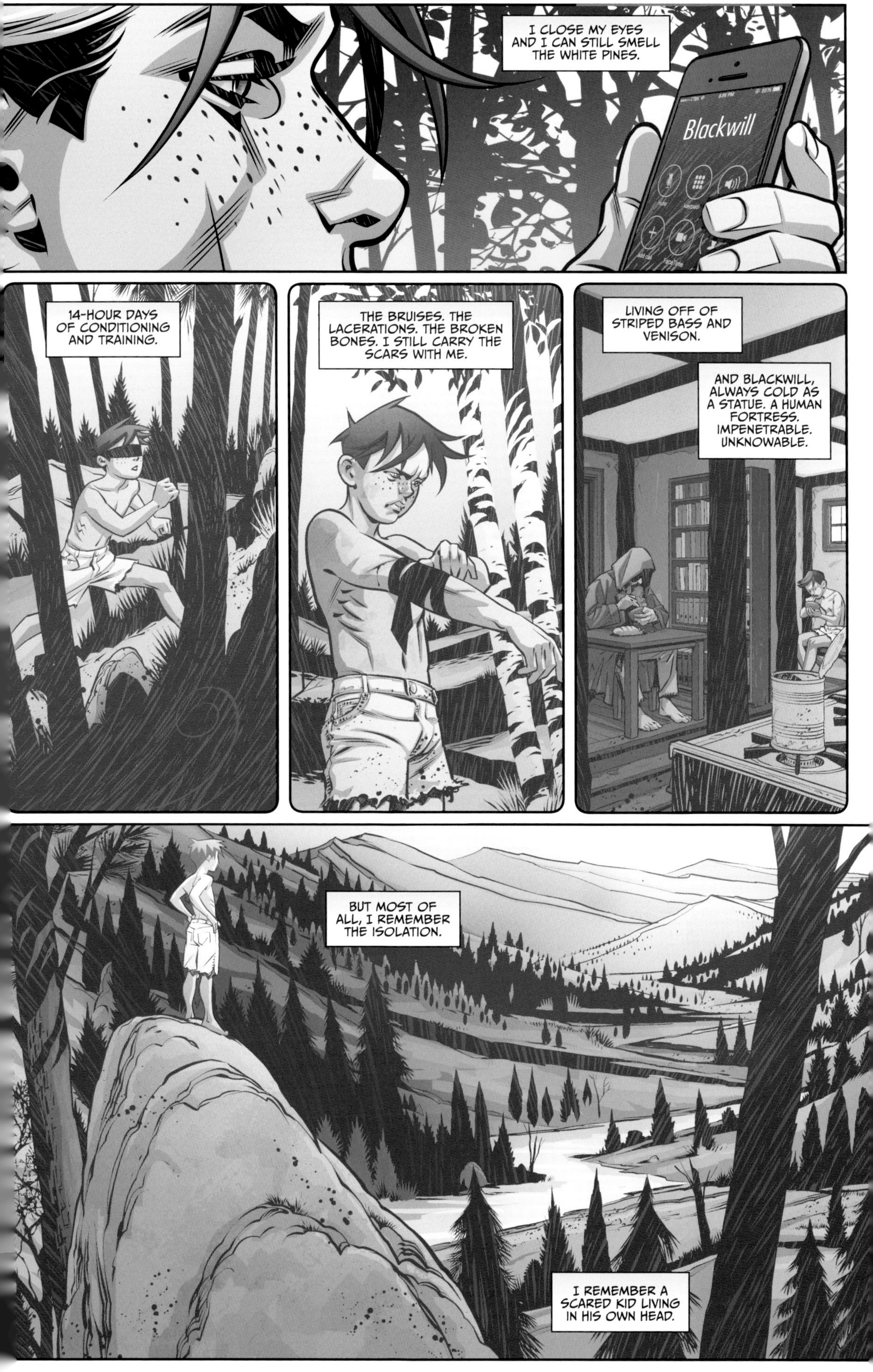
I CLOSE MY EYES AND I CAN STILL SMELL THE WHITE PINES.
Blackwill
14-HOUR DAYS OF CONDITIONING AND TRAINING.
THE BRUISES. THE LACERATIONS. THE BROKEN BONES. I STILL CARRY THE SCARS WITH ME.
LIVING OFF OF STRIPED BASS AND VENISON.
AND BLACKWILL, ALWAYS COLD AS A STATUE. A HUMAN FORTRESS. IMPENETRABLE. UNKNOWABLE.
BUT MOST OF ALL, I REMEMBER THE ISOLATION.
I REMEMBER A SCARED KID LIVING IN HIS OWN HEAD.

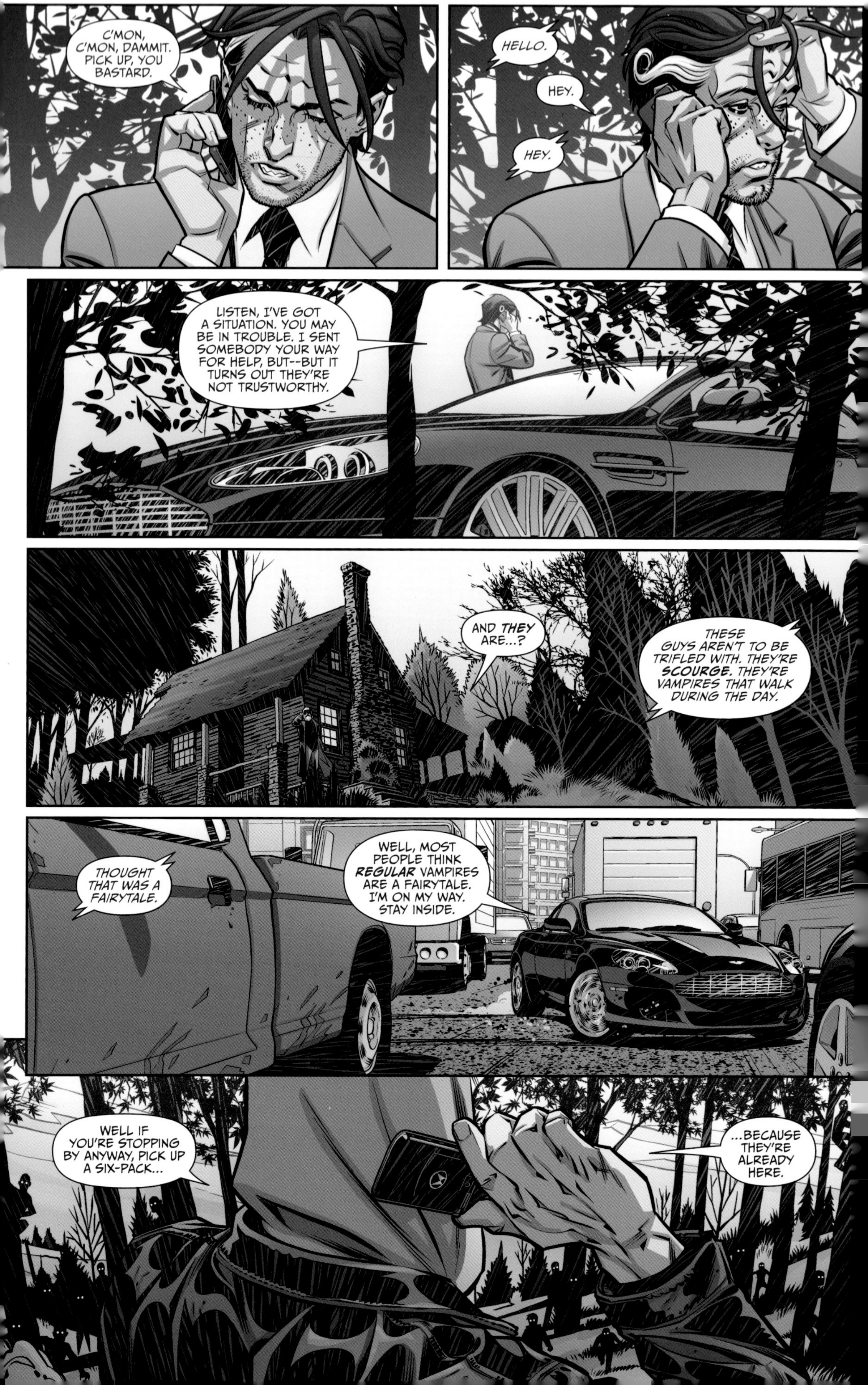
C'MON, C'MON, DAMMIT. PICK UP, YOU BASTARD.
HELLO.
HEY.
HEY.
LISTEN, I'VE GOT A SITUATION. YOU MAY BE IN TROUBLE. I SENT SOMEBODY YOUR WAY FOR HELP, BUT--BUT IT TURNS OUT THEY'RE NOT TRUSTWORTHY.
AND THEY ARE...?
THESE GUYS AREN'T TO BE TRIFLED WITH. THEY'RE SCOURGE. THEY'RE VAMPIRES THAT WALK DURING THE DAY.
THOUGHT THAT WAS A FAIRYTALE.
WELL, MOST PEOPLE THINK REGULAR VAMPIRES ARE A FAIRYTALE. I'M ON MY WAY. STAY INSIDE.
WELL IF YOU'RE STOPPING BY ANYWAY, PICK UP A SIX-PACK...
...BECAUSE THEY'RE ALREADY HERE.

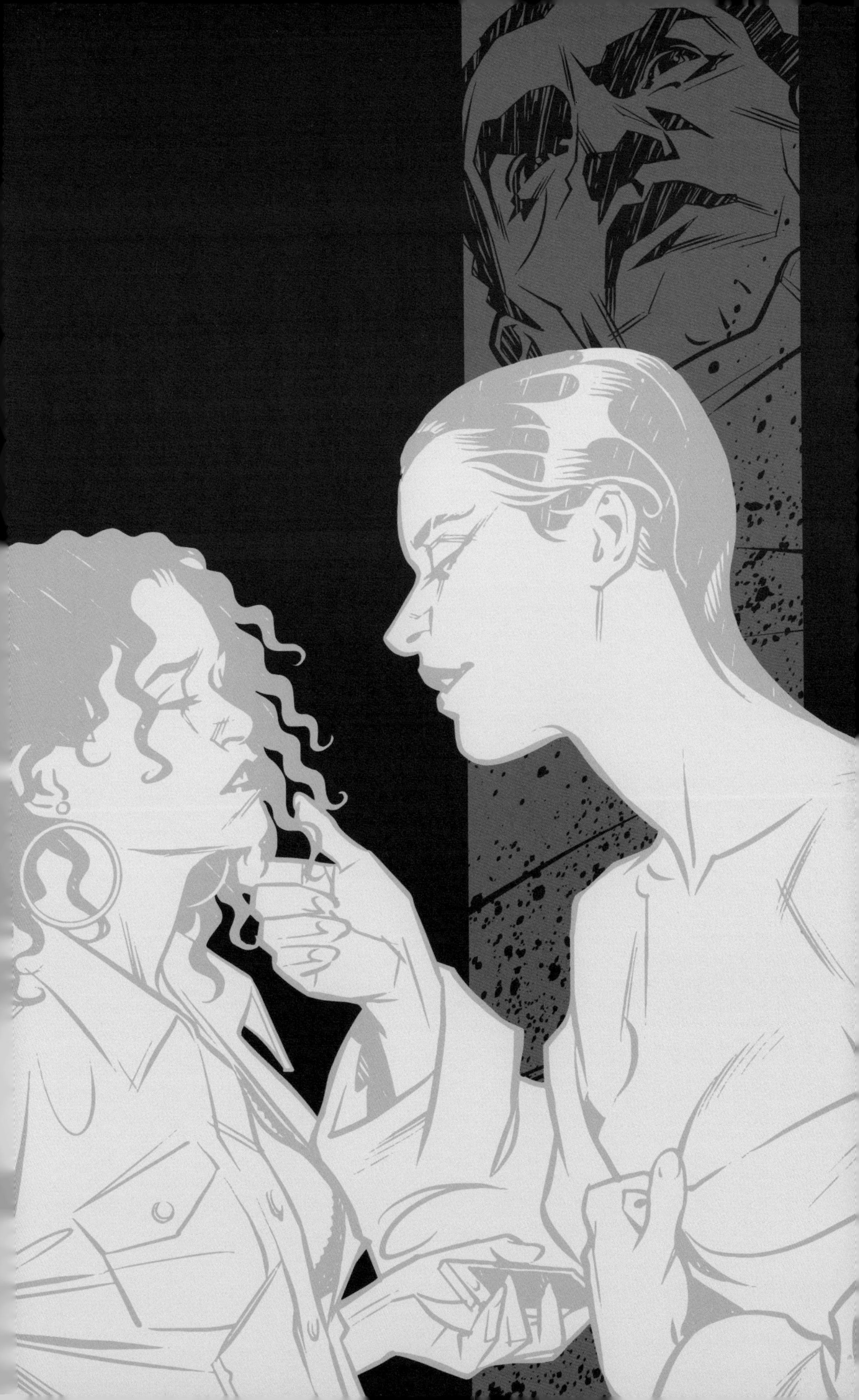

# CHAPTER SIX

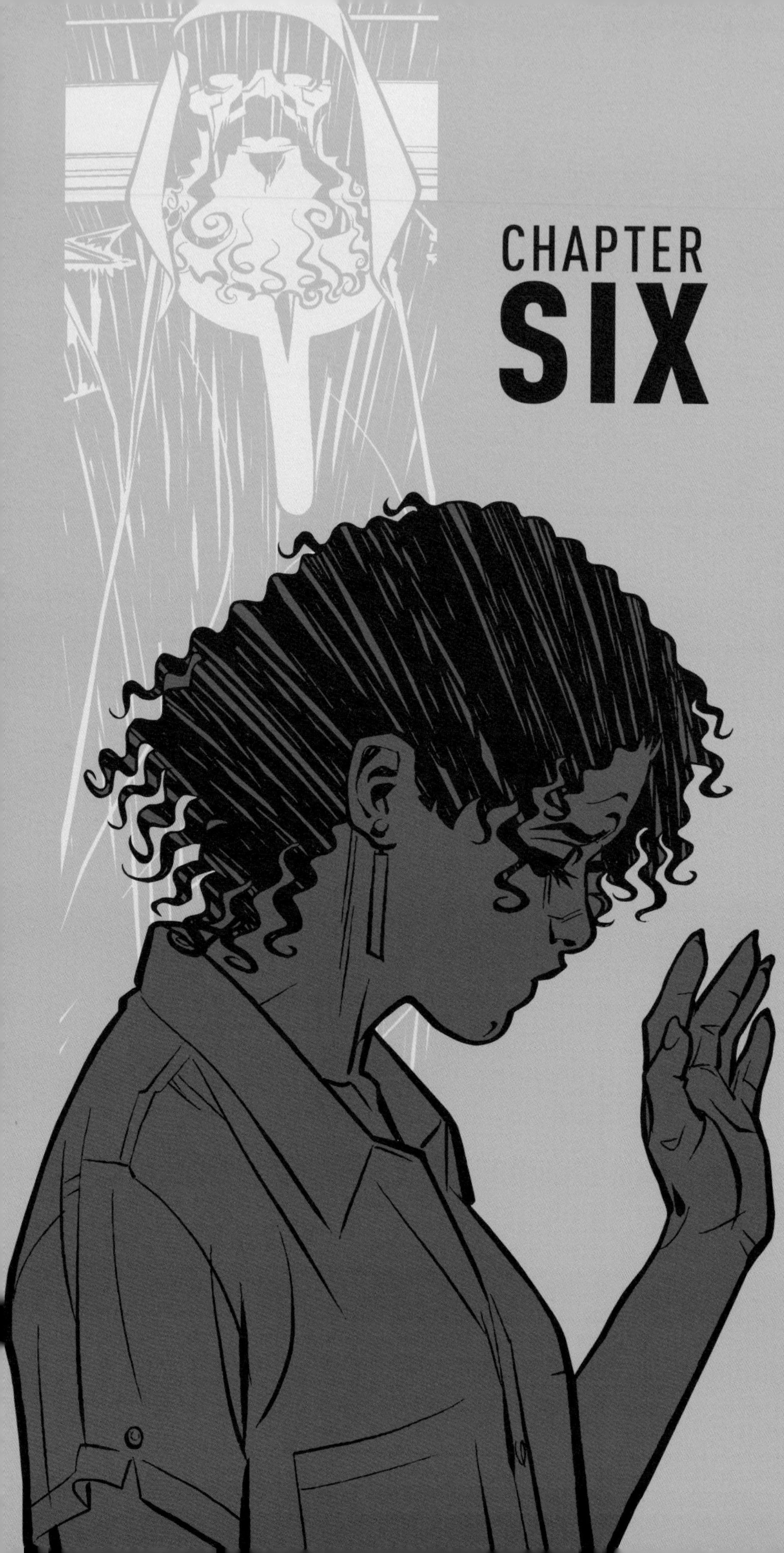

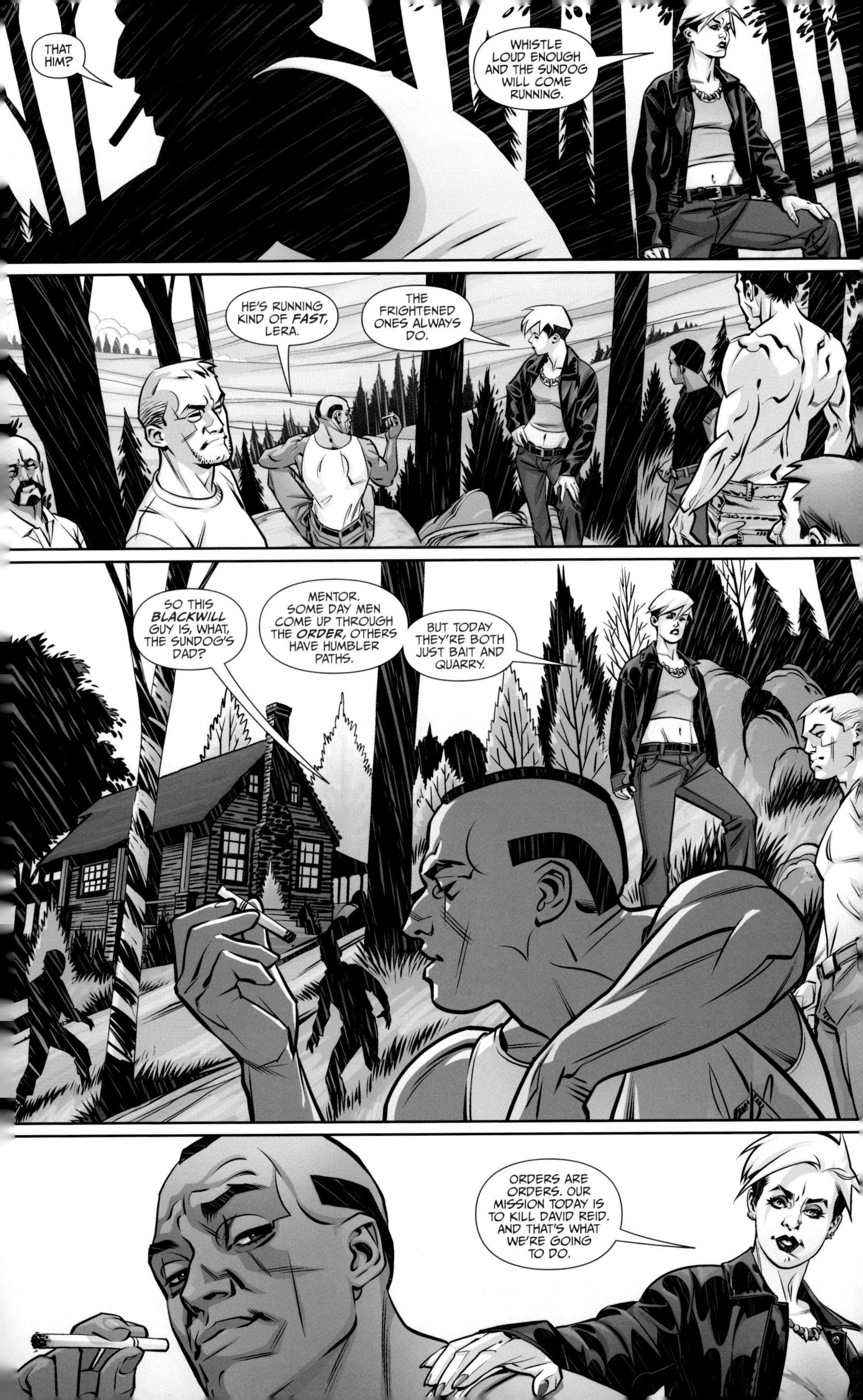
THAT HIM?
WHISTLE LOUD ENOUGH AND THE SUNDOG WILL COME RUNNING.
HE'S RUNNING KIND OF FAST, LERA.
THE FRIGHTENED ONES ALWAYS DO.
SO THIS BLACKWILL GUY IS, WHAT, THE SUNDOG'S DAD?
MENTOR. SOME DAY MEN COME UP THROUGH THE ORDER, OTHERS HAVE HUMBLER PATHS.
BUT TODAY THEY'RE BOTH JUST BAIT AND QUARRY.
ORDERS ARE ORDERS. OUR MISSION TODAY IS TO KILL DAVID REID. AND THAT'S WHAT WE'RE GOING TO DO.

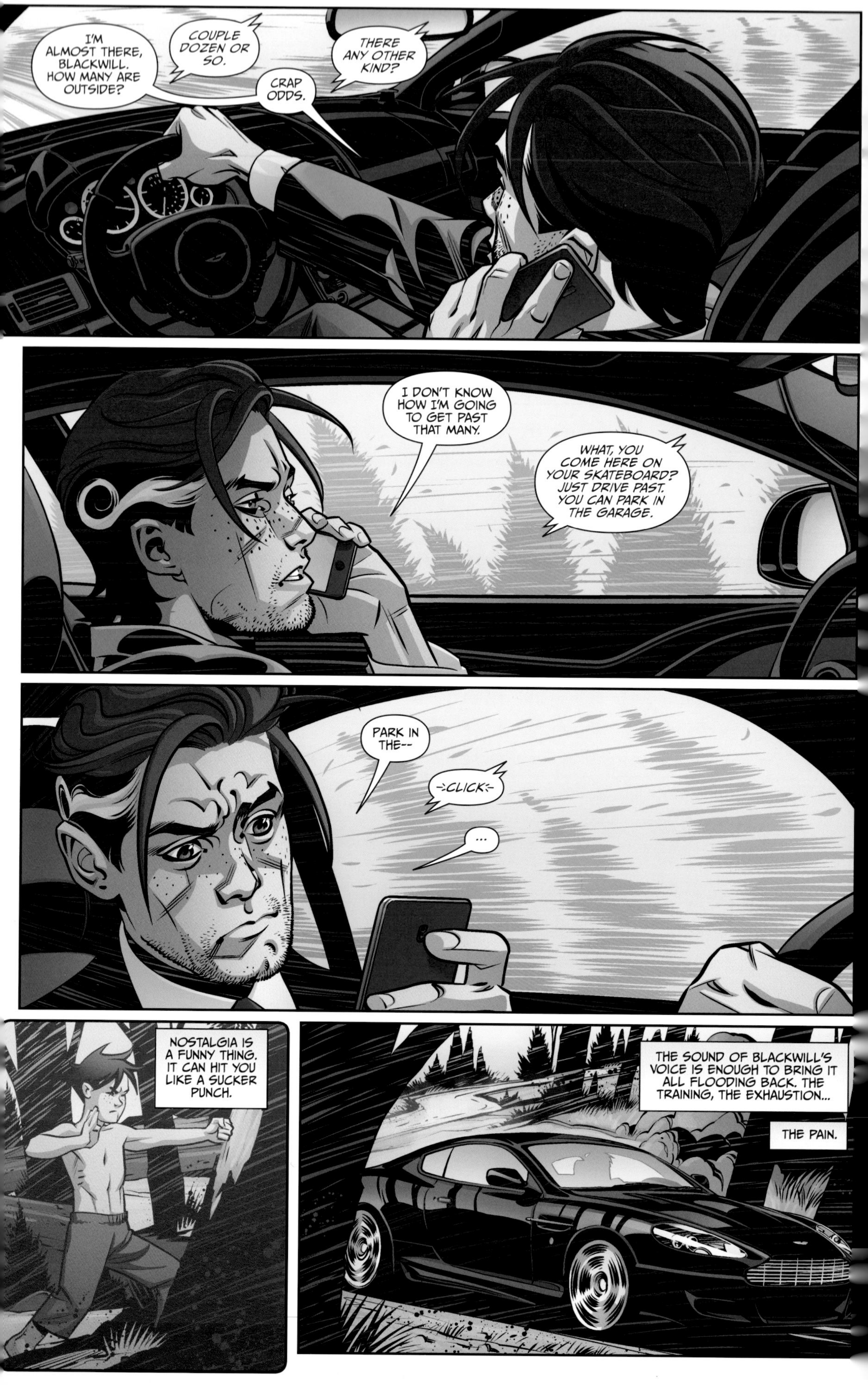
I'M ALMOST THERE, BLACKWILL. HOW MANY ARE OUTSIDE?
COUPLE DOZEN OR SO.
CRAP ODDS.
THERE ANY OTHER KIND?
I DON'T KNOW HOW I'M GOING TO GET PAST THAT MANY.
WHAT, YOU COME HERE ON YOUR SKATEBOARD? JUST DRIVE PAST. YOU CAN PARK IN THE GARAGE.
PARK IN THE--
-CLICK-
...
NOSTALGIA IS A FUNNY THING. IT CAN HIT YOU LIKE A SUCKER PUNCH.
THE SOUND OF BLACKWILL'S VOICE IS ENOUGH TO BRING IT ALL FLOODING BACK. THE TRAINING, THE EXHAUSTION...
THE PAIN.

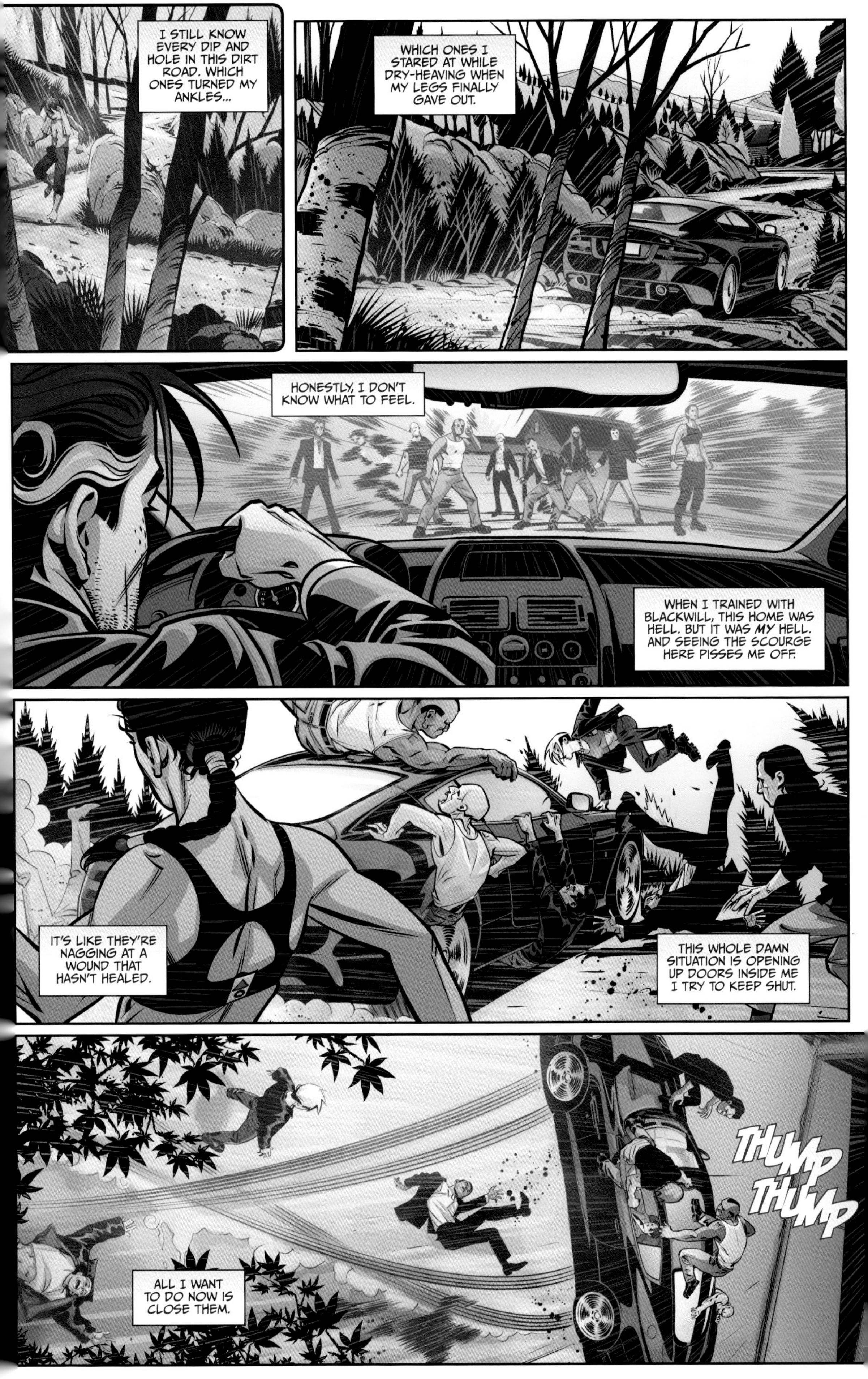
I STILL KNOW EVERY DIP AND HOLE IN THIS DIRT ROAD. WHICH ONES TURNED MY ANKLES...
WHICH ONES I STARED AT WHILE DRY-HEAVING WHEN MY LEGS FINALLY GAVE OUT.
HONESTLY, I DON'T KNOW WHAT TO FEEL.
WHEN I TRAINED WITH BLACKWILL, THIS HOME WAS HELL. BUT IT WAS *MY* HELL. AND SEEING THE SCOURGE HERE PISSES ME OFF.
IT'S LIKE THEY'RE NAGGING AT A WOUND THAT HASN'T HEALED.
THIS WHOLE DAMN SITUATION IS OPENING UP DOORS INSIDE ME I TRY TO KEEP SHUT.
ALL I WANT TO DO NOW IS CLOSE THEM.
THUMP
THUMP

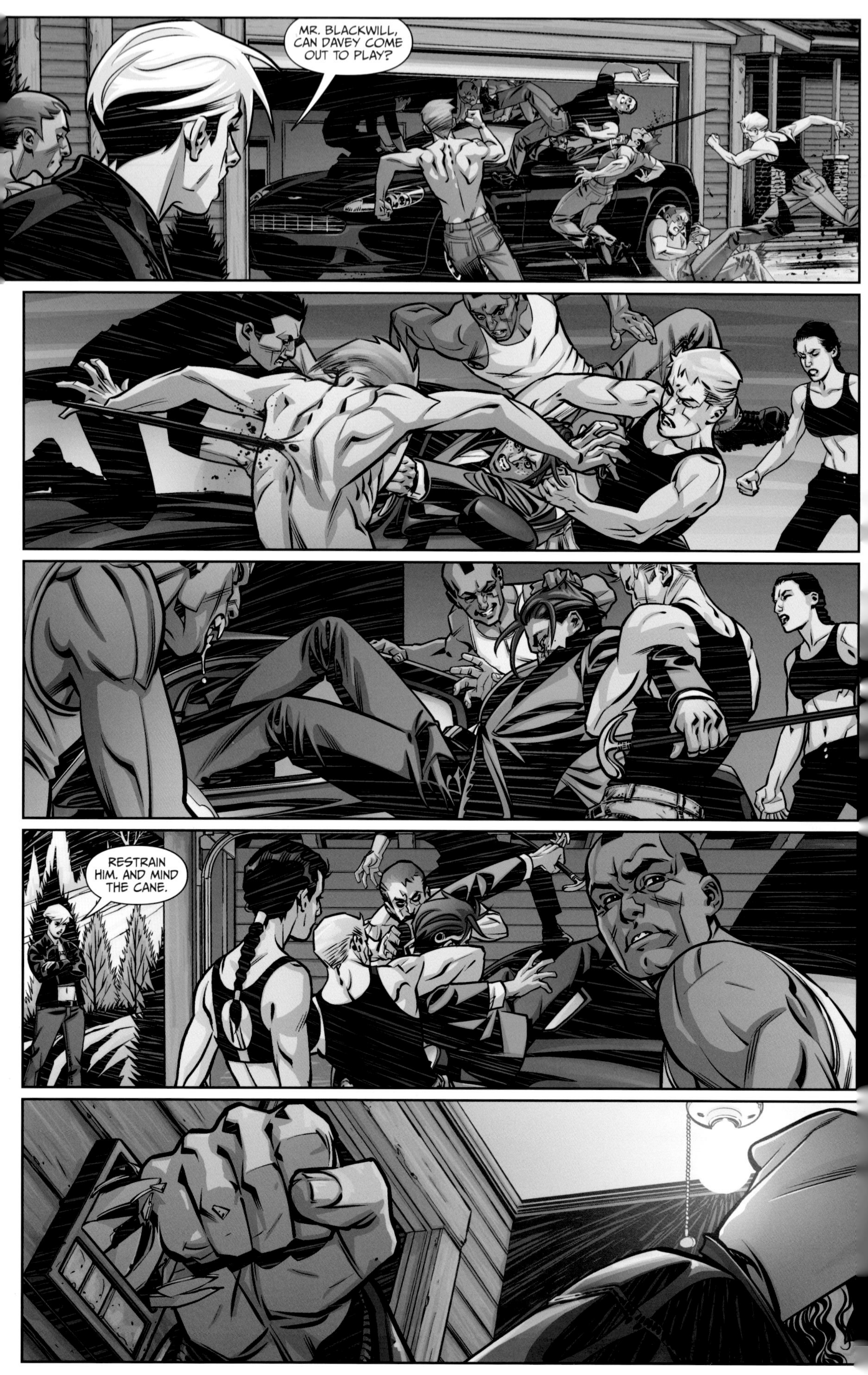
MR. BLACKWILL, CAN DAVEY COME OUT TO PLAY?
RESTRAIN HIM. AND MIND THE CANE.

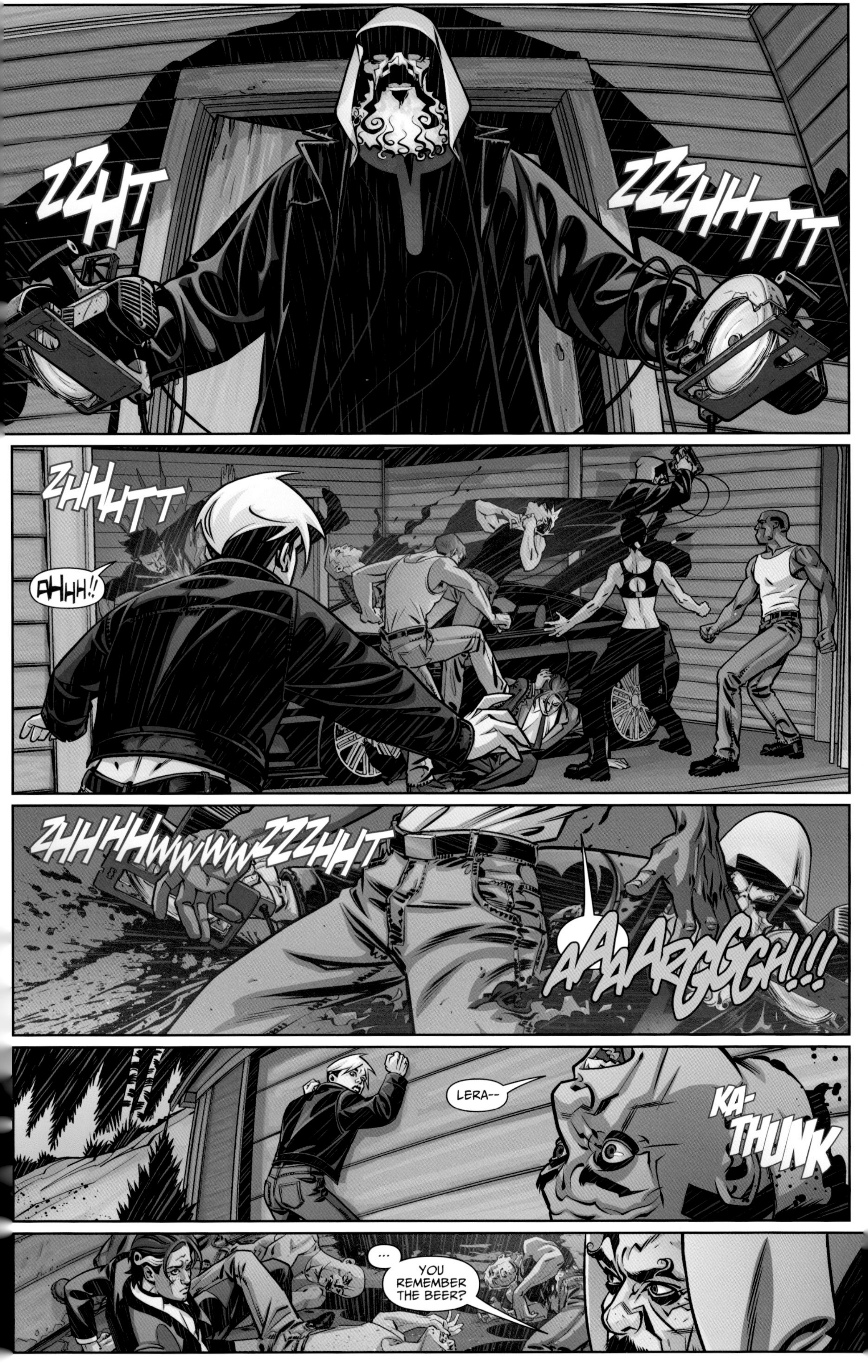
ZZHT
ZZZHHTTT
ZHHHTT
AHHH!!
ZHHHHWWWWZZZHHT
AAAARGGGH!!!
LERA--
KA-THUNK
...
YOU REMEMBER THE BEER?

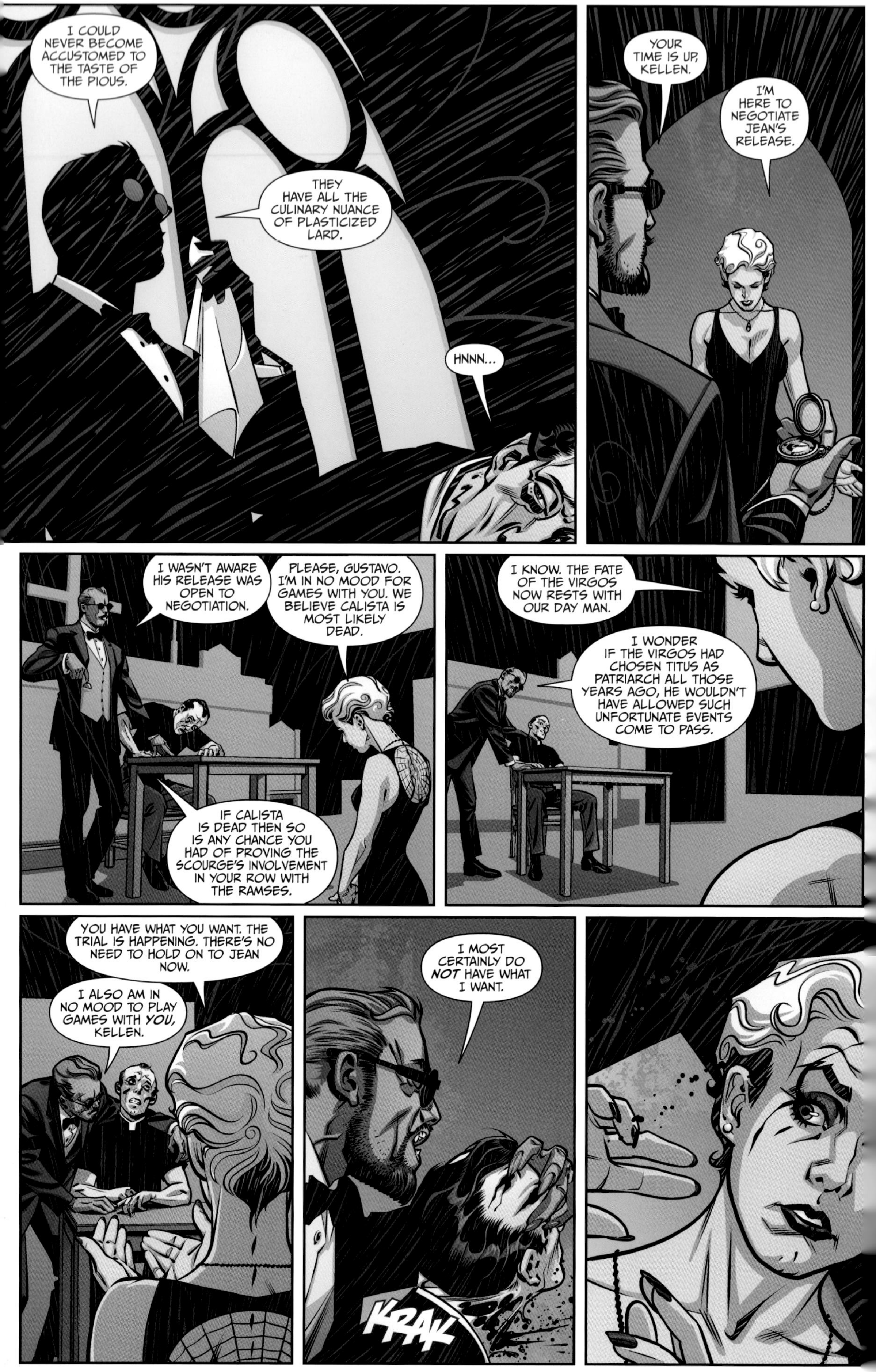
I COULD NEVER BECOME ACCUSTOMED TO THE TASTE OF THE PIOUS.
THEY HAVE ALL THE CULINARY NUANCE OF PLASTICIZED LARD.
HNNN...
YOUR TIME IS UP, KELLEN.
I'M HERE TO NEGOTIATE JEAN'S RELEASE.
I WASN'T AWARE HIS RELEASE WAS OPEN TO NEGOTIATION.
PLEASE, GUSTAVO. I'M IN NO MOOD FOR GAMES WITH YOU. WE BELIEVE CALISTA IS MOST LIKELY DEAD.
IF CALISTA IS DEAD THEN SO IS ANY CHANCE YOU HAD OF PROVING THE SCOURGE'S INVOLVEMENT IN YOUR ROW WITH THE RAMSES.
I KNOW. THE FATE OF THE VIRGOS NOW RESTS WITH OUR DAY MAN.
I WONDER IF THE VIRGOS HAD CHOSEN TITUS AS PATRIARCH ALL THOSE YEARS AGO, HE WOULDN'T HAVE ALLOWED SUCH UNFORTUNATE EVENTS COME TO PASS.
YOU HAVE WHAT YOU WANT. THE TRIAL IS HAPPENING. THERE'S NO NEED TO HOLD ON TO JEAN NOW.
I ALSO AM IN NO MOOD TO PLAY GAMES WITH *YOU,* KELLEN.
I MOST CERTAINLY DO ***NOT*** HAVE WHAT I WANT.
KRAK

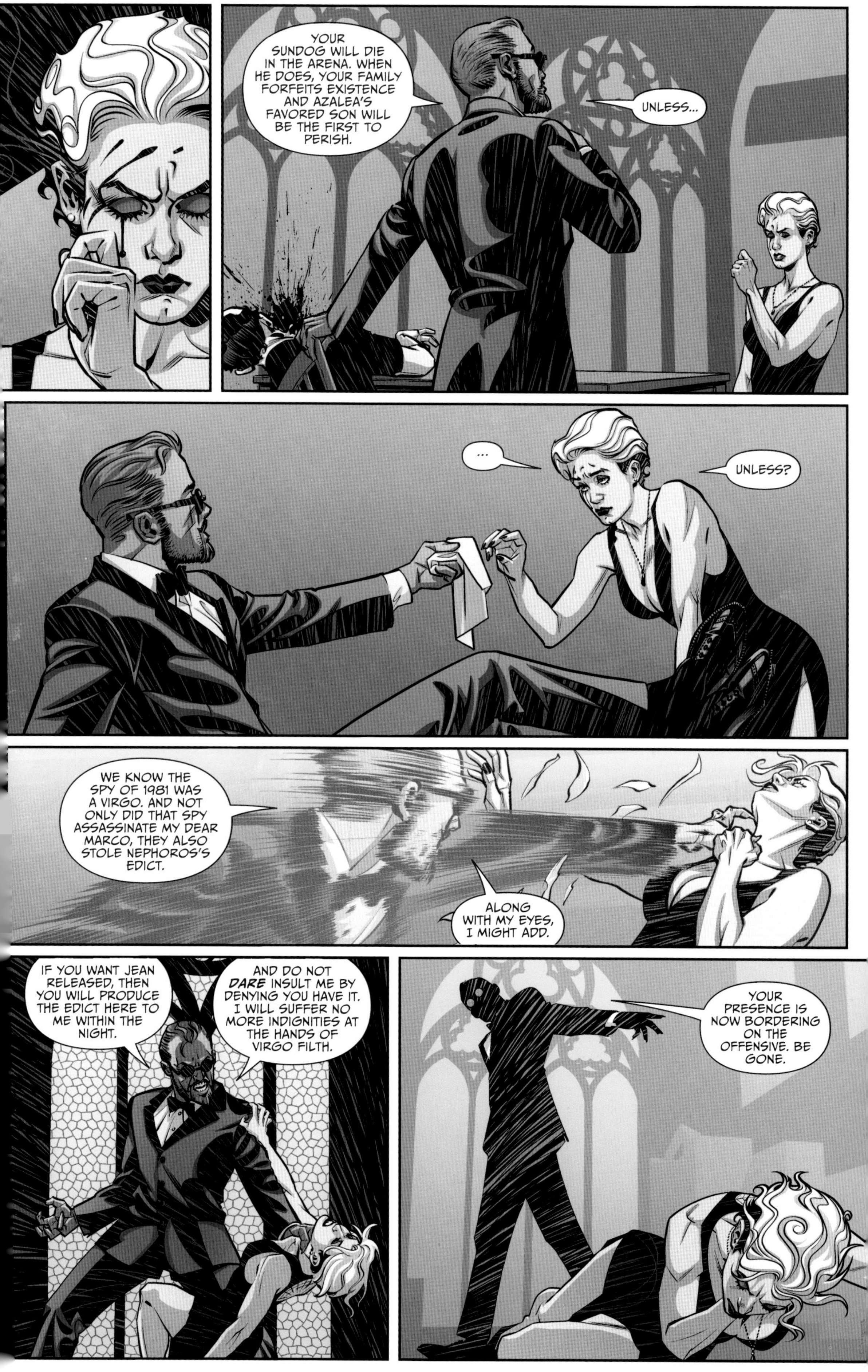
YOUR SUNDOG WILL DIE IN THE ARENA. WHEN HE DOES, YOUR FAMILY FORFEITS EXISTENCE AND AZALEA'S FAVORED SON WILL BE THE FIRST TO PERISH.
UNLESS...
...
UNLESS?
WE KNOW THE SPY OF 1981 WAS A VIRGO. AND NOT ONLY DID THAT SPY ASSASSINATE MY DEAR MARCO, THEY ALSO STOLE NEPHOROS'S EDICT.
ALONG WITH MY EYES, I MIGHT ADD.
IF YOU WANT JEAN RELEASED, THEN YOU WILL PRODUCE THE EDICT HERE TO ME WITHIN THE NIGHT.
AND DO NOT *DARE* INSULT ME BY DENYING YOU HAVE IT. I WILL SUFFER NO MORE INDIGNITIES AT THE HANDS OF VIRGO FILTH.
YOUR PRESENCE IS NOW BORDERING ON THE OFFENSIVE. BE GONE.

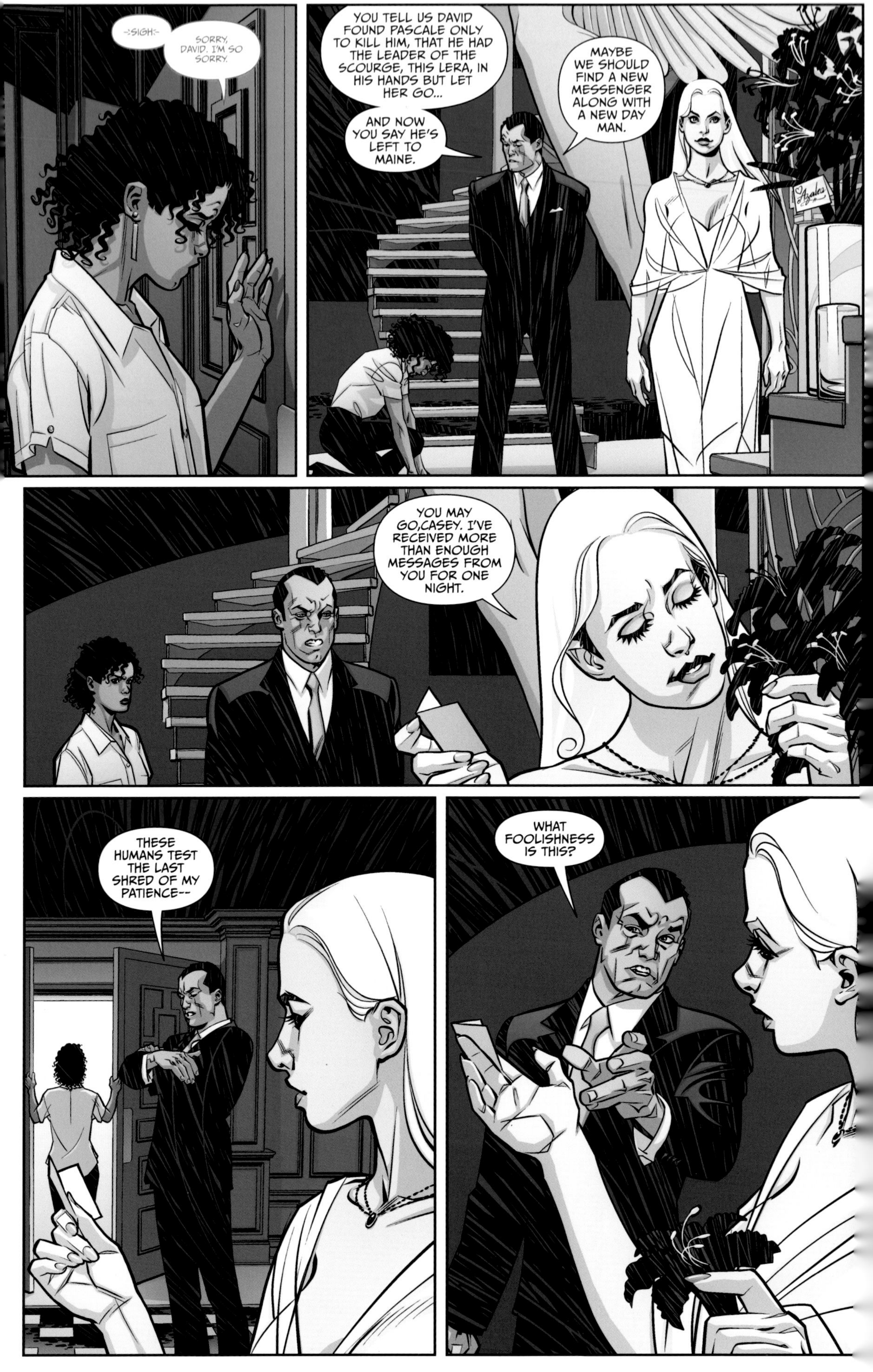
-:SIGH:-
SORRY, DAVID. I'M SO SORRY.
YOU TELL US DAVID FOUND PASCALE ONLY TO KILL HIM, THAT HE HAD THE LEADER OF THE SCOURGE, THIS LERA, IN HIS HANDS BUT LET HER GO...
AND NOW YOU SAY HE'S LEFT TO MAINE.
MAYBE WE SHOULD FIND A NEW MESSENGER ALONG WITH A NEW DAY MAN.
YOU MAY GO,CASEY. I'VE RECEIVED MORE THAN ENOUGH MESSAGES FROM YOU FOR ONE NIGHT.
THESE HUMANS TEST THE LAST SHRED OF MY PATIENCE--
WHAT FOOLISHNESS IS THIS?

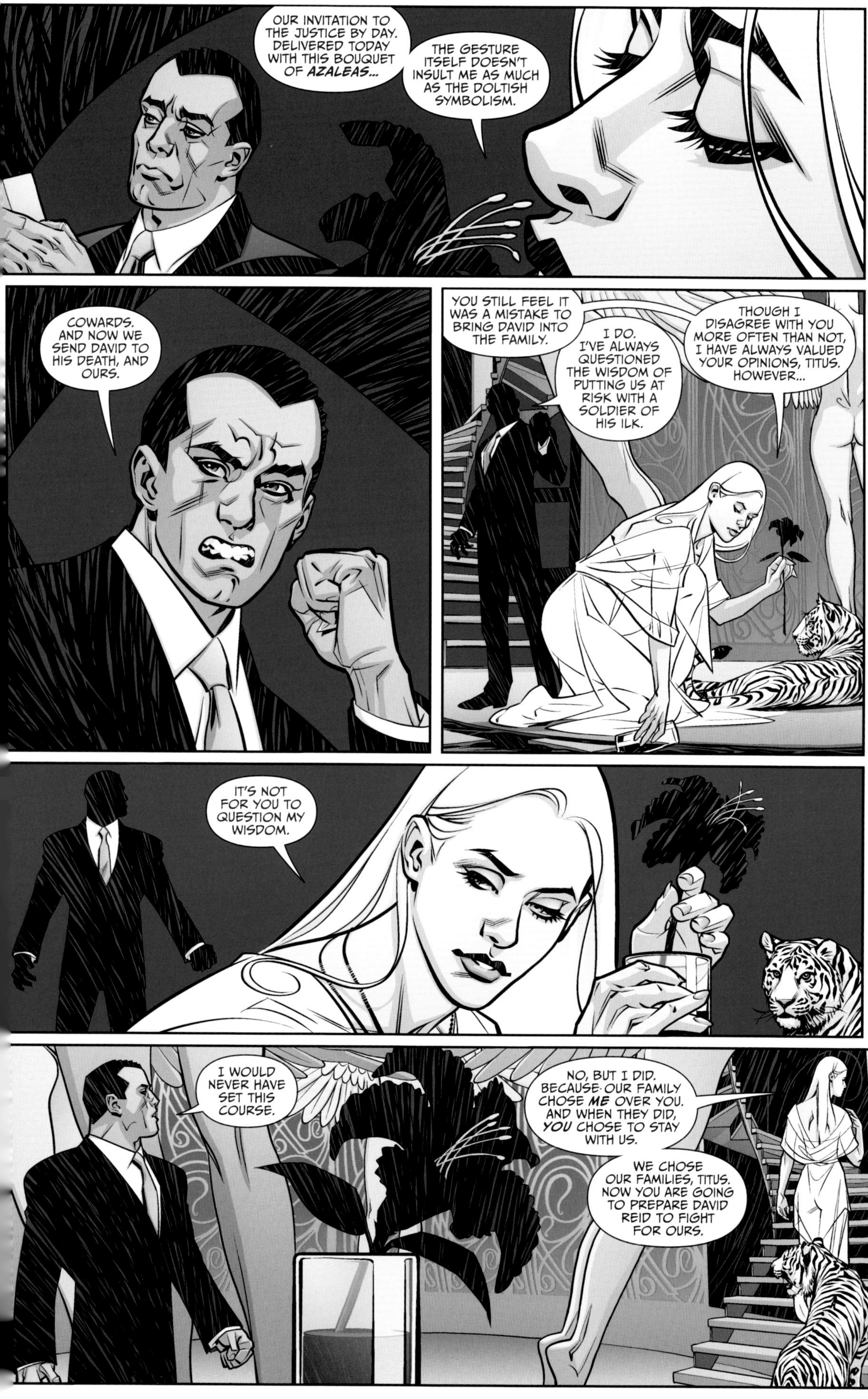
OUR INVITATION TO THE JUSTICE BY DAY. DELIVERED TODAY WITH THIS BOUQUET OF *AZALEAS*...
THE GESTURE ITSELF DOESN'T INSULT ME AS MUCH AS THE DOLTISH SYMBOLISM.
COWARDS. AND NOW WE SEND DAVID TO HIS DEATH, AND OURS.
YOU STILL FEEL IT WAS A MISTAKE TO BRING DAVID INTO THE FAMILY.
I DO. I'VE ALWAYS QUESTIONED THE WISDOM OF PUTTING US AT RISK WITH A SOLDIER OF HIS ILK.
THOUGH I DISAGREE WITH YOU MORE OFTEN THAN NOT, I HAVE ALWAYS VALUED YOUR OPINIONS, TITUS. HOWEVER...
IT'S NOT FOR YOU TO QUESTION MY WISDOM.
I WOULD NEVER HAVE SET THIS COURSE.
NO, BUT I DID. BECAUSE OUR FAMILY CHOSE *ME* OVER YOU. AND WHEN THEY DID, *YOU* CHOSE TO STAY WITH US.
WE CHOSE OUR FAMILIES, TITUS. NOW YOU ARE GOING TO PREPARE DAVID REID TO FIGHT FOR OURS.

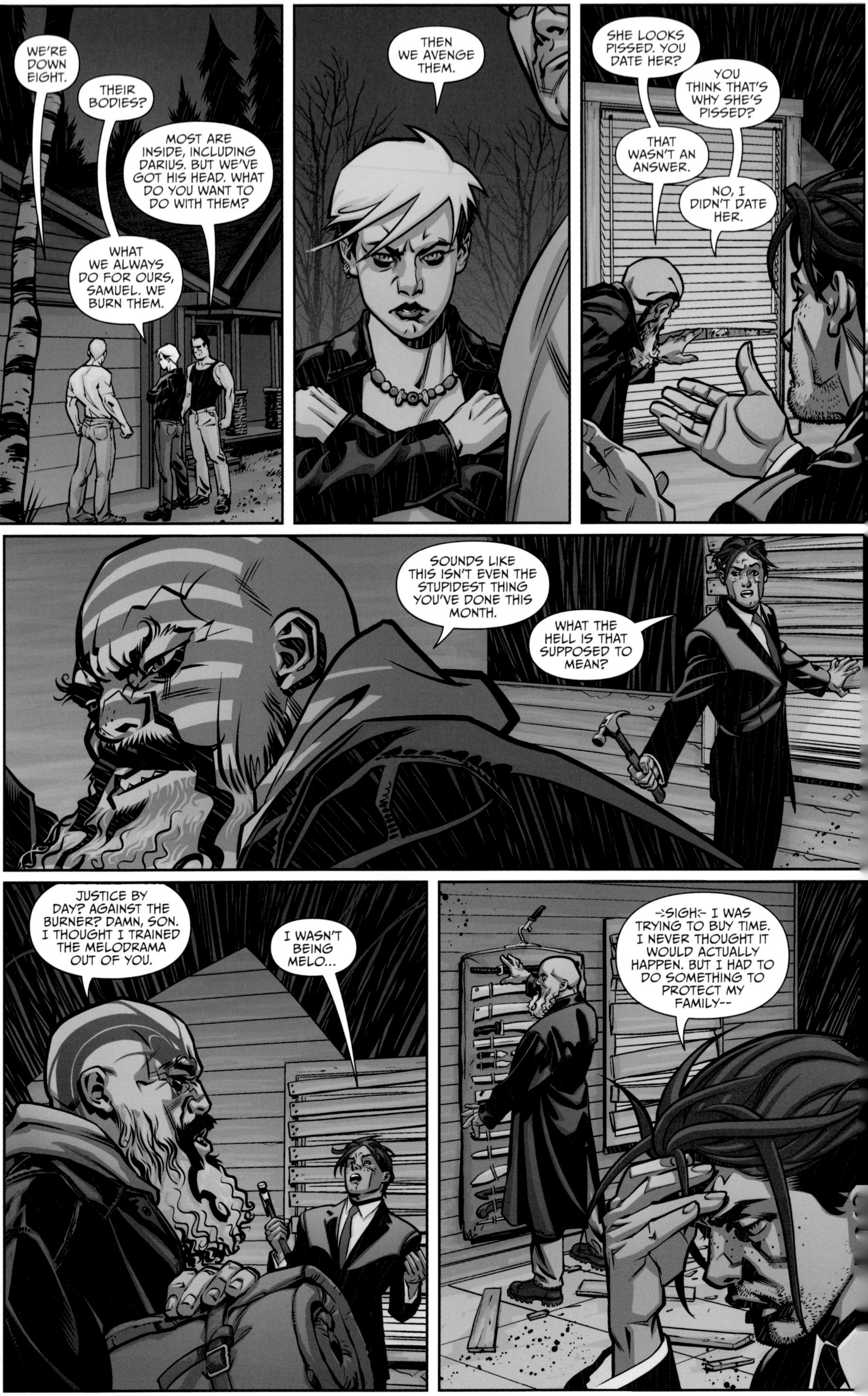
WE'RE DOWN EIGHT.
THEIR BODIES?
MOST ARE INSIDE, INCLUDING DARIUS. BUT WE'VE GOT HIS HEAD. WHAT DO YOU WANT TO DO WITH THEM?
WHAT WE ALWAYS DO FOR OURS, SAMUEL. WE BURN THEM.
THEN WE AVENGE THEM.
SHE LOOKS PISSED. YOU DATE HER?
YOU THINK THAT'S WHY SHE'S PISSED?
THAT WASN'T AN ANSWER.
NO, I DIDN'T DATE HER.
SOUNDS LIKE THIS ISN'T EVEN THE STUPIDEST THING YOU'VE DONE THIS MONTH.
WHAT THE HELL IS THAT SUPPOSED TO MEAN?
JUSTICE BY DAY? AGAINST THE BURNER? DAMN, SON. I THOUGHT I TRAINED THE MELODRAMA OUT OF YOU.
I WASN'T BEING MELO...
-SIGH- I WAS TRYING TO BUY TIME. I NEVER THOUGHT IT WOULD ACTUALLY HAPPEN. BUT I HAD TO DO SOMETHING TO PROTECT MY FAMILY--

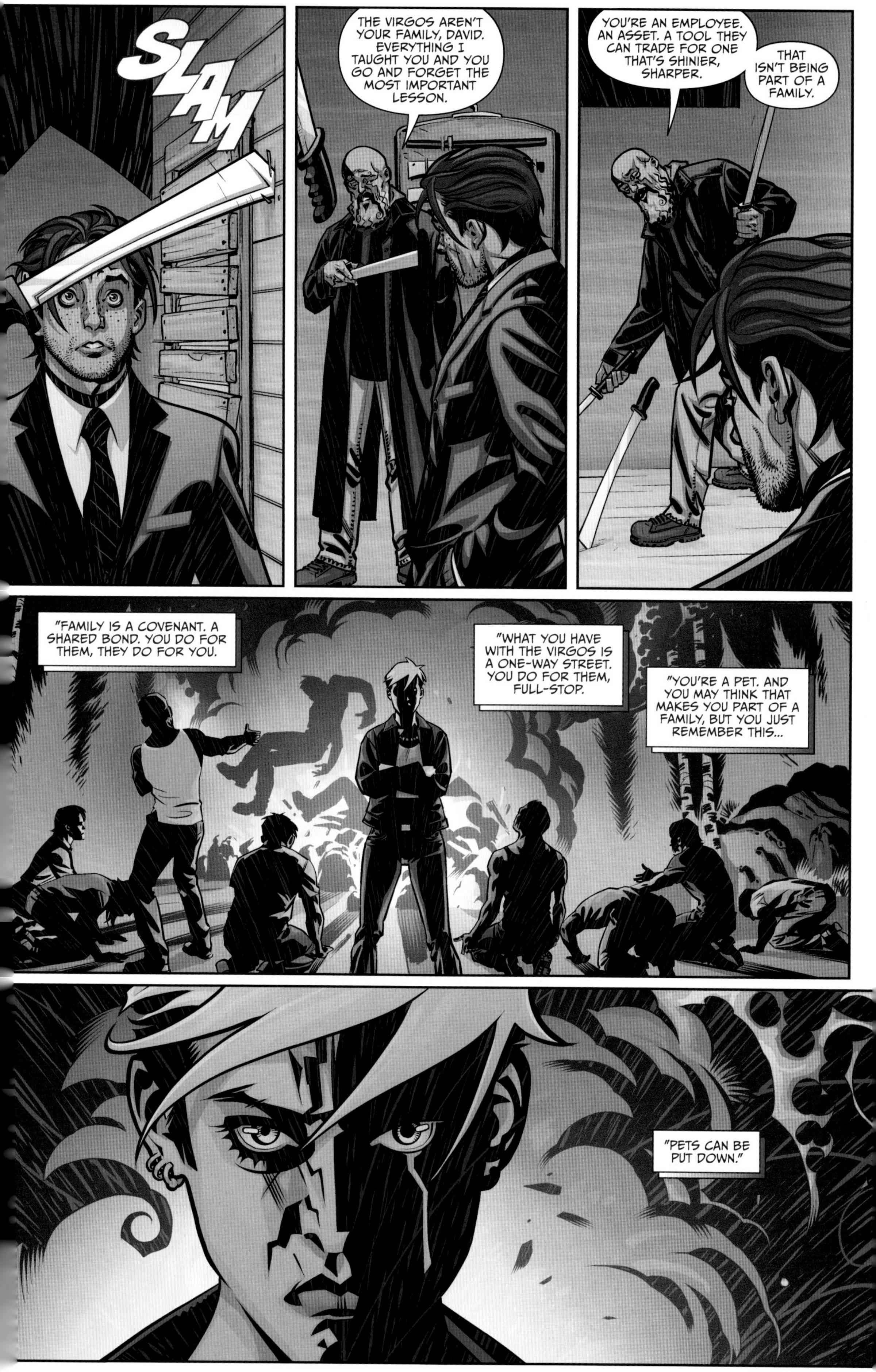
SLAM
THE VIRGOS AREN'T YOUR FAMILY, DAVID. EVERYTHING I TAUGHT YOU AND YOU GO AND FORGET THE MOST IMPORTANT LESSON.
YOU'RE AN EMPLOYEE. AN ASSET. A TOOL THEY CAN TRADE FOR ONE THAT'S SHINIER, SHARPER.
THAT ISN'T BEING PART OF A FAMILY.
"FAMILY IS A COVENANT. A SHARED BOND. YOU DO FOR THEM, THEY DO FOR YOU.
"WHAT YOU HAVE WITH THE VIRGOS IS A ONE-WAY STREET. YOU DO FOR THEM, FULL-STOP.
"YOU'RE A PET. AND YOU MAY THINK THAT MAKES YOU PART OF A FAMILY, BUT YOU JUST REMEMBER THIS...
"PETS CAN BE PUT DOWN."

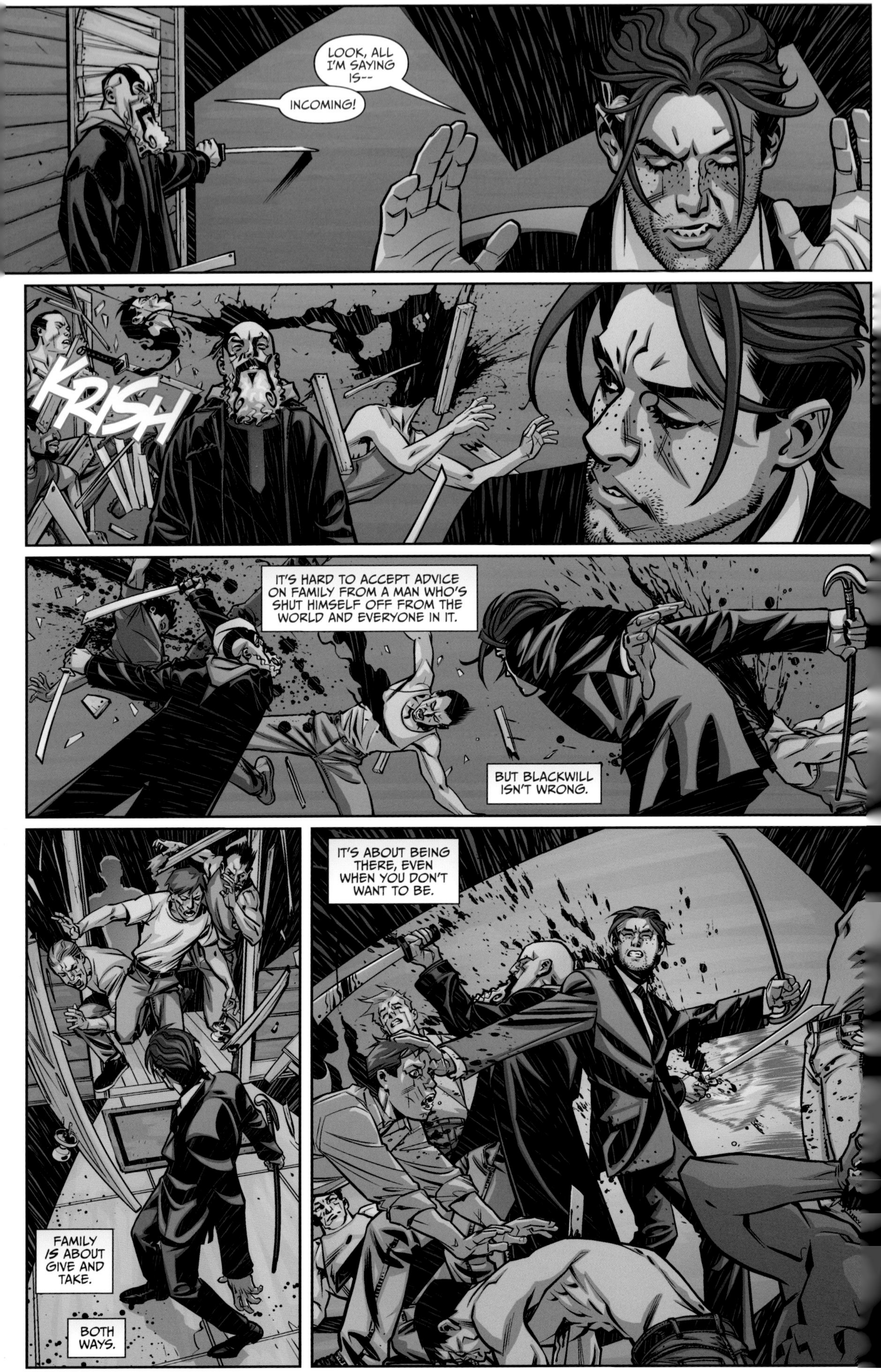

LOOK, ALL I'M SAYING IS--
INCOMING!
KRISH
IT'S HARD TO ACCEPT ADVICE ON FAMILY FROM A MAN WHO'S SHUT HIMSELF OFF FROM THE WORLD AND EVERYONE IN IT.
BUT BLACKWILL ISN'T WRONG.
FAMILY *IS* ABOUT GIVE AND TAKE.
BOTH WAYS.
IT'S ABOUT BEING THERE, EVEN WHEN YOU DON'T WANT TO BE.

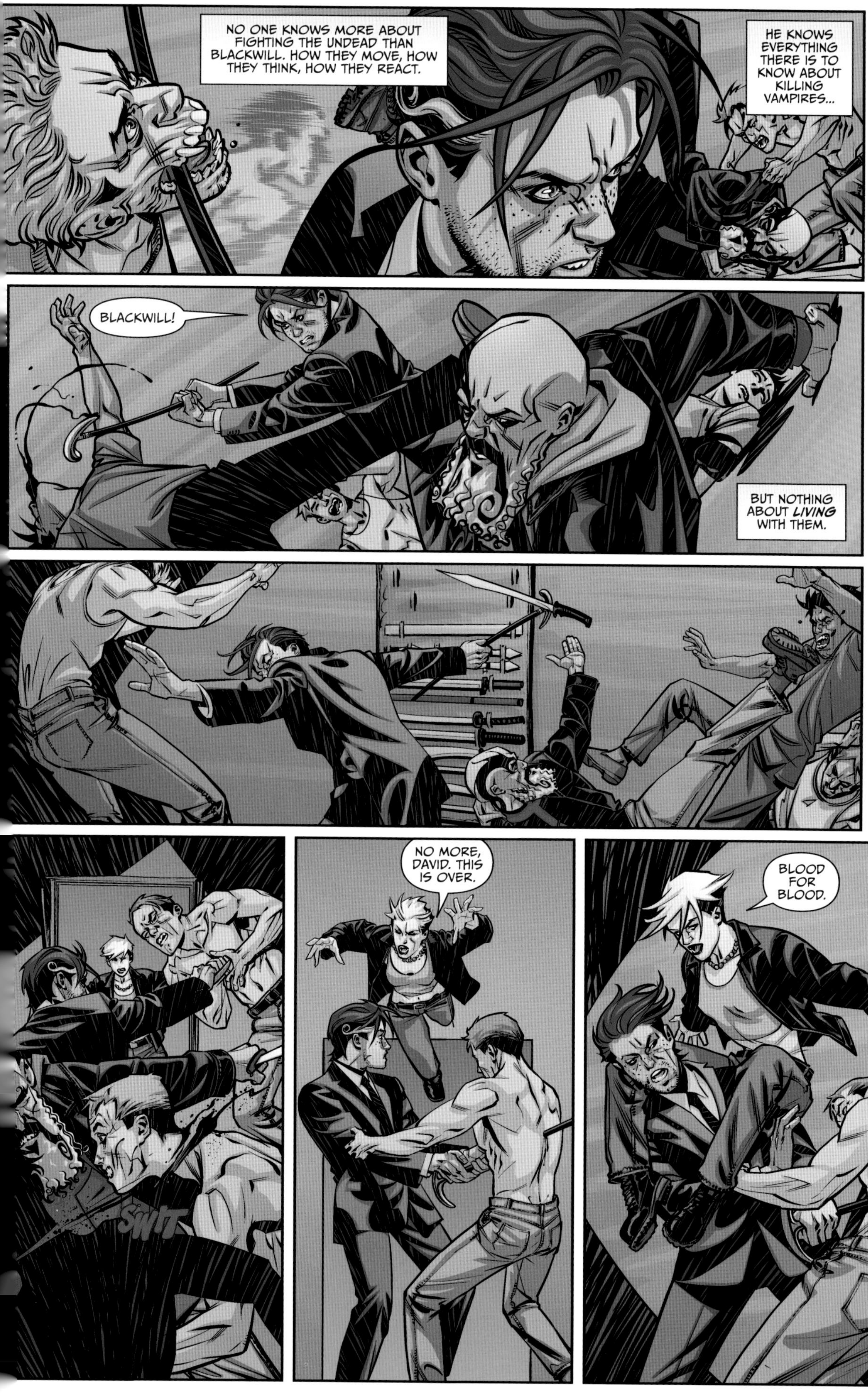
NO ONE KNOWS MORE ABOUT FIGHTING THE UNDEAD THAN BLACKWILL. HOW THEY MOVE, HOW THEY THINK, HOW THEY REACT.
HE KNOWS EVERYTHING THERE IS TO KNOW ABOUT KILLING VAMPIRES...
BLACKWILL!
BUT NOTHING ABOUT *LIVING* WITH THEM.
SWIT
NO MORE, DAVID. THIS IS OVER.
BLOOD FOR BLOOD.

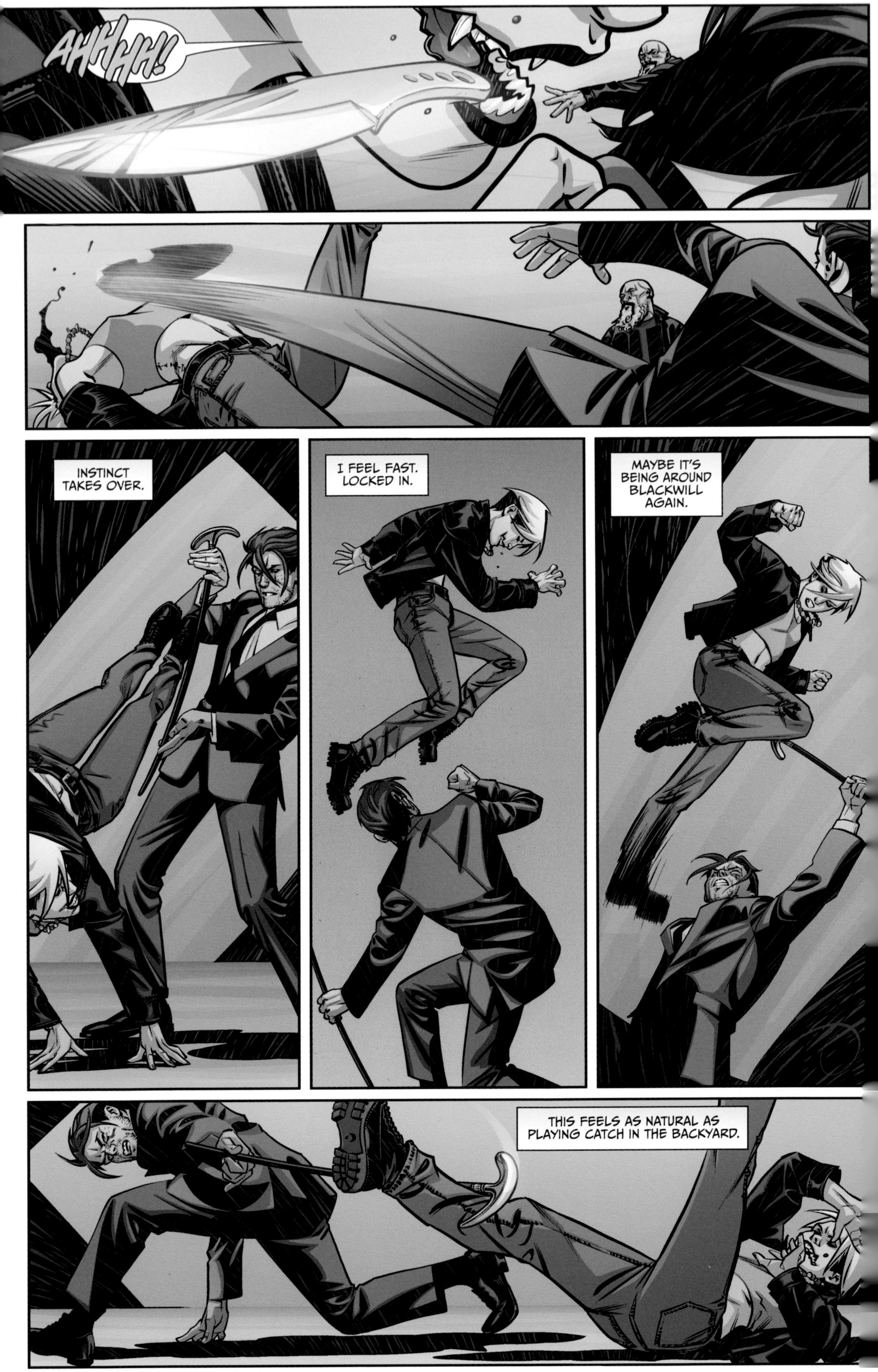
AHHHH!
INSTINCT TAKES OVER.
I FEEL FAST. LOCKED IN.
MAYBE IT'S BEING AROUND BLACKWILL AGAIN.
THIS FEELS AS NATURAL AS PLAYING CATCH IN THE BACKYARD.

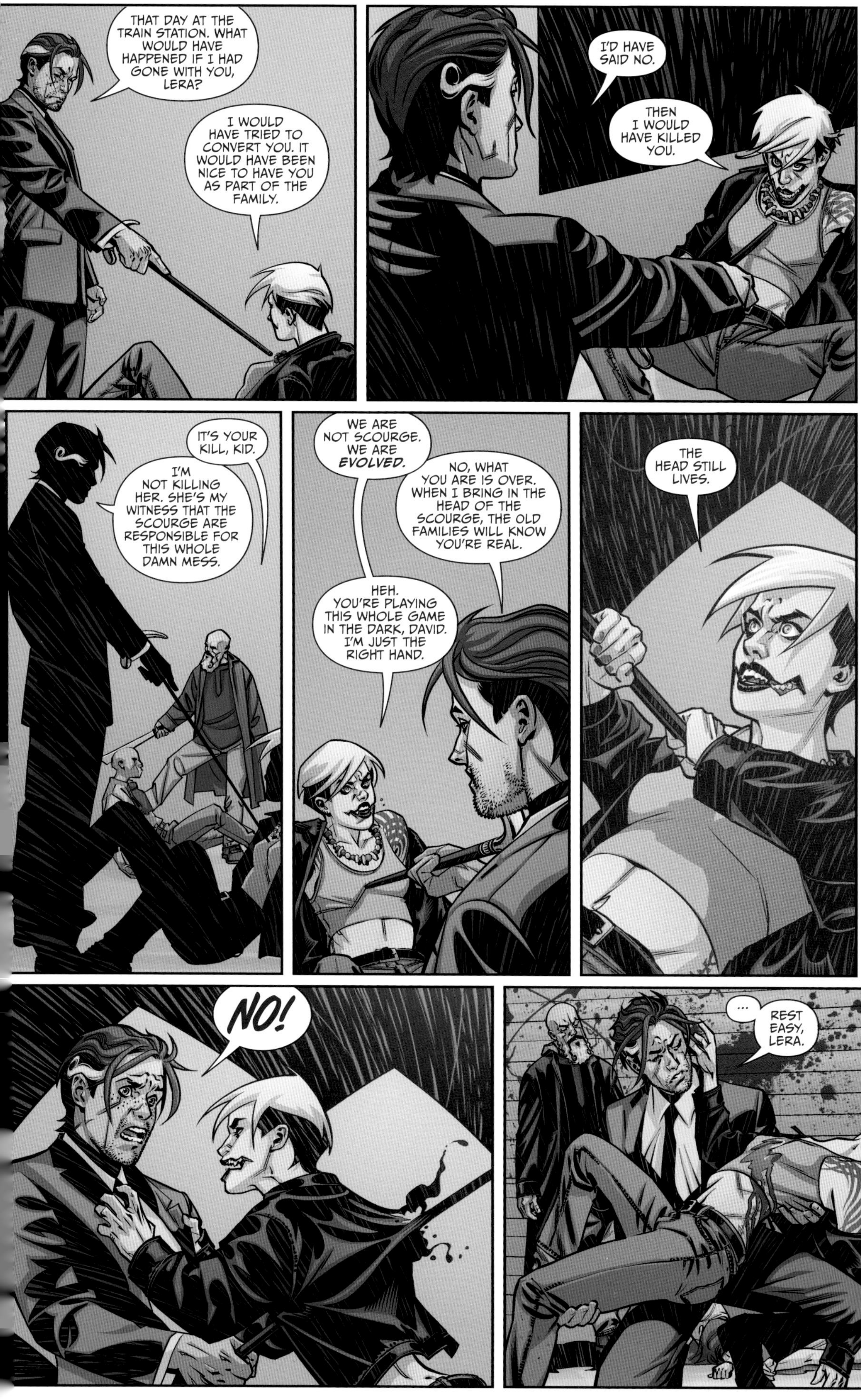
THAT DAY AT THE TRAIN STATION. WHAT WOULD HAVE HAPPENED IF I HAD GONE WITH YOU, LERA?
I WOULD HAVE TRIED TO CONVERT YOU. IT WOULD HAVE BEEN NICE TO HAVE YOU AS PART OF THE FAMILY.
I'D HAVE SAID NO.
THEN I WOULD HAVE KILLED YOU.
IT'S YOUR KILL, KID.
I'M NOT KILLING HER. SHE'S MY WITNESS THAT THE SCOURGE ARE RESPONSIBLE FOR THIS WHOLE DAMN MESS.
WE ARE NOT SCOURGE. WE ARE *EVOLVED.*
NO, WHAT YOU ARE IS OVER. WHEN I BRING IN THE HEAD OF THE SCOURGE, THE OLD FAMILIES WILL KNOW YOU'RE REAL.
HEH. YOU'RE PLAYING THIS WHOLE GAME IN THE DARK, DAVID. I'M JUST THE RIGHT HAND.
THE HEAD STILL LIVES.
NO!
...
REST EASY, LERA.

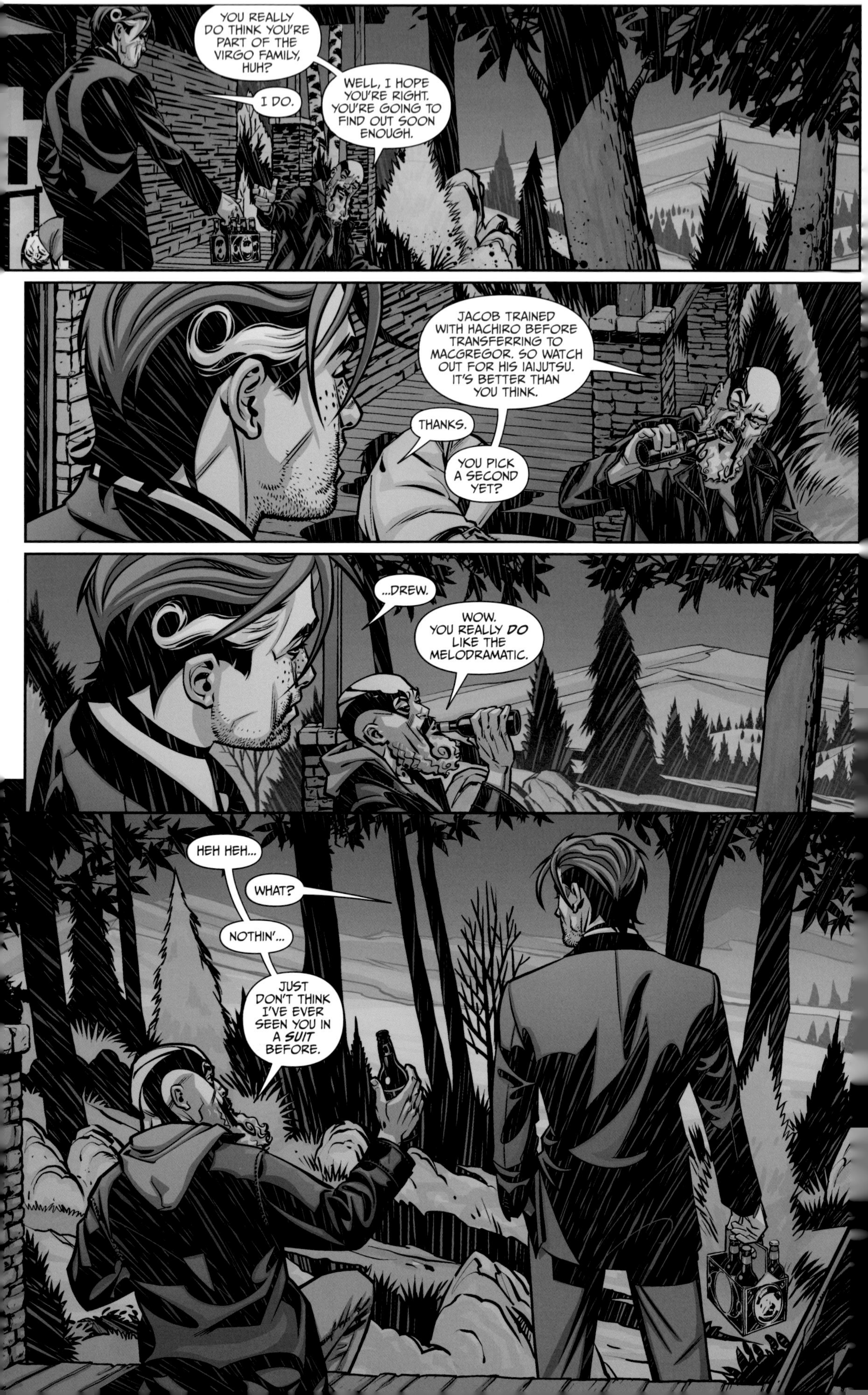
YOU REALLY DO THINK YOU'RE PART OF THE VIRGO FAMILY, HUH?
I DO.
WELL, I HOPE YOU'RE RIGHT. YOU'RE GOING TO FIND OUT SOON ENOUGH.
JACOB TRAINED WITH HACHIRO BEFORE TRANSFERRING TO MACGREGOR. SO WATCH OUT FOR HIS IAIJUTSU. IT'S BETTER THAN YOU THINK.
THANKS.
YOU PICK A SECOND YET?
...DREW.
WOW. YOU REALLY *DO* LIKE THE MELODRAMATIC.
HEH HEH...
WHAT?
NOTHIN'...
JUST DON'T THINK I'VE EVER SEEN YOU IN A *SUIT* BEFORE.

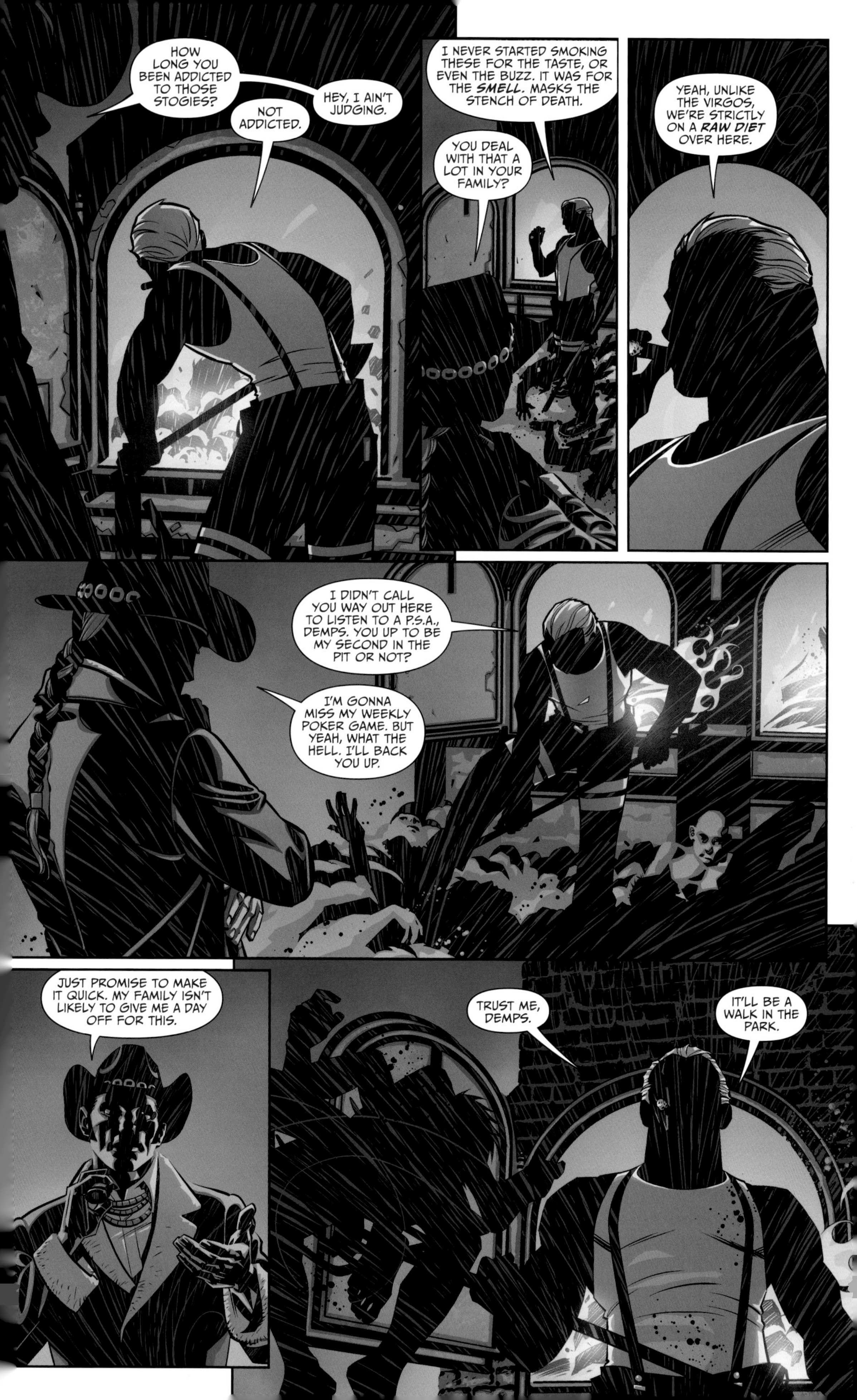
HOW LONG YOU BEEN ADDICTED TO THOSE STOGIES?
NOT ADDICTED.
HEY, I AIN'T JUDGING.
I NEVER STARTED SMOKING THESE FOR THE TASTE, OR EVEN THE BUZZ. IT WAS FOR THE SMELL. MASKS THE STENCH OF DEATH.
YOU DEAL WITH THAT A LOT IN YOUR FAMILY?
YEAH, UNLIKE THE VIRGOS, WE'RE STRICTLY ON A RAW DIET OVER HERE.
I DIDN'T CALL YOU WAY OUT HERE TO LISTEN TO A P.S.A., DEMPS. YOU UP TO BE MY SECOND IN THE PIT OR NOT?
I'M GONNA MISS MY WEEKLY POKER GAME. BUT YEAH, WHAT THE HELL. I'LL BACK YOU UP.
JUST PROMISE TO MAKE IT QUICK. MY FAMILY ISN'T LIKELY TO GIVE ME A DAY OFF FOR THIS.
TRUST ME, DEMPS.
IT'LL BE A WALK IN THE PARK.

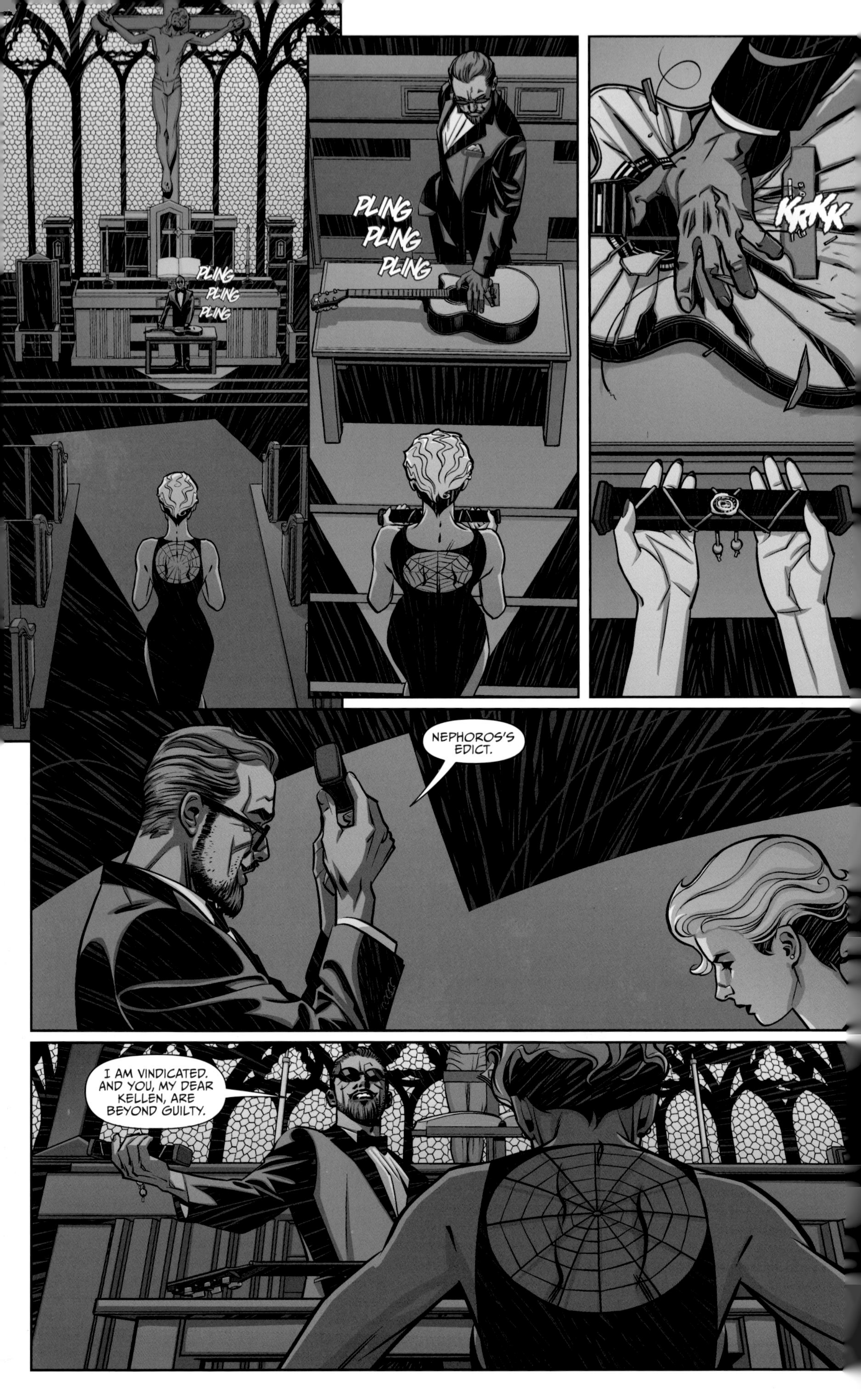
PLING
PLING
PLING
PLING
PLING
PLING
KRKK
NEPHOROS'S EDICT.
I AM VINDICATED. AND YOU, MY DEAR KELLEN, ARE BEYOND GUILTY.

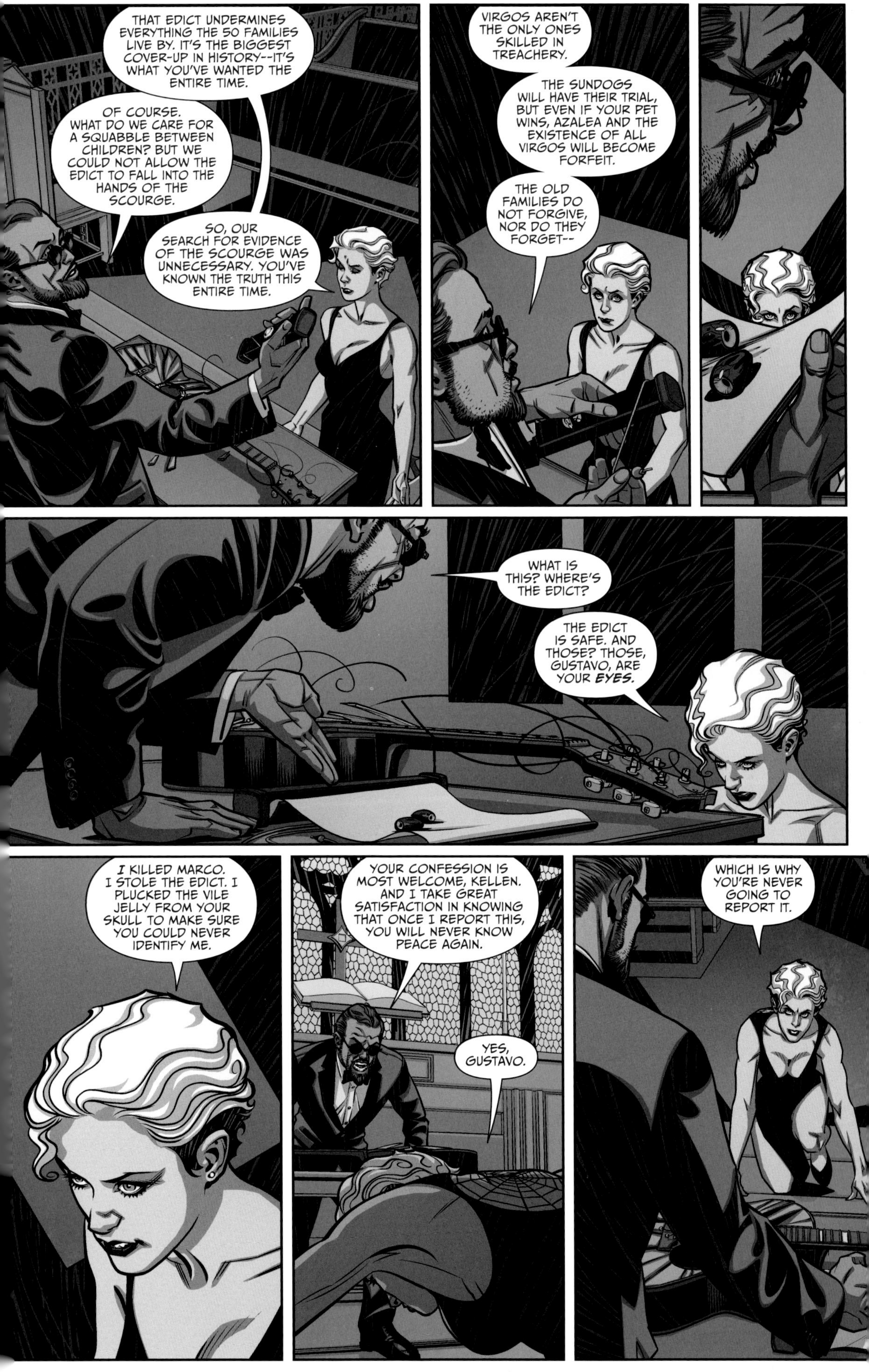
THAT EDICT UNDERMINES EVERYTHING THE 50 FAMILIES LIVE BY. IT'S THE BIGGEST COVER-UP IN HISTORY--IT'S WHAT YOU'VE WANTED THE ENTIRE TIME.
OF COURSE. WHAT DO WE CARE FOR A SQUABBLE BETWEEN CHILDREN? BUT WE COULD NOT ALLOW THE EDICT TO FALL INTO THE HANDS OF THE SCOURGE.
SO, OUR SEARCH FOR EVIDENCE OF THE SCOURGE WAS UNNECESSARY. YOU'VE KNOWN THE TRUTH THIS ENTIRE TIME.
VIRGOS AREN'T THE ONLY ONES SKILLED IN TREACHERY.
THE SUNDOGS WILL HAVE THEIR TRIAL, BUT EVEN IF YOUR PET WINS, AZALEA AND THE EXISTENCE OF ALL VIRGOS WILL BECOME FORFEIT.
THE OLD FAMILIES DO NOT FORGIVE, NOR DO THEY FORGET--
WHAT IS THIS? WHERE'S THE EDICT?
THE EDICT IS SAFE. AND THOSE? THOSE, GUSTAVO, ARE YOUR ***EYES.***
*I* KILLED MARCO. I STOLE THE EDICT. I PLUCKED THE VILE JELLY FROM YOUR SKULL TO MAKE SURE YOU COULD NEVER IDENTIFY ME.
YOUR CONFESSION IS MOST WELCOME, KELLEN. AND I TAKE GREAT SATISFACTION IN KNOWING THAT ONCE I REPORT THIS, YOU WILL NEVER KNOW PEACE AGAIN.
YES, GUSTAVO.
WHICH IS WHY YOU'RE NEVER GOING TO REPORT IT.

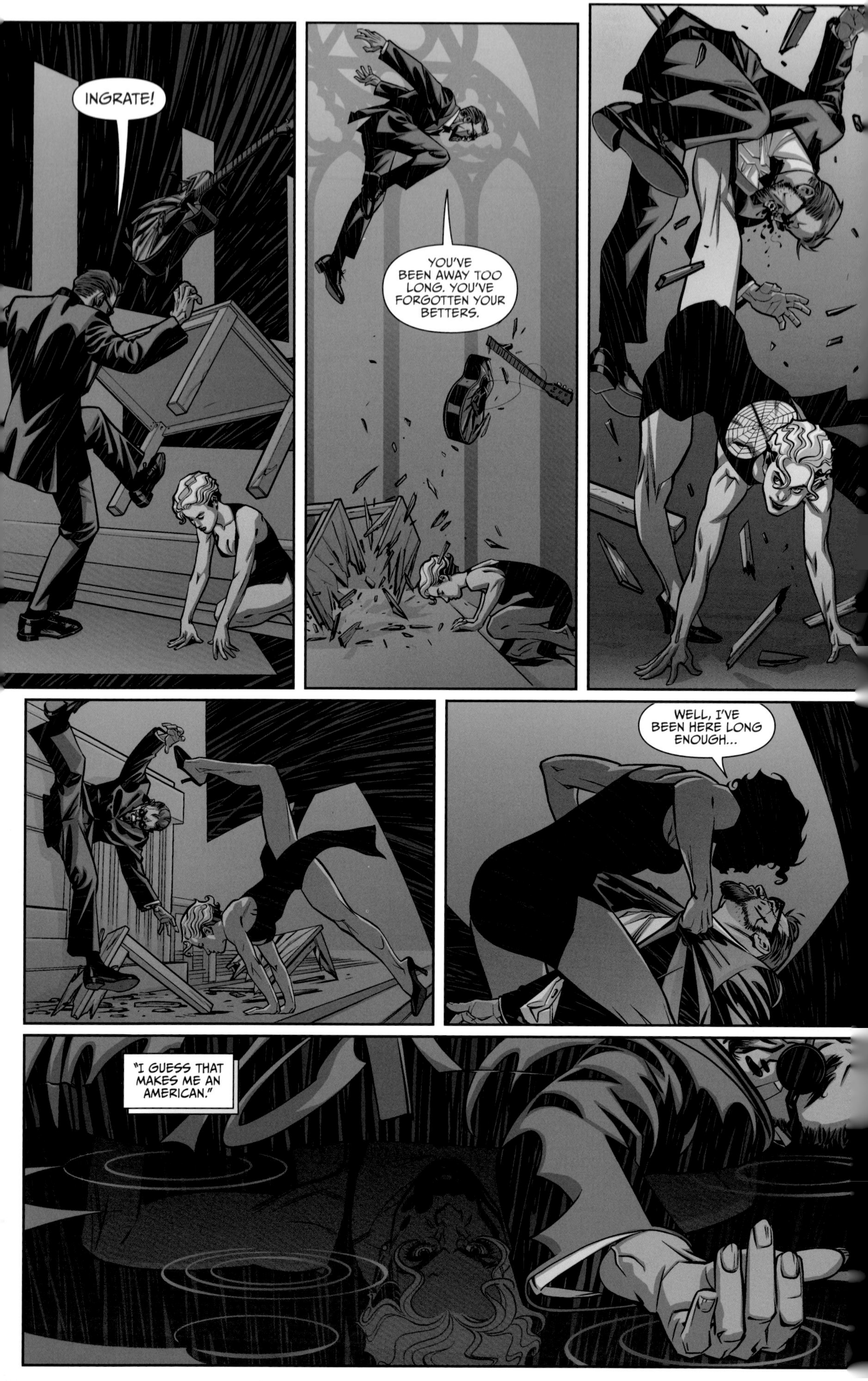
INGRATE!
YOU'VE BEEN AWAY TOO LONG. YOU'VE FORGOTTEN YOUR BETTERS.
WELL, I'VE BEEN HERE LONG ENOUGH...
"I GUESS THAT MAKES ME AN AMERICAN."

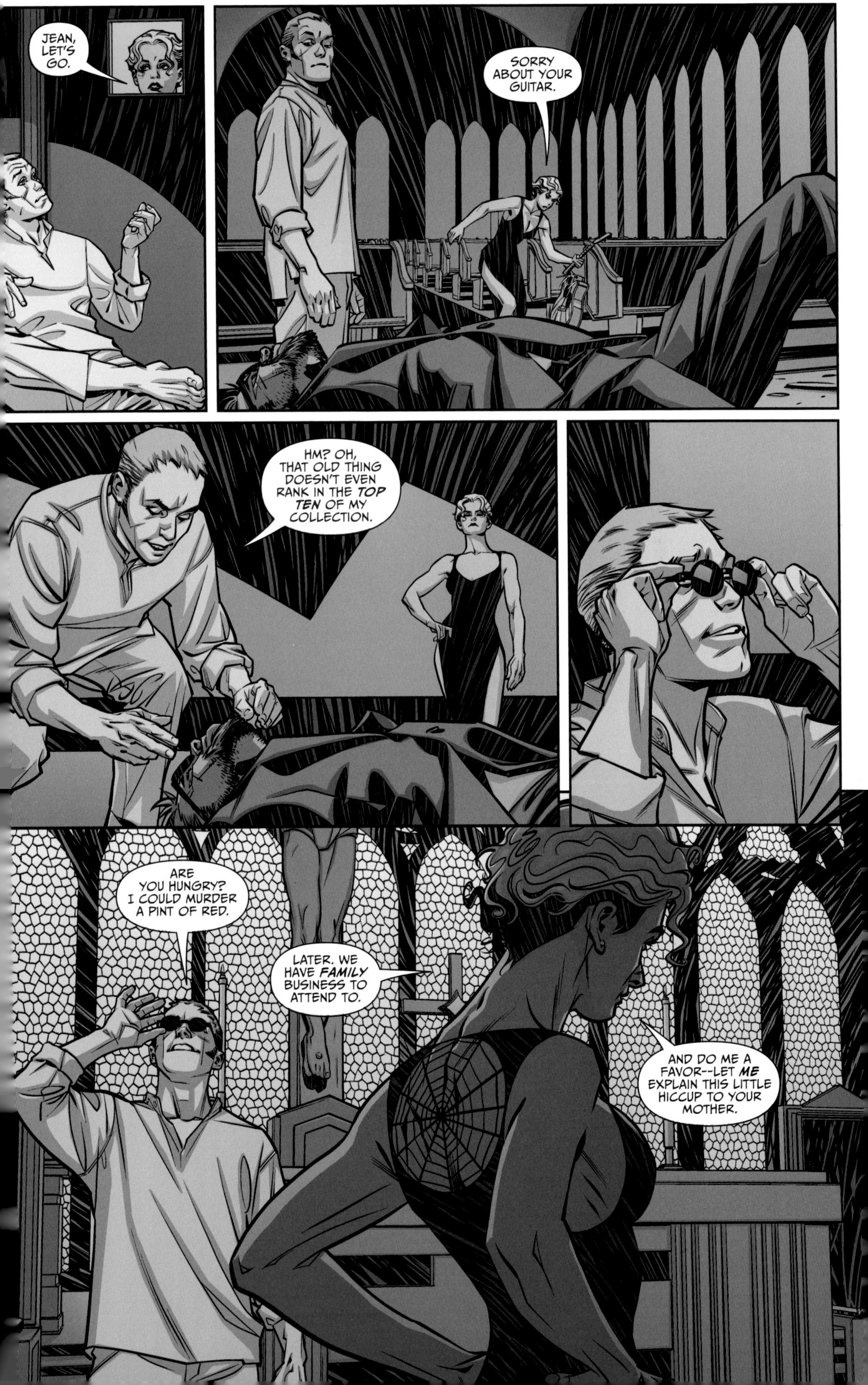
JEAN, LET'S GO.
SORRY ABOUT YOUR GUITAR.
HM? OH, THAT OLD THING DOESN'T EVEN RANK IN THE TOP TEN OF MY COLLECTION.
ARE YOU HUNGRY? I COULD MURDER A PINT OF RED.
LATER. WE HAVE FAMILY BUSINESS TO ATTEND TO.
AND DO ME A FAVOR--LET ME EXPLAIN THIS LITTLE HICCUP TO YOUR MOTHER.

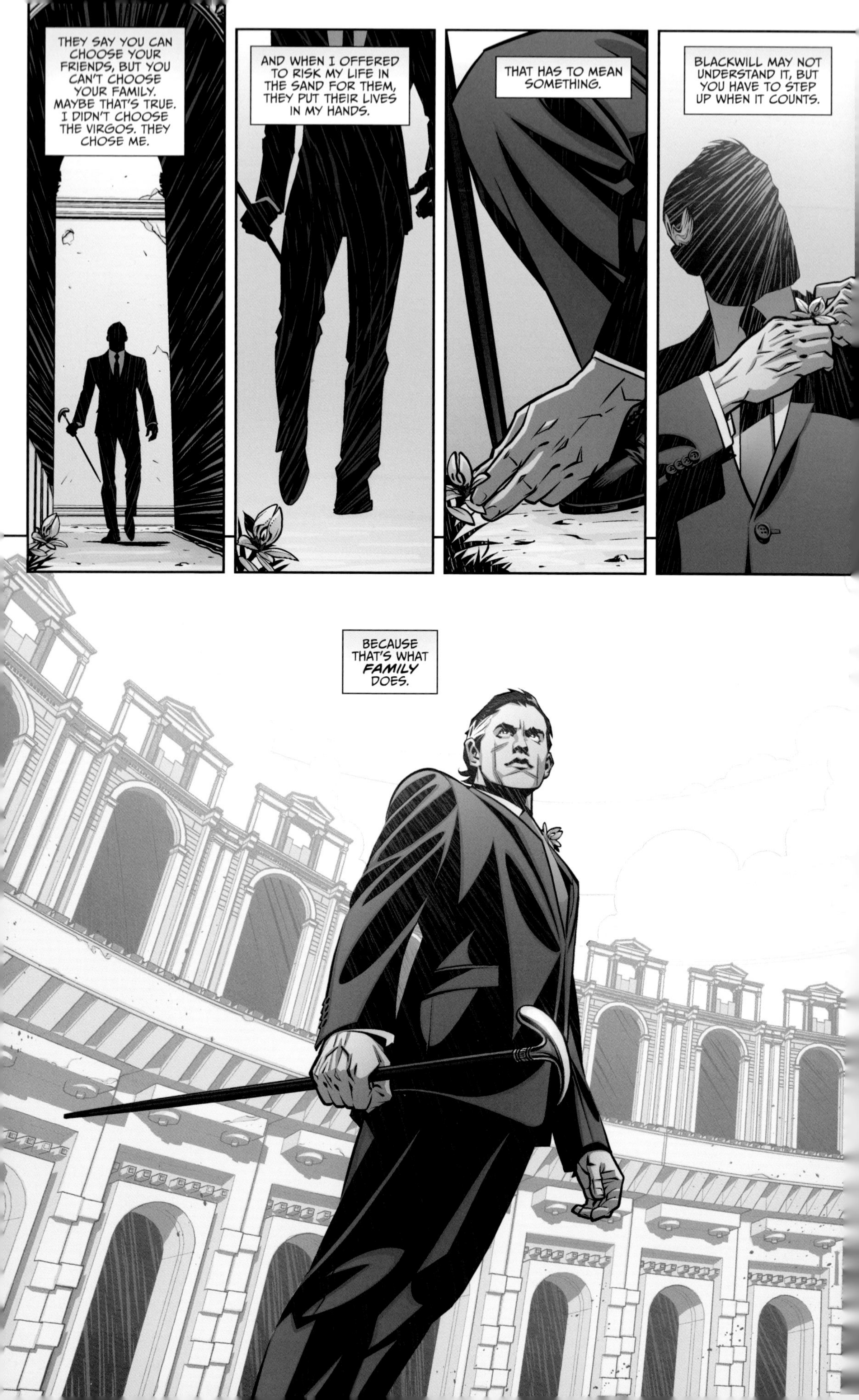
THEY SAY YOU CAN CHOOSE YOUR FRIENDS, BUT YOU CAN'T CHOOSE YOUR FAMILY. MAYBE THAT'S TRUE. I DIDN'T CHOOSE THE VIRGOS. THEY CHOSE ME.
AND WHEN I OFFERED TO RISK MY LIFE IN THE SAND FOR THEM, THEY PUT THEIR LIVES IN MY HANDS.
THAT HAS TO MEAN SOMETHING.
BLACKWILL MAY NOT UNDERSTAND IT, BUT YOU HAVE TO STEP UP WHEN IT COUNTS.
BECAUSE THAT'S WHAT *FAMILY* DOES.

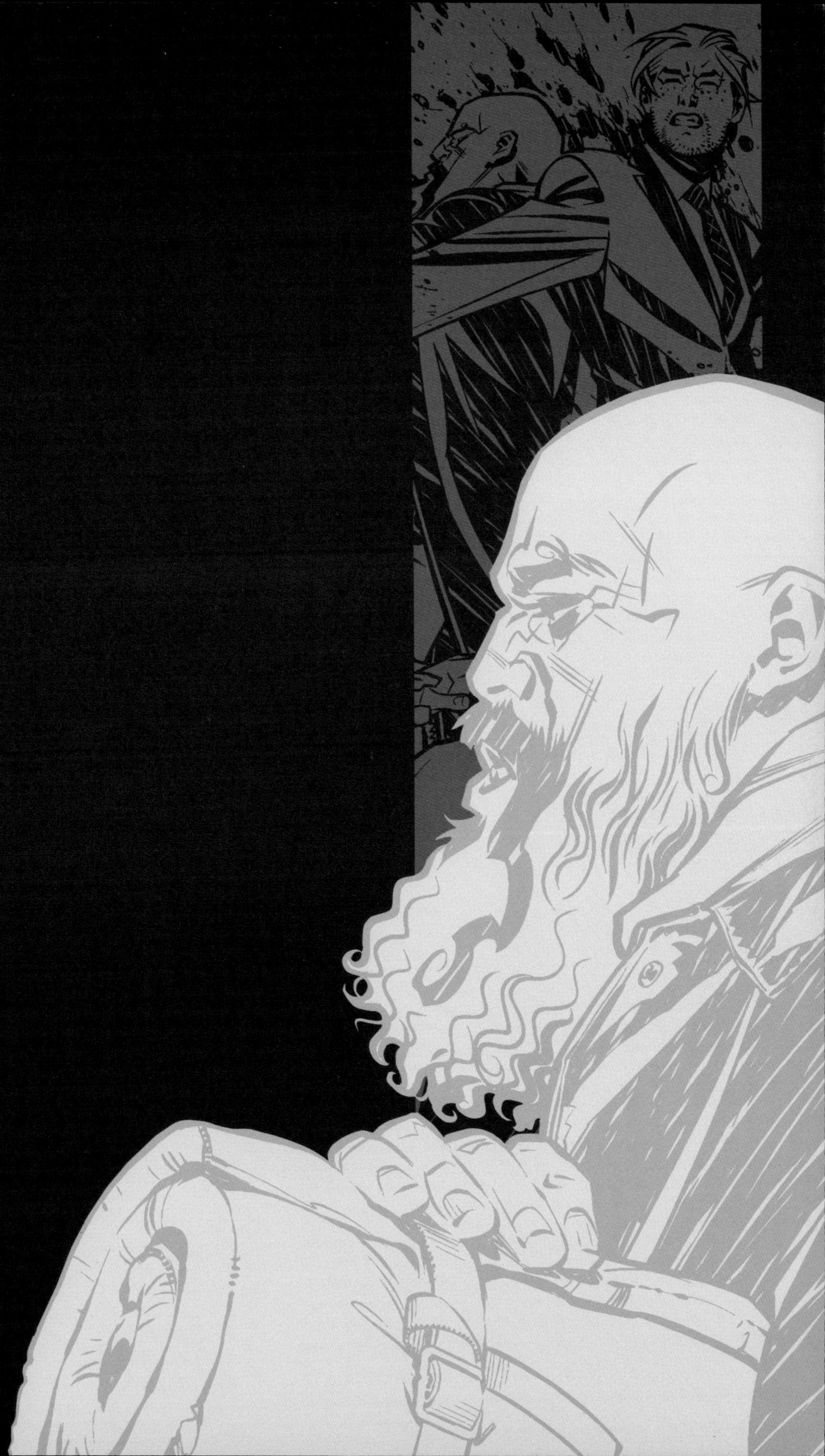

# CHAPTER SEVEN

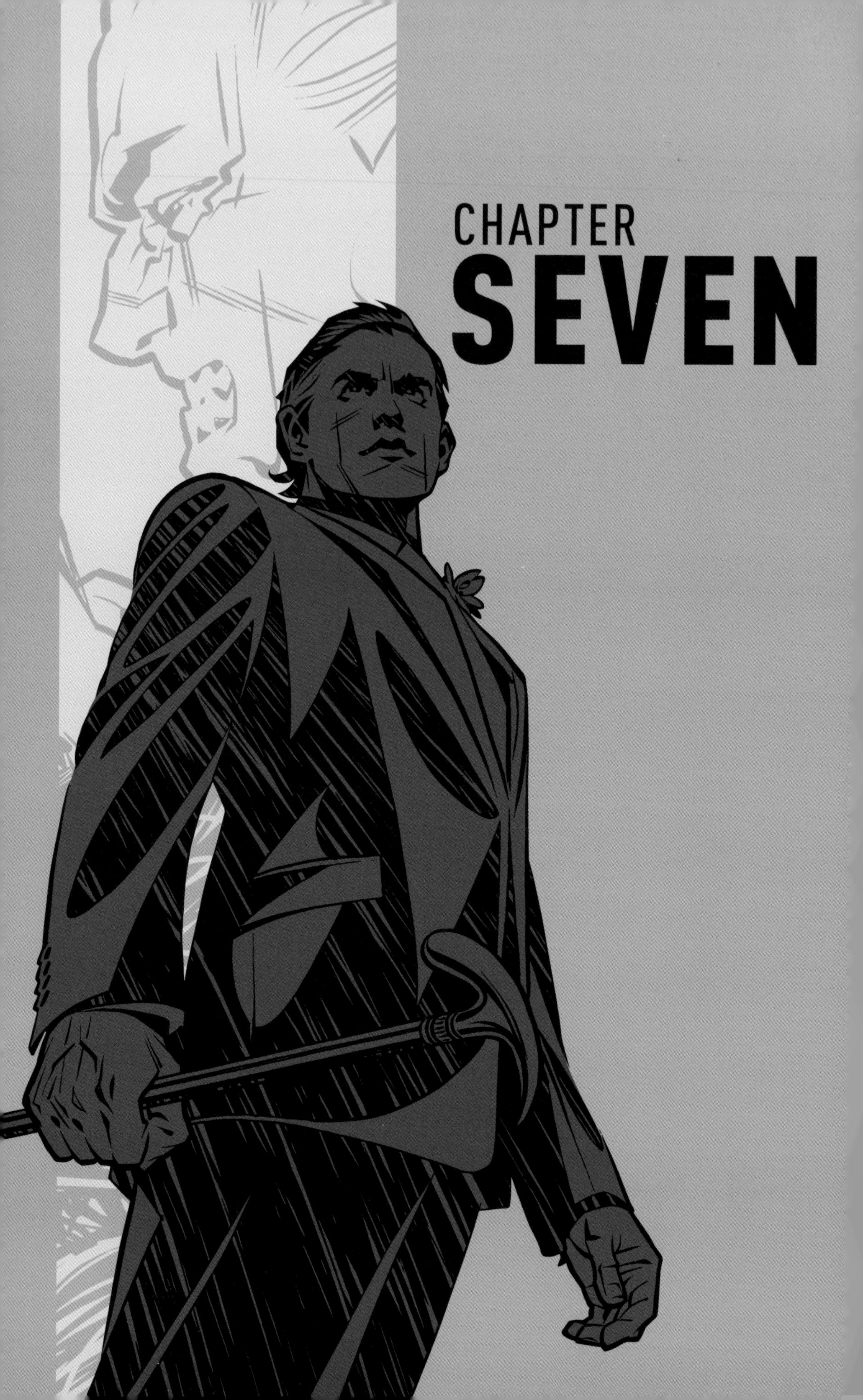

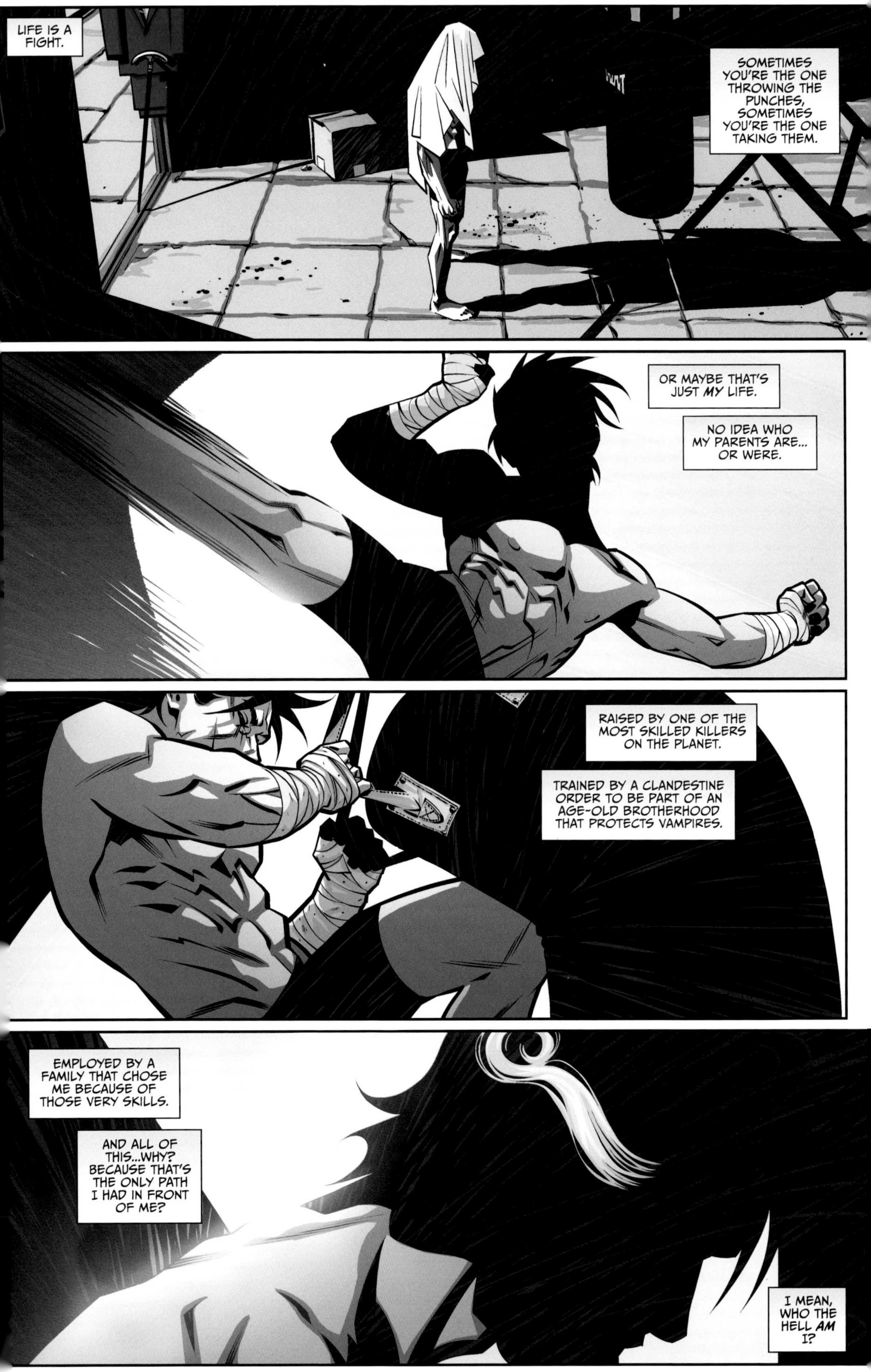
LIFE IS A FIGHT.
SOMETIMES YOU'RE THE ONE THROWING THE PUNCHES, SOMETIMES YOU'RE THE ONE TAKING THEM.
OR MAYBE THAT'S JUST *MY* LIFE.
NO IDEA WHO MY PARENTS ARE... OR WERE.
RAISED BY ONE OF THE MOST SKILLED KILLERS ON THE PLANET.
TRAINED BY A CLANDESTINE ORDER TO BE PART OF AN AGE-OLD BROTHERHOOD THAT PROTECTS VAMPIRES.
EMPLOYED BY A FAMILY THAT CHOSE ME BECAUSE OF THOSE VERY SKILLS.
AND ALL OF THIS...WHY? BECAUSE THAT'S THE ONLY PATH I HAD IN FRONT OF ME?
I MEAN, WHO THE HELL *AM* I?

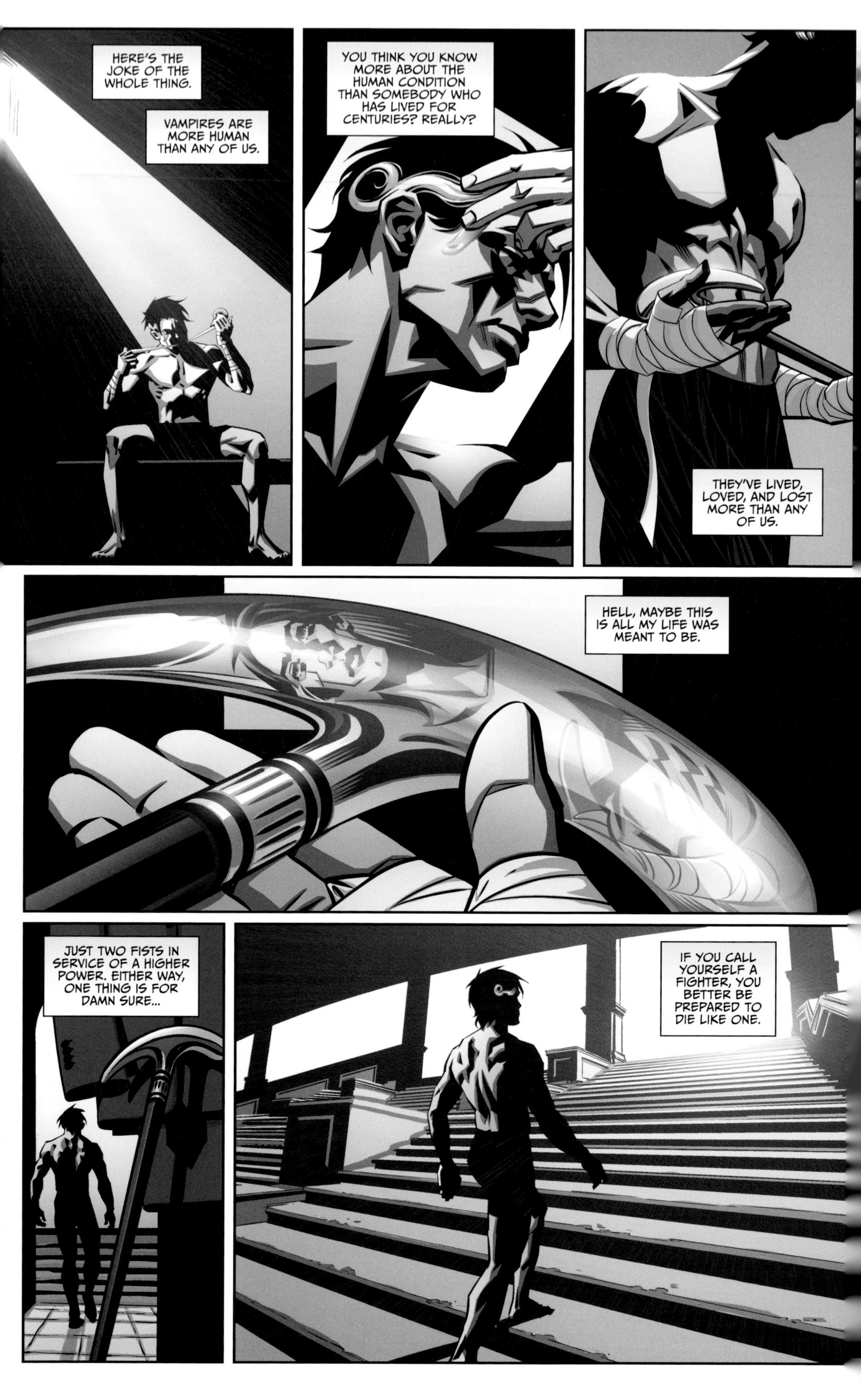
HERE'S THE JOKE OF THE WHOLE THING.
VAMPIRES ARE MORE HUMAN THAN ANY OF US.
YOU THINK YOU KNOW MORE ABOUT THE HUMAN CONDITION THAN SOMEBODY WHO HAS LIVED FOR CENTURIES? REALLY?
THEY'VE LIVED, LOVED, AND LOST MORE THAN ANY OF US.
HELL, MAYBE THIS IS ALL MY LIFE WAS MEANT TO BE.
JUST TWO FISTS IN SERVICE OF A HIGHER POWER. EITHER WAY, ONE THING IS FOR DAMN SURE...
IF YOU CALL YOURSELF A FIGHTER, YOU BETTER BE PREPARED TO DIE LIKE ONE.

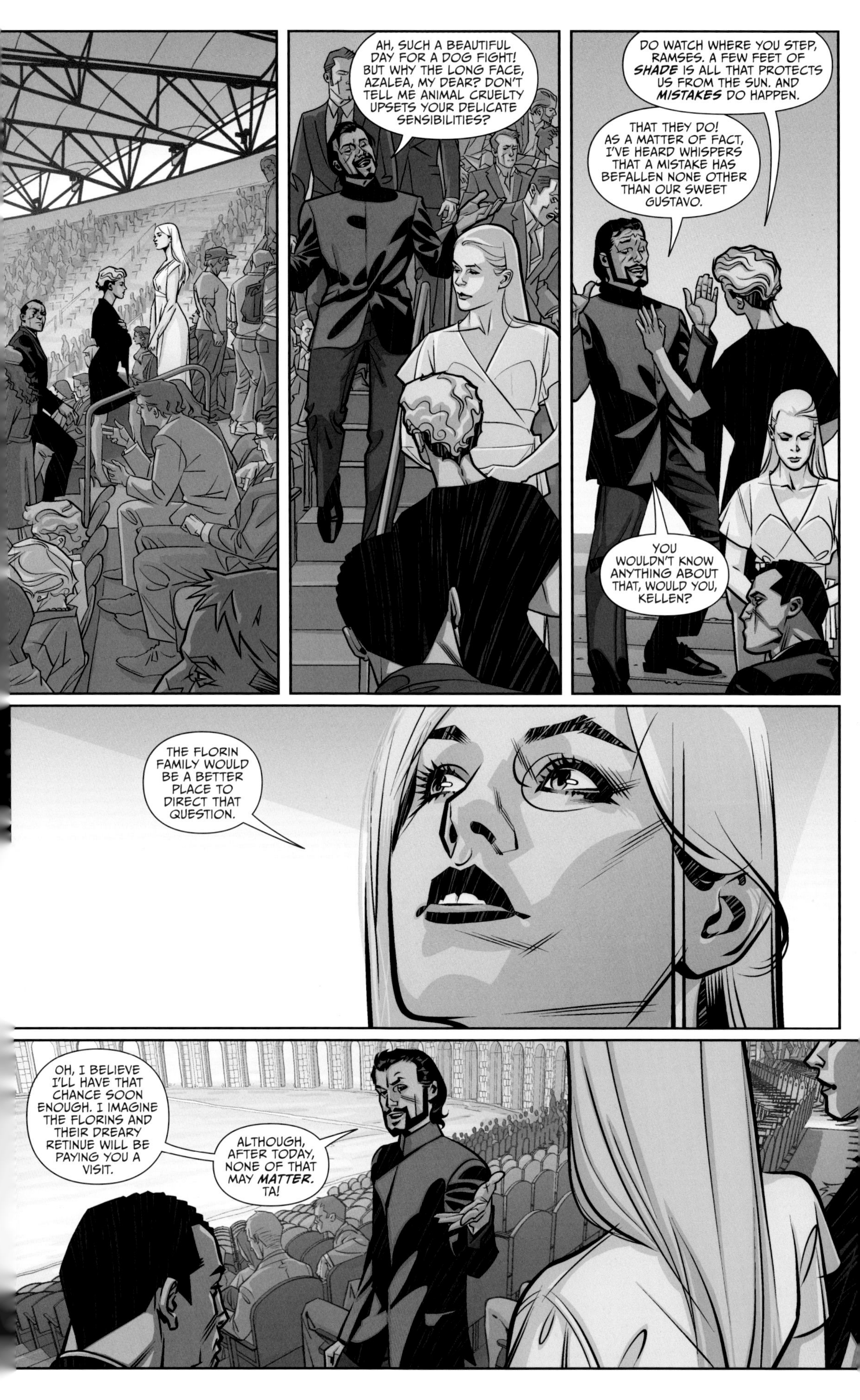
AH, SUCH A BEAUTIFUL DAY FOR A DOG FIGHT! BUT WHY THE LONG FACE, AZALEA, MY DEAR? DON'T TELL ME ANIMAL CRUELTY UPSETS YOUR DELICATE SENSIBILITIES?
DO WATCH WHERE YOU STEP, RAMSES. A FEW FEET OF SHADE IS ALL THAT PROTECTS US FROM THE SUN. AND MISTAKES DO HAPPEN.
THAT THEY DO! AS A MATTER OF FACT, I'VE HEARD WHISPERS THAT A MISTAKE HAS BEFALLEN NONE OTHER THAN OUR SWEET GUSTAVO.
YOU WOULDN'T KNOW ANYTHING ABOUT THAT, WOULD YOU, KELLEN?
THE FLORIN FAMILY WOULD BE A BETTER PLACE TO DIRECT THAT QUESTION.
OH, I BELIEVE I'LL HAVE THAT CHANCE SOON ENOUGH. I IMAGINE THE FLORINS AND THEIR DREARY RETINUE WILL BE PAYING YOU A VISIT.
ALTHOUGH, AFTER TODAY, NONE OF THAT MAY MATTER. TA!

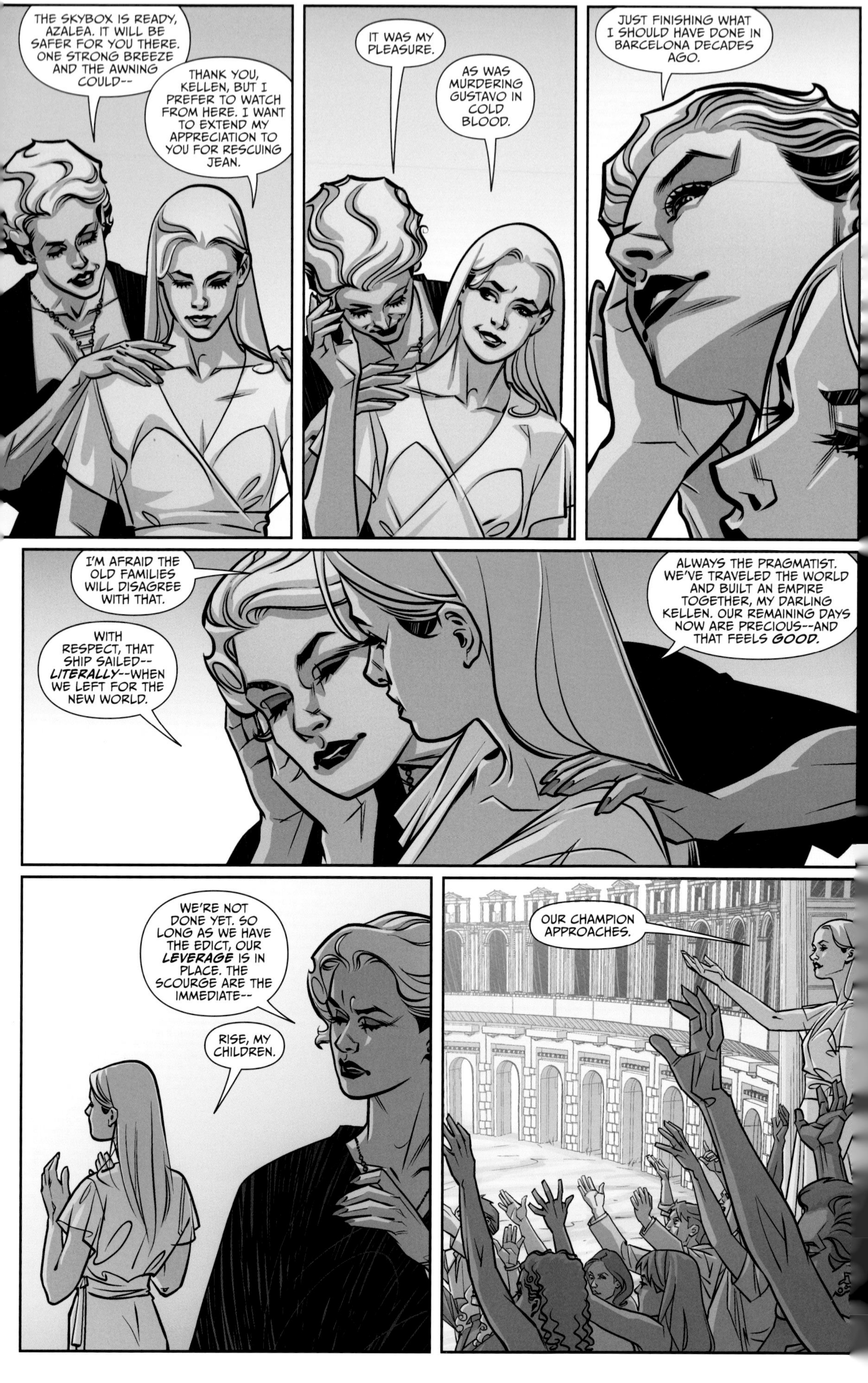
THE SKYBOX IS READY, AZALEA. IT WILL BE SAFER FOR YOU THERE. ONE STRONG BREEZE AND THE AWNING COULD--
THANK YOU, KELLEN, BUT I PREFER TO WATCH FROM HERE. I WANT TO EXTEND MY APPRECIATION TO YOU FOR RESCUING JEAN.
IT WAS MY PLEASURE.
AS WAS MURDERING GUSTAVO IN COLD BLOOD.
JUST FINISHING WHAT I SHOULD HAVE DONE IN BARCELONA DECADES AGO.
I'M AFRAID THE OLD FAMILIES WILL DISAGREE WITH THAT.
WITH RESPECT, THAT SHIP SAILED--*LITERALLY*--WHEN WE LEFT FOR THE NEW WORLD.
ALWAYS THE PRAGMATIST. WE'VE TRAVELED THE WORLD AND BUILT AN EMPIRE TOGETHER, MY DARLING KELLEN. OUR REMAINING DAYS NOW ARE PRECIOUS--AND THAT FEELS *GOOD.*
WE'RE NOT DONE YET. SO LONG AS WE HAVE THE EDICT, OUR *LEVERAGE* IS IN PLACE. THE SCOURGE ARE THE IMMEDIATE--
RISE, MY CHILDREN.
OUR CHAMPION APPROACHES.

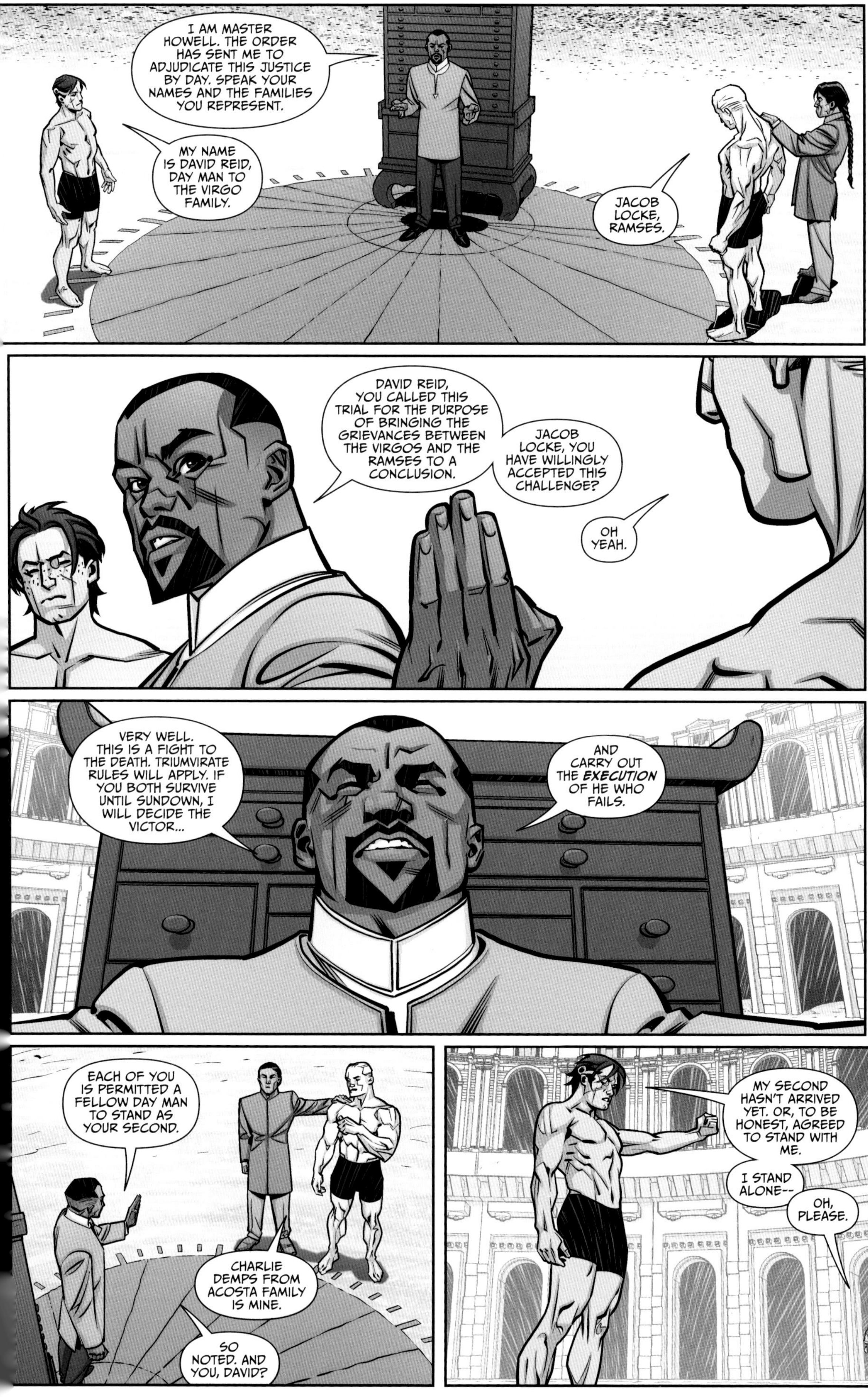
I AM MASTER HOWELL. THE ORDER HAS SENT ME TO ADJUDICATE THIS JUSTICE BY DAY. SPEAK YOUR NAMES AND THE FAMILIES YOU REPRESENT.
MY NAME IS DAVID REID, DAY MAN TO THE VIRGO FAMILY.
JACOB LOCKE, RAMSES.
DAVID REID, YOU CALLED THIS TRIAL FOR THE PURPOSE OF BRINGING THE GRIEVANCES BETWEEN THE VIRGOS AND THE RAMSES TO A CONCLUSION.
JACOB LOCKE, YOU HAVE WILLINGLY ACCEPTED THIS CHALLENGE?
OH YEAH.
VERY WELL. THIS IS A FIGHT TO THE DEATH. TRIUMVIRATE RULES WILL APPLY. IF YOU BOTH SURVIVE UNTIL SUNDOWN, I WILL DECIDE THE VICTOR...
AND CARRY OUT THE ***EXECUTION*** OF HE WHO FAILS.
EACH OF YOU IS PERMITTED A FELLOW DAY MAN TO STAND AS YOUR SECOND.
CHARLIE DEMPS FROM ACOSTA FAMILY IS MINE.
SO NOTED. AND YOU, DAVID?
MY SECOND HASN'T ARRIVED YET. OR, TO BE HONEST, AGREED TO STAND WITH ME.
I STAND ALONE--
OH, PLEASE.

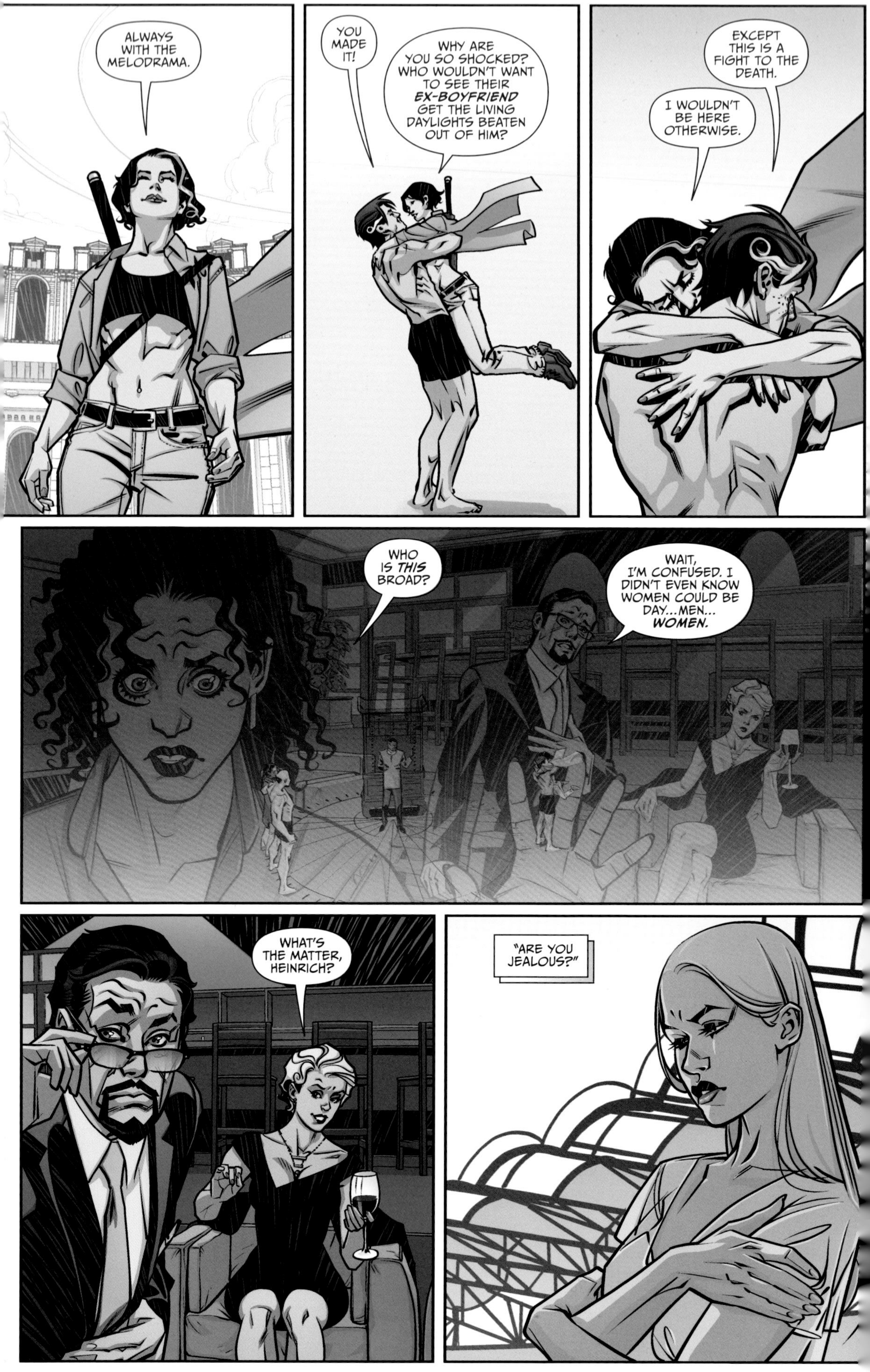
ALWAYS WITH THE MELODRAMA.
YOU MADE IT!
WHY ARE YOU SO SHOCKED? WHO WOULDN'T WANT TO SEE THEIR EX-BOYFRIEND GET THE LIVING DAYLIGHTS BEATEN OUT OF HIM?
EXCEPT THIS IS A FIGHT TO THE DEATH.
I WOULDN'T BE HERE OTHERWISE.
WHO IS THIS BROAD?
WAIT, I'M CONFUSED. I DIDN'T EVEN KNOW WOMEN COULD BE DAY...MEN... WOMEN.
WHAT'S THE MATTER, HEINRICH?
"ARE YOU JEALOUS?"

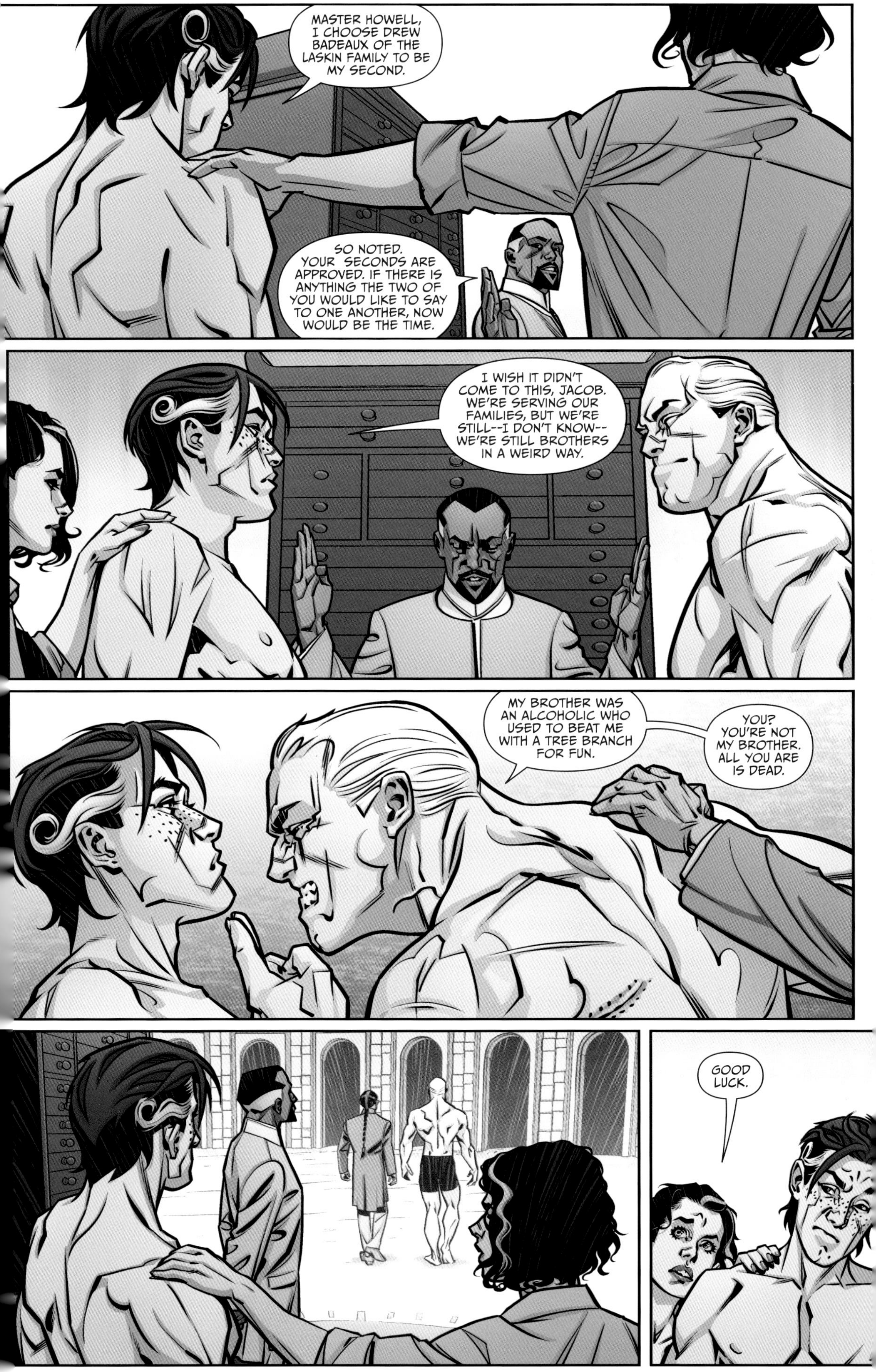
MASTER HOWELL, I CHOOSE DREW BADEAUX OF THE LASKIN FAMILY TO BE MY SECOND.
SO NOTED. YOUR SECONDS ARE APPROVED. IF THERE IS ANYTHING THE TWO OF YOU WOULD LIKE TO SAY TO ONE ANOTHER, NOW WOULD BE THE TIME.
I WISH IT DIDN'T COME TO THIS, JACOB. WE'RE SERVING OUR FAMILIES, BUT WE'RE STILL--I DON'T KNOW--WE'RE STILL BROTHERS IN A WEIRD WAY.
MY BROTHER WAS AN ALCOHOLIC WHO USED TO BEAT ME WITH A TREE BRANCH FOR FUN.
YOU? YOU'RE NOT MY BROTHER. ALL YOU ARE IS DEAD.
GOOD LUCK.

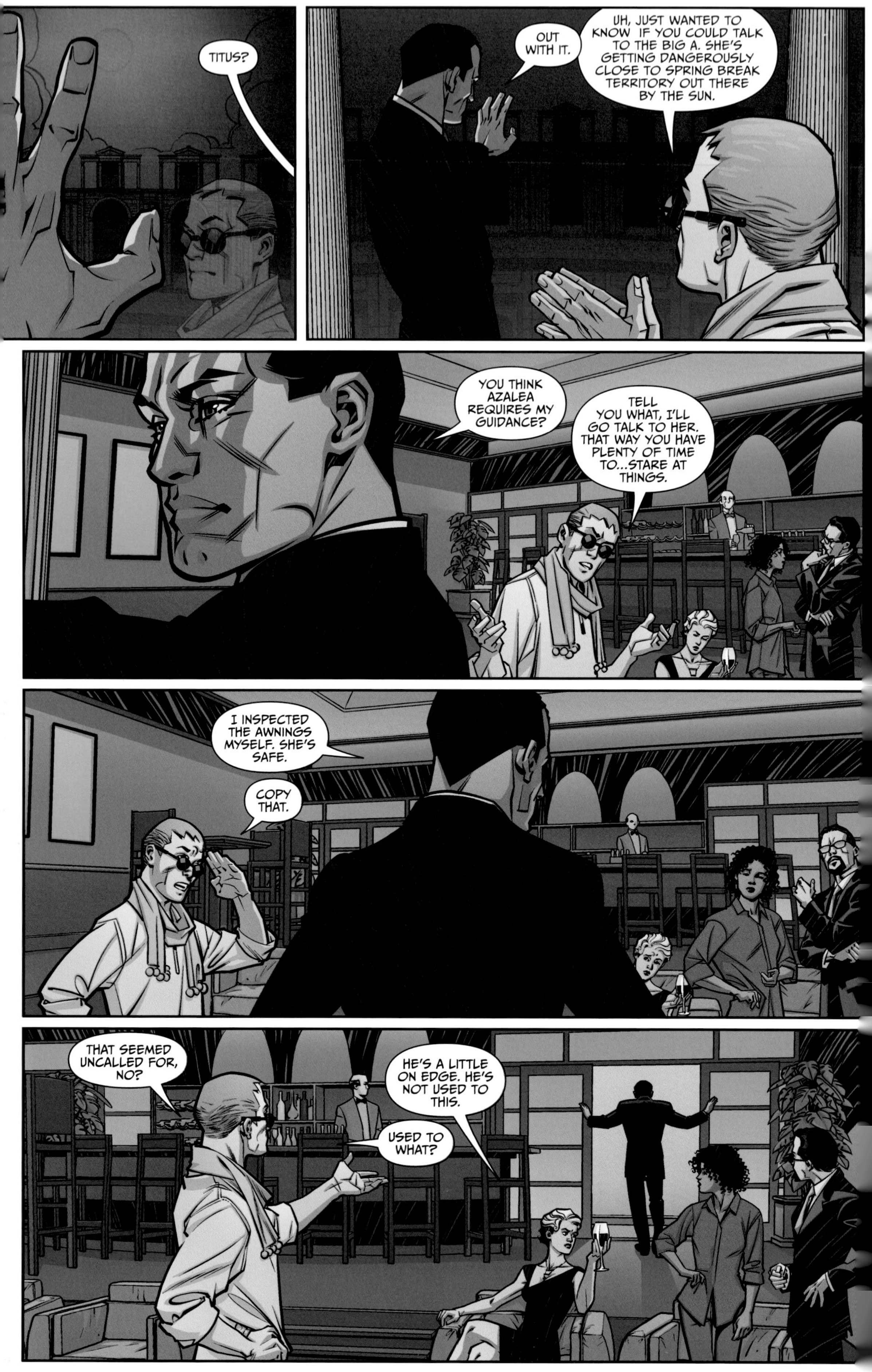
TITUS?
OUT WITH IT.
UH, JUST WANTED TO KNOW IF YOU COULD TALK TO THE BIG A. SHE'S GETTING DANGEROUSLY CLOSE TO SPRING BREAK TERRITORY OUT THERE BY THE SUN.
YOU THINK AZALEA REQUIRES MY GUIDANCE?
TELL YOU WHAT, I'LL GO TALK TO HER. THAT WAY YOU HAVE PLENTY OF TIME TO...STARE AT THINGS.
I INSPECTED THE AWNINGS MYSELF. SHE'S SAFE.
COPY THAT.
THAT SEEMED UNCALLED FOR, NO?
HE'S A LITTLE ON EDGE. HE'S NOT USED TO THIS.
USED TO WHAT?

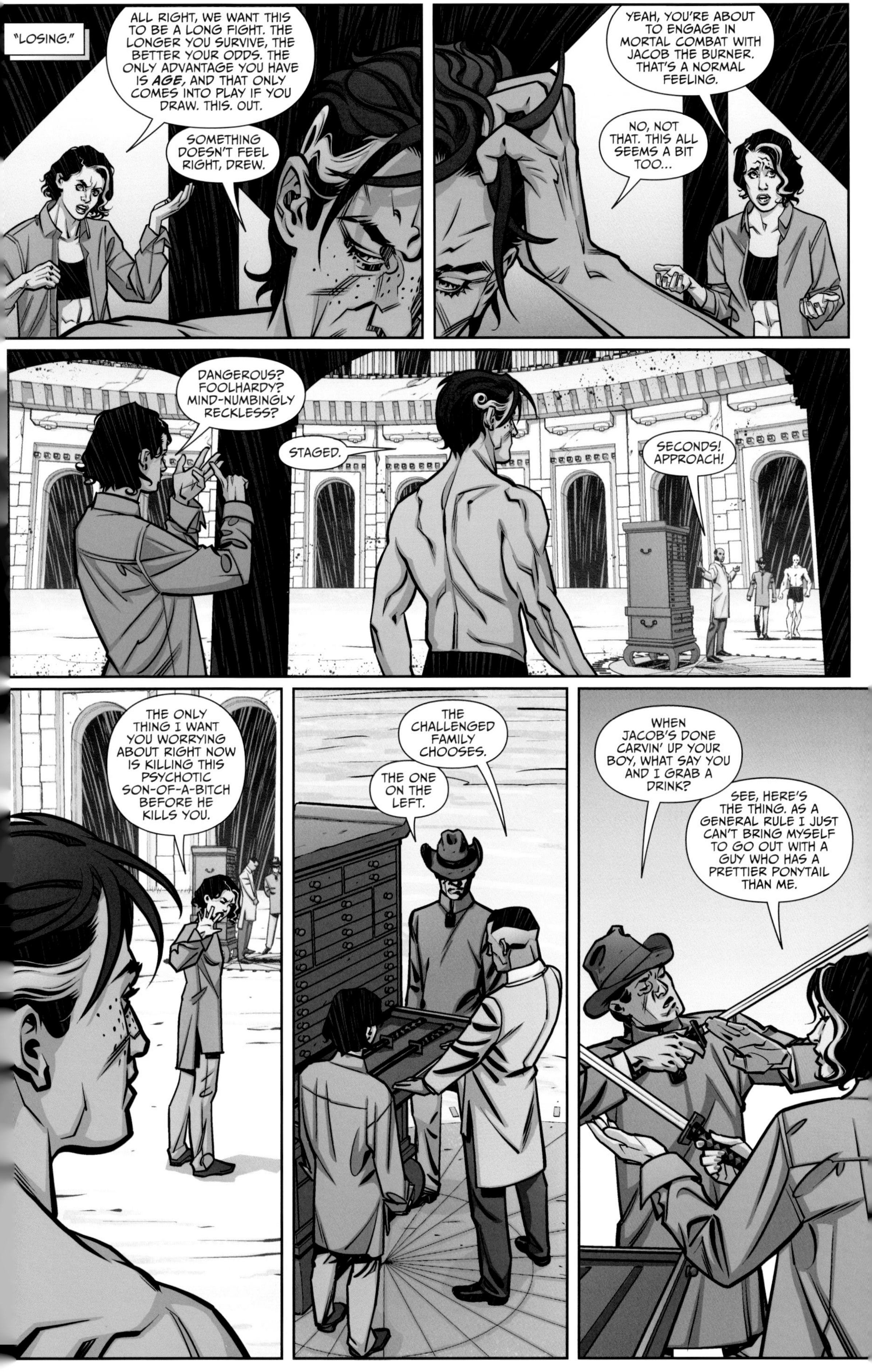
"LOSING."
ALL RIGHT, WE WANT THIS TO BE A LONG FIGHT. THE LONGER YOU SURVIVE, THE BETTER YOUR ODDS. THE ONLY ADVANTAGE YOU HAVE IS AGE, AND THAT ONLY COMES INTO PLAY IF YOU DRAW. THIS. OUT.
SOMETHING DOESN'T FEEL RIGHT, DREW.
YEAH, YOU'RE ABOUT TO ENGAGE IN MORTAL COMBAT WITH JACOB THE BURNER. THAT'S A NORMAL FEELING.
NO, NOT THAT. THIS ALL SEEMS A BIT TOO...
DANGEROUS? FOOLHARDY? MIND-NUMBINGLY RECKLESS?
STAGED.
SECONDS! APPROACH!
THE ONLY THING I WANT YOU WORRYING ABOUT RIGHT NOW IS KILLING THIS PSYCHOTIC SON-OF-A-BITCH BEFORE HE KILLS YOU.
THE CHALLENGED FAMILY CHOOSES.
THE ONE ON THE LEFT.
WHEN JACOB'S DONE CARVIN' UP YOUR BOY, WHAT SAY YOU AND I GRAB A DRINK?
SEE, HERE'S THE THING. AS A GENERAL RULE I JUST CAN'T BRING MYSELF TO GO OUT WITH A GUY WHO HAS A PRETTIER PONYTAIL THAN ME.

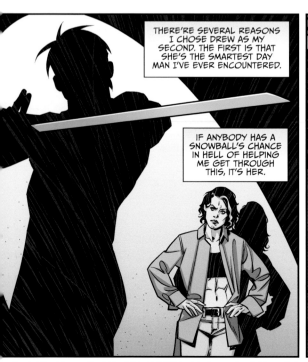

THERE'RE SEVERAL REASONS I CHOSE DREW AS MY SECOND. THE FIRST IS THAT SHE'S THE SMARTEST DAY MAN I'VE EVER ENCOUNTERED.

IF ANYBODY HAS A SNOWBALL'S CHANCE IN HELL OF HELPING ME GET THROUGH THIS, IT'S HER.

BUT THE BIGGEST REASON IS I DON'T WANT TO DIE ALONE.

YES, THE VIRGOS ARE MY FAMILY. AND I EVEN CONSIDER CASEY A TRUE FRIEND.

BUT DREW IS SOMEONE I CHOSE TO BE A PART OF MY LIFE. A PARTNER. AN EQUAL.

AND SHE WANTED ME IN HER LIFE BECAUSE OF WHO I WAS...

NOT WHAT I COULD DO FOR HER.

IF I'M GOING TO DIE IN THE SAND TODAY, I WANT TO HAVE AT LEAST ONE PERSON HERE WHO WILL MOURN ME AS A MAN FIRST--NOT A DAY MAN.

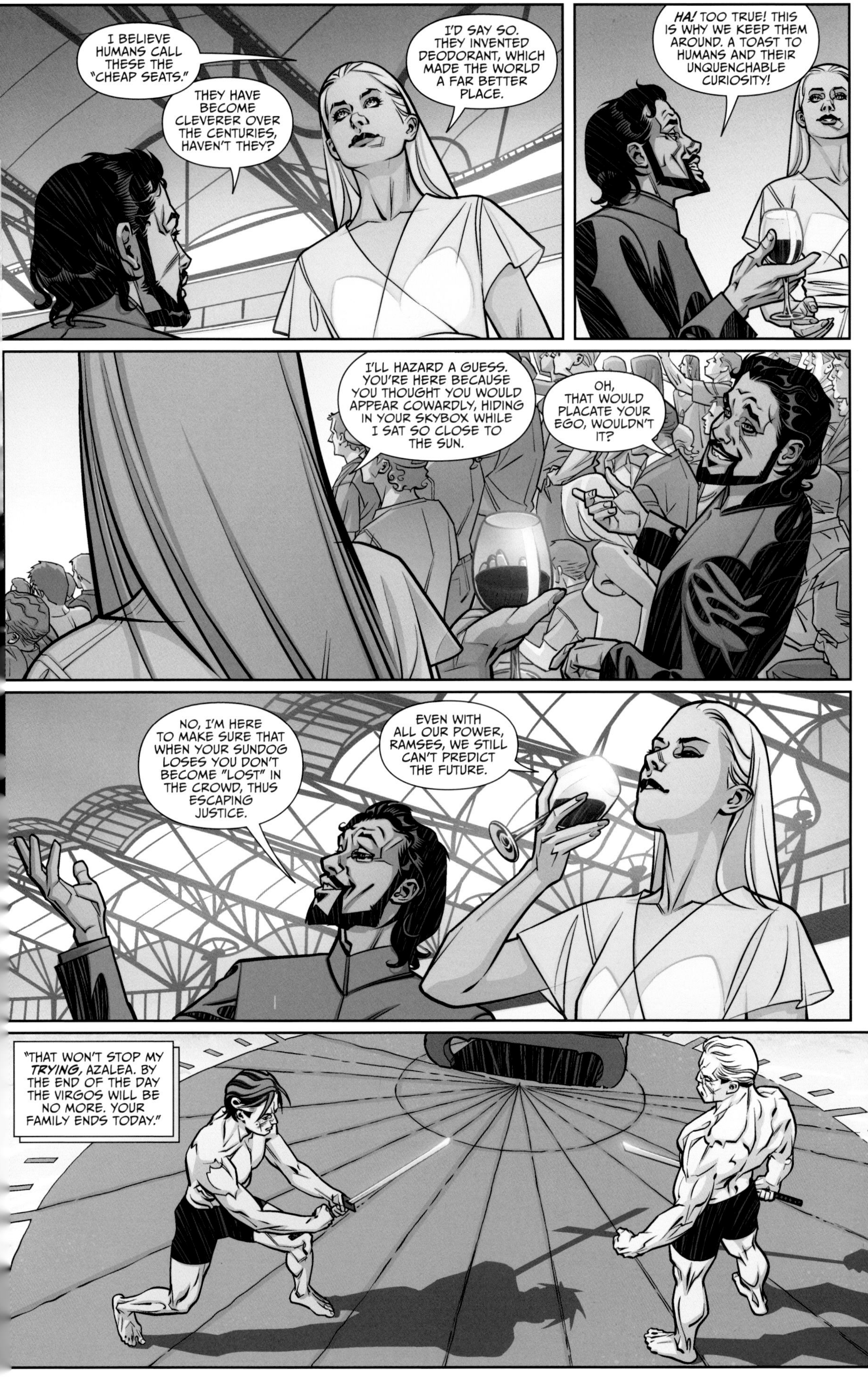
I BELIEVE HUMANS CALL THESE THE "CHEAP SEATS."
THEY HAVE BECOME CLEVERER OVER THE CENTURIES, HAVEN'T THEY?
I'D SAY SO. THEY INVENTED DEODORANT, WHICH MADE THE WORLD A FAR BETTER PLACE.
HA! TOO TRUE! THIS IS WHY WE KEEP THEM AROUND. A TOAST TO HUMANS AND THEIR UNQUENCHABLE CURIOSITY!
I'LL HAZARD A GUESS. YOU'RE HERE BECAUSE YOU THOUGHT YOU WOULD APPEAR COWARDLY, HIDING IN YOUR SKYBOX WHILE I SAT SO CLOSE TO THE SUN.
OH, THAT WOULD PLACATE YOUR EGO, WOULDN'T IT?
NO, I'M HERE TO MAKE SURE THAT WHEN YOUR SUNDOG LOSES YOU DON'T BECOME "LOST" IN THE CROWD, THUS ESCAPING JUSTICE.
EVEN WITH ALL OUR POWER, RAMSES, WE STILL CAN'T PREDICT THE FUTURE.
"THAT WON'T STOP MY TRYING, AZALEA. BY THE END OF THE DAY THE VIRGOS WILL BE NO MORE. YOUR FAMILY ENDS TODAY."

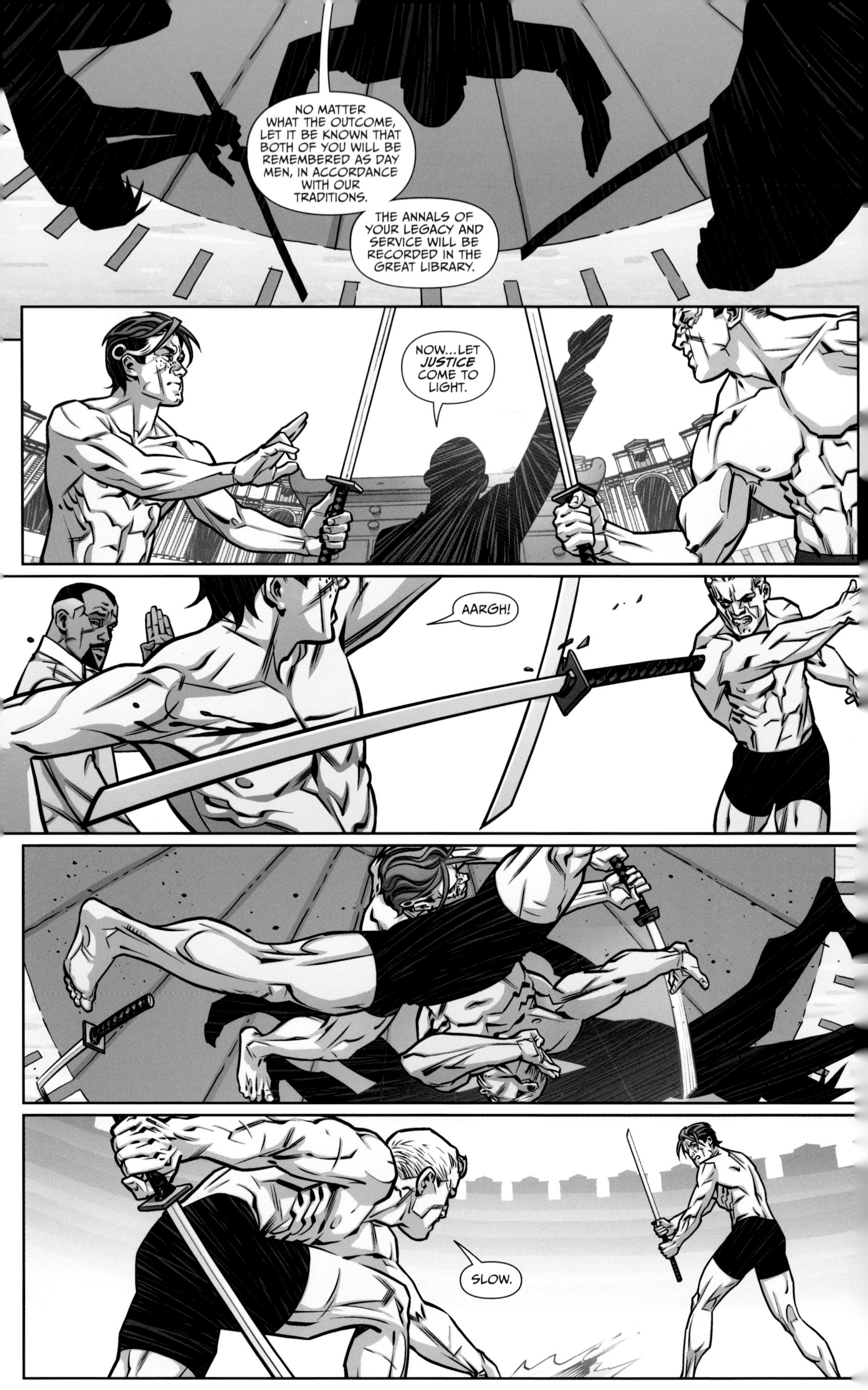
NO MATTER WHAT THE OUTCOME, LET IT BE KNOWN THAT BOTH OF YOU WILL BE REMEMBERED AS DAY MEN, IN ACCORDANCE WITH OUR TRADITIONS.
THE ANNALS OF YOUR LEGACY AND SERVICE WILL BE RECORDED IN THE GREAT LIBRARY.
NOW...LET *JUSTICE* COME TO LIGHT.
AARGH!
SLOW.

HO! *MAGNIFICENT* DISPLAY OF AGILITY! A TRUE MASTER!

HE'S FASTER THAN MOST MEN HIS SIZE.

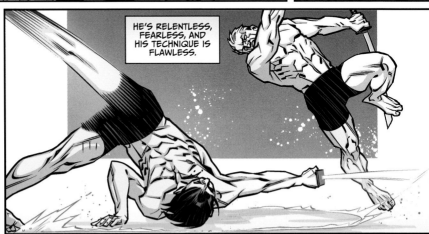

HE'S RELENTLESS, FEARLESS, AND HIS TECHNIQUE IS FLAWLESS.

GOTTA MAKE THIS A FIGHT. RIGHT *NOW.*

LEAVE MY LEFT SIDE EXPOSED EVER SO SLIGHTLY. BAIT HIM.

HOPE THAT HE MAKES THE MISTAKE SO MANY OTHERS HAVE...

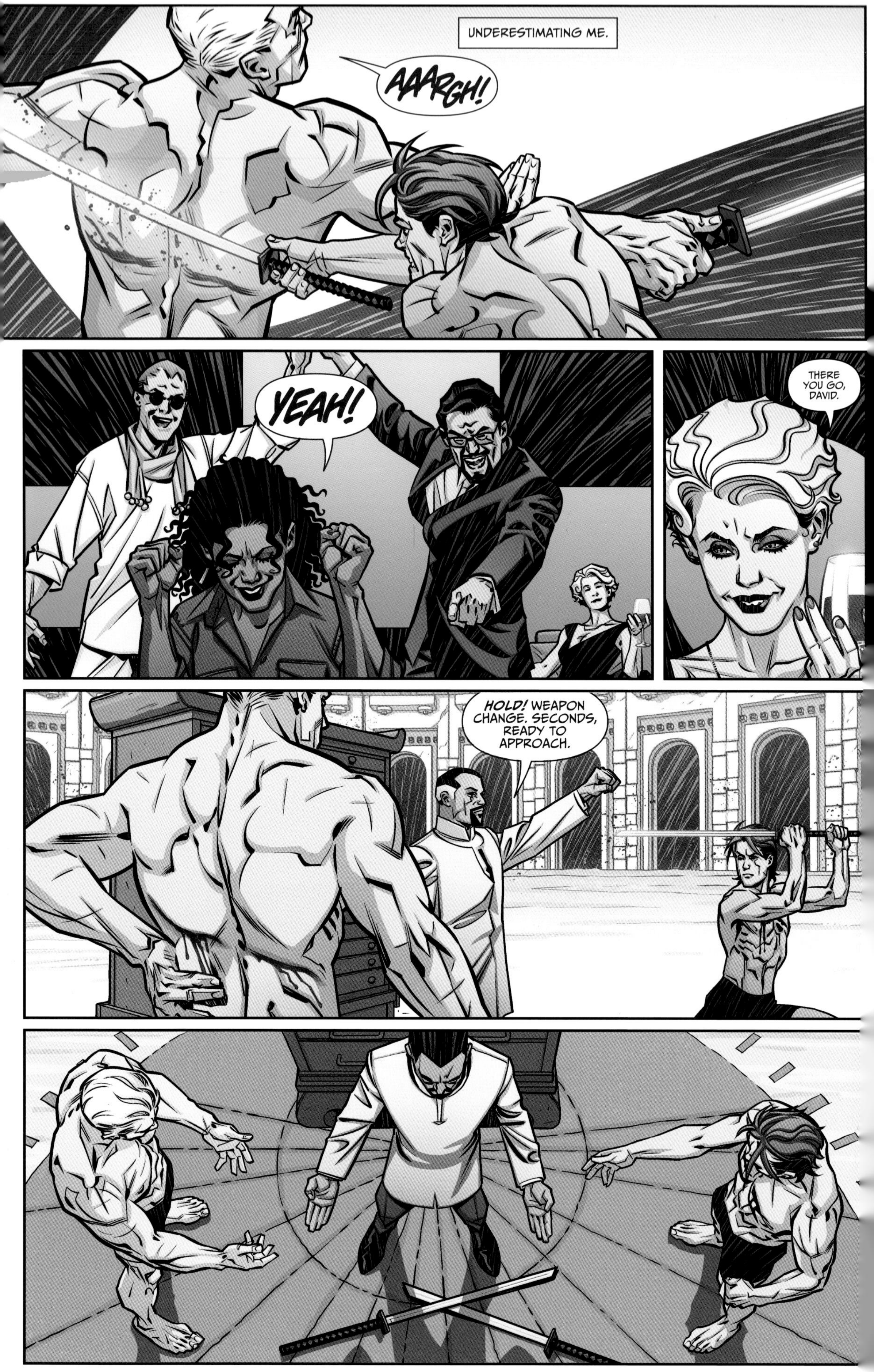
UNDERESTIMATING ME.
AAARGH!
YEAH!
THERE YOU GO, DAVID.
HOLD! WEAPON CHANGE. SECONDS, READY TO APPROACH.

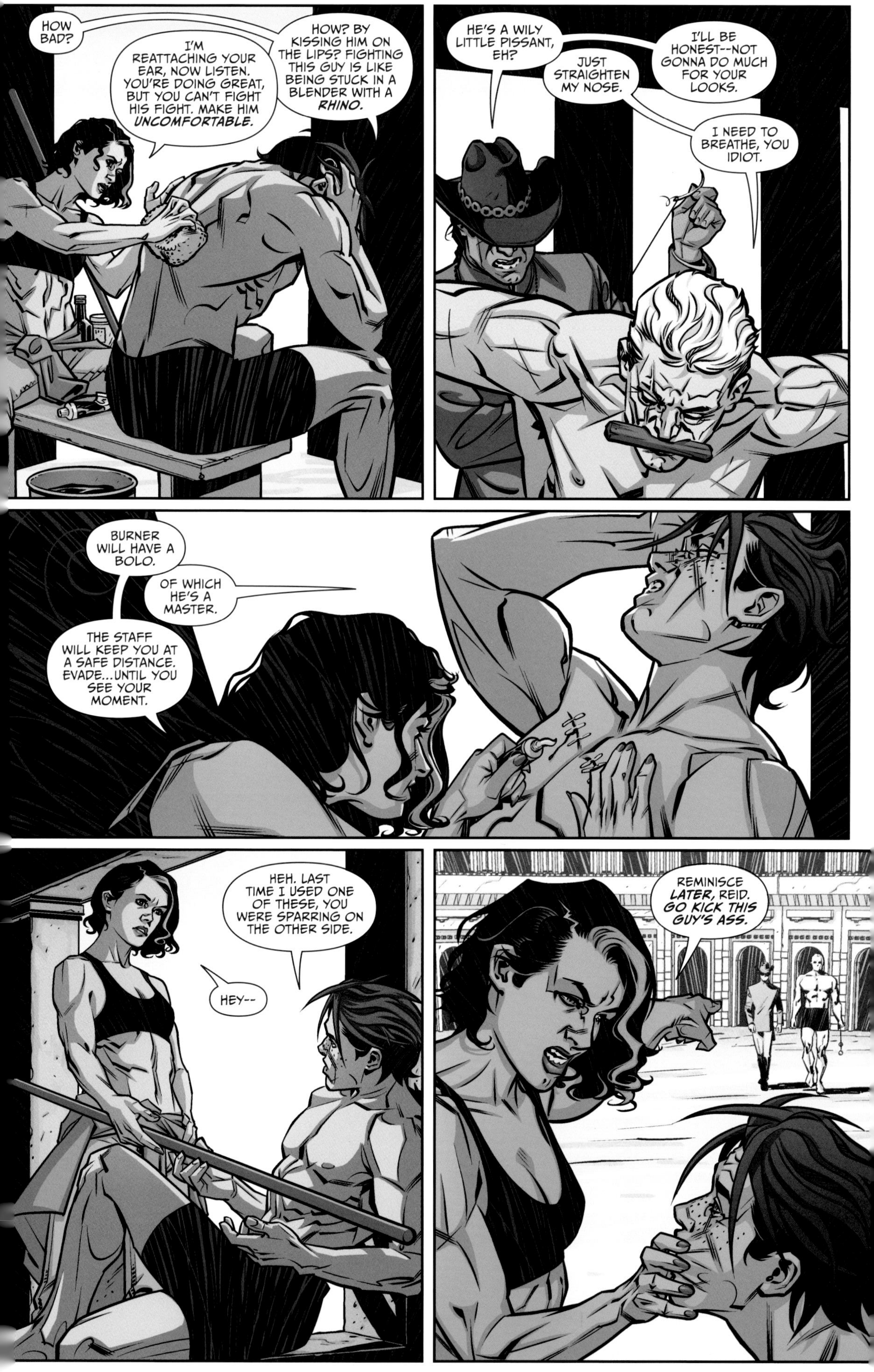
HOW BAD?
I'M REATTACHING YOUR EAR, NOW LISTEN. YOU'RE DOING GREAT, BUT YOU CAN'T FIGHT HIS FIGHT. MAKE HIM UNCOMFORTABLE.
HOW? BY KISSING HIM ON THE LIPS? FIGHTING THIS GUY IS LIKE BEING STUCK IN A BLENDER WITH A RHINO.
HE'S A WILY LITTLE PISSANT, EH?
I'LL BE HONEST--NOT GONNA DO MUCH FOR YOUR LOOKS.
JUST STRAIGHTEN MY NOSE.
I NEED TO BREATHE, YOU IDIOT.
BURNER WILL HAVE A BOLO.
OF WHICH HE'S A MASTER.
THE STAFF WILL KEEP YOU AT A SAFE DISTANCE. EVADE...UNTIL YOU SEE YOUR MOMENT.
HEH. LAST TIME I USED ONE OF THESE, YOU WERE SPARRING ON THE OTHER SIDE.
HEY--
REMINISCE LATER, REID. GO KICK THIS GUY'S ASS.

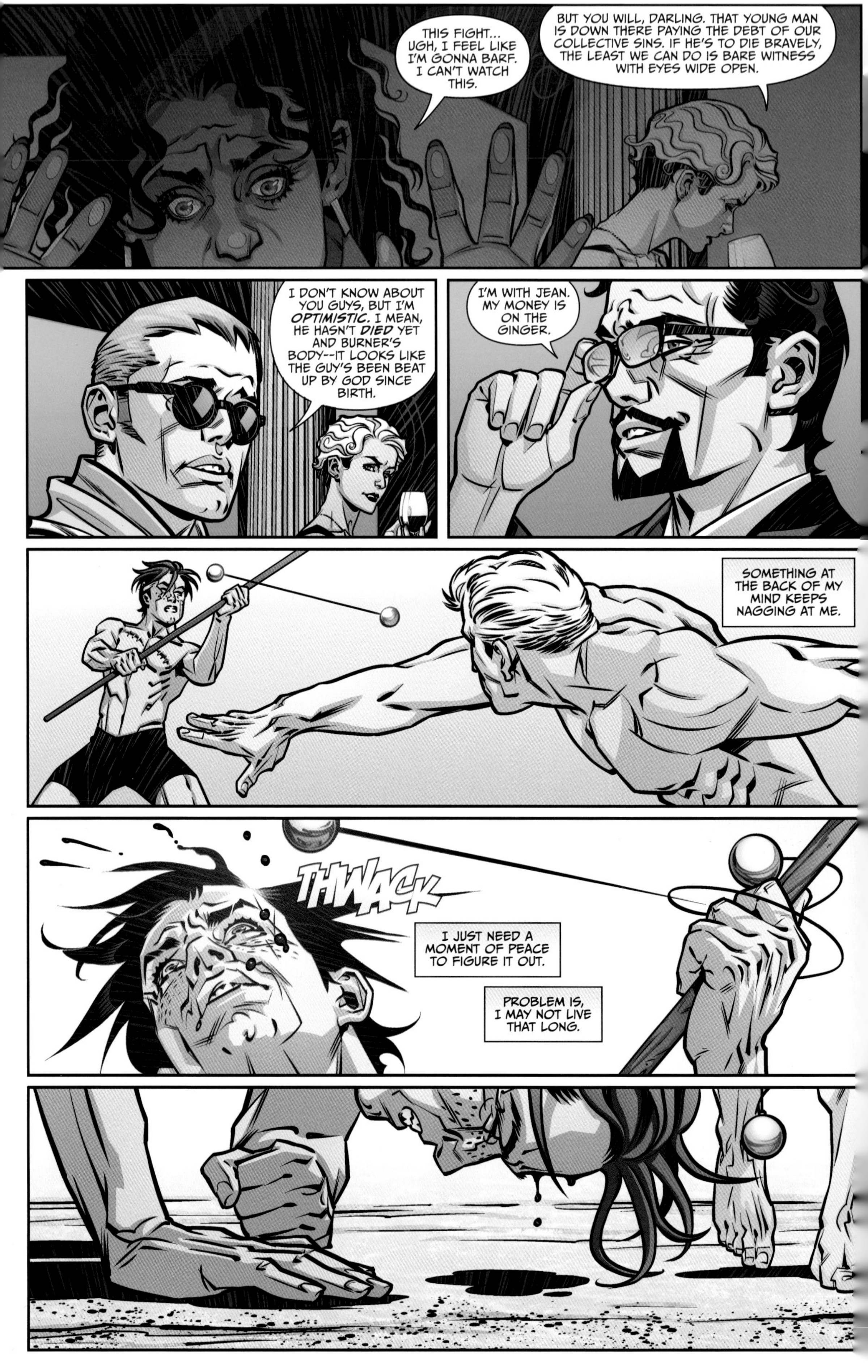
THIS FIGHT... UGH, I FEEL LIKE I'M GONNA BARF. I CAN'T WATCH THIS.
BUT YOU WILL, DARLING. THAT YOUNG MAN IS DOWN THERE PAYING THE DEBT OF OUR COLLECTIVE SINS. IF HE'S TO DIE BRAVELY, THE LEAST WE CAN DO IS BARE WITNESS WITH EYES WIDE OPEN.
I DON'T KNOW ABOUT YOU GUYS, BUT I'M *OPTIMISTIC.* I MEAN, HE HASN'T *DIED* YET AND BURNER'S BODY--IT LOOKS LIKE THE GUY'S BEEN BEAT UP BY GOD SINCE BIRTH.
I'M WITH JEAN. MY MONEY IS ON THE GINGER.
SOMETHING AT THE BACK OF MY MIND KEEPS NAGGING AT ME.
THWACK
I JUST NEED A MOMENT OF PEACE TO FIGURE IT OUT.
PROBLEM IS, I MAY NOT LIVE THAT LONG.

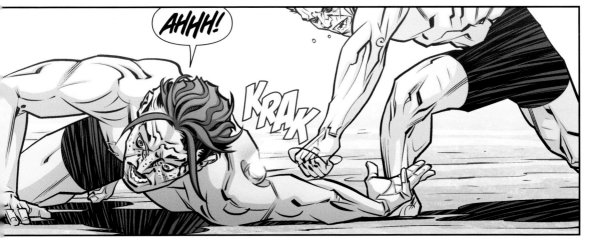

AHHH!

KRAK

YOU... SHOULD HAVE...DIED IN THAT FIRE.

AH, YES. FINALLY. AVERT YOUR EYES, AZALEA, THIS IS GOING TO BE RATHER UNPLEASANT.

I TASTE BLOOD, MOST OF IT MINE. IT'S FILLING MY MOUTH, MY NOSE, DRAINING INTO MY LUNGS.

I'M DROWNING IN THE SAND.

TWO...MAYBE THREE MORE BREATHS. MAKE THEM COUNT.

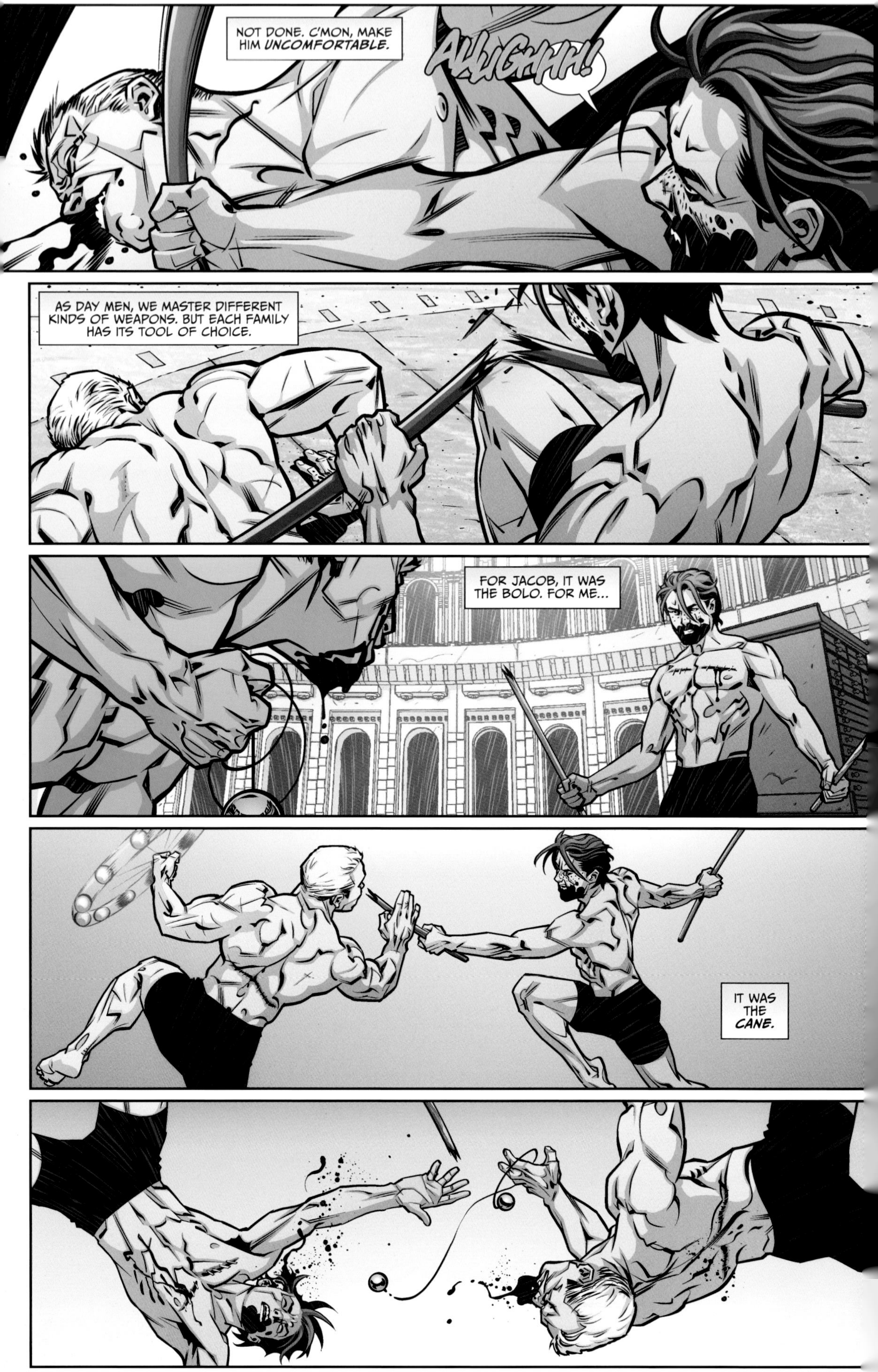
NOT DONE. C'MON, MAKE HIM *UNCOMFORTABLE.*
AUUGHHH!
AS DAY MEN, WE MASTER DIFFERENT KINDS OF WEAPONS. BUT EACH FAMILY HAS ITS TOOL OF CHOICE.
FOR JACOB, IT WAS THE BOLO. FOR ME...
IT WAS THE *CANE.*

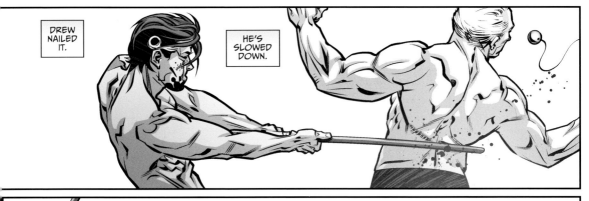

DREW NAILED IT.

HE'S SLOWED DOWN.

JUST A HALF OF A FRACTION.

BUT WE TRADE IN MILLISECONDS AS DAY MEN.

WE LIVE OR DIE BETWEEN HEARTBEATS.

BETTER YOU THAN ONE OF THEM. THEY NEVER GOT ME. HEHE...

GO AHEAD AND FLIP THE SWITCH, KID. I'M READY.

I HEAR THE VIRGOS CHEERING, THE RAMSES CURSING.

AND IT'S IN THIS MOMENT THAT I FIGURE IT OUT.

GET UP, JACOB.

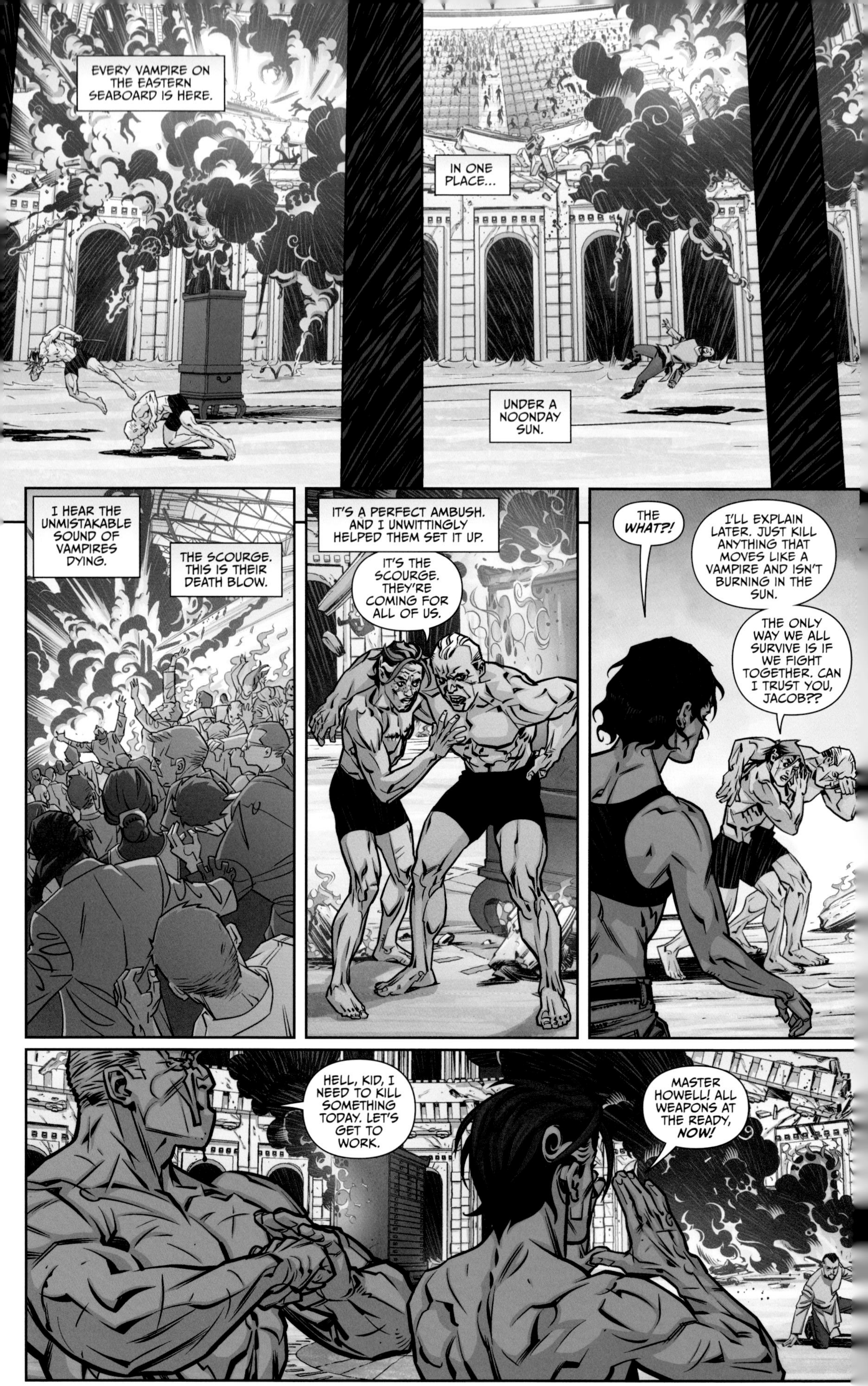
EVERY VAMPIRE ON THE EASTERN SEABOARD IS HERE.
IN ONE PLACE...
UNDER A NOONDAY SUN.
I HEAR THE UNMISTAKABLE SOUND OF VAMPIRES DYING.
THE SCOURGE. THIS IS THEIR DEATH BLOW.
IT'S A PERFECT AMBUSH. AND I UNWITTINGLY HELPED THEM SET IT UP.
IT'S THE SCOURGE. THEY'RE COMING FOR ALL OF US.
THE WHAT?!
I'LL EXPLAIN LATER. JUST KILL ANYTHING THAT MOVES LIKE A VAMPIRE AND ISN'T BURNING IN THE SUN.
THE ONLY WAY WE ALL SURVIVE IS IF WE FIGHT TOGETHER. CAN I TRUST YOU, JACOB??
HELL, KID, I NEED TO KILL SOMETHING TODAY. LET'S GET TO WORK.
MASTER HOWELL! ALL WEAPONS AT THE READY, NOW!

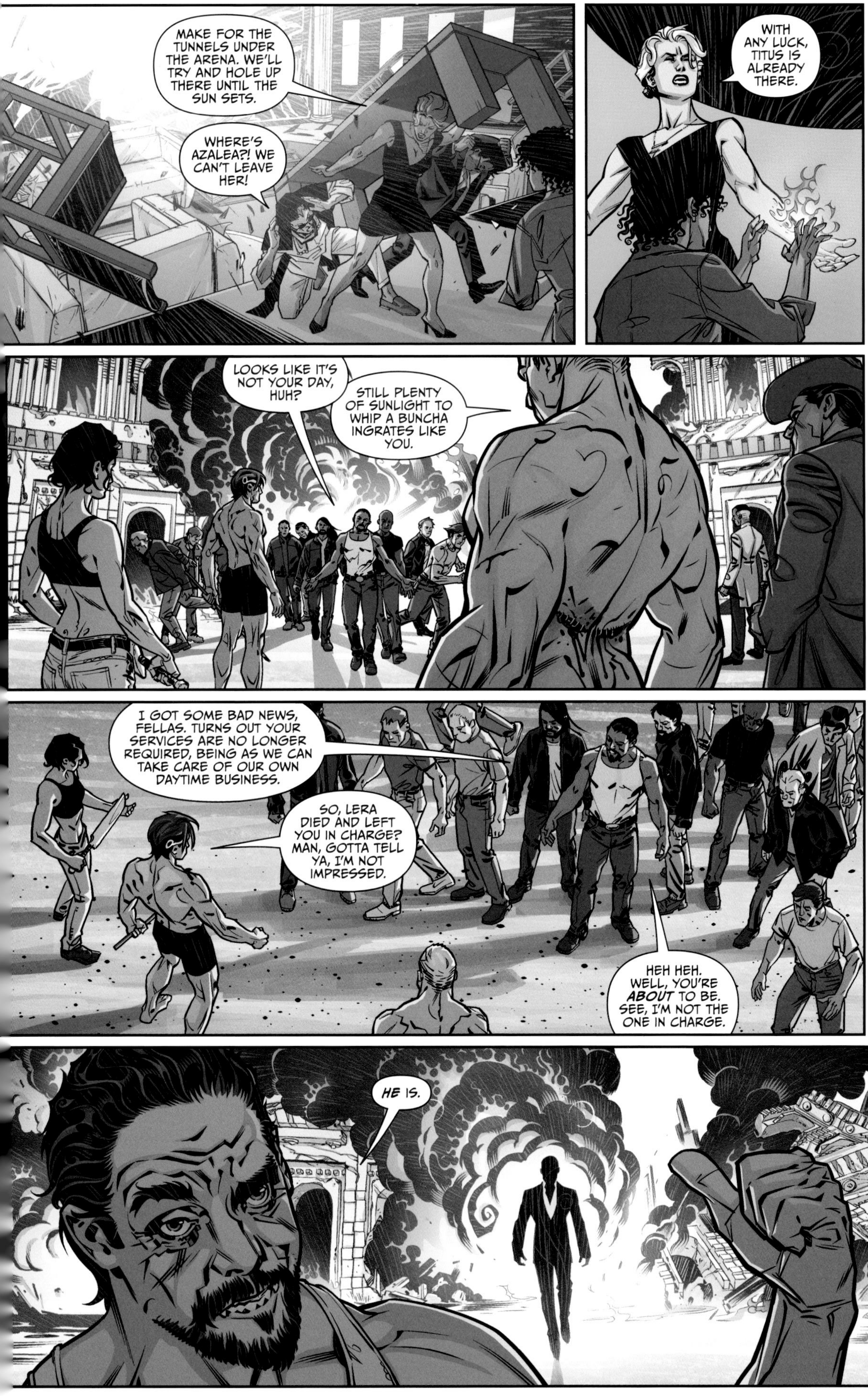
MAKE FOR THE TUNNELS UNDER THE ARENA. WE'LL TRY AND HOLE UP THERE UNTIL THE SUN SETS.
WHERE'S AZALEA?! WE CAN'T LEAVE HER!
WITH ANY LUCK, TITUS IS ALREADY THERE.
LOOKS LIKE IT'S NOT YOUR DAY, HUH?
STILL PLENTY OF SUNLIGHT TO WHIP A BUNCHA INGRATES LIKE YOU.
I GOT SOME BAD NEWS, FELLAS. TURNS OUT YOUR SERVICES ARE NO LONGER REQUIRED, BEING AS WE CAN TAKE CARE OF OUR OWN DAYTIME BUSINESS.
SO, LERA DIED AND LEFT YOU IN CHARGE? MAN, GOTTA TELL YA, I'M NOT IMPRESSED.
HEH HEH. WELL, YOU'RE *ABOUT* TO BE. SEE, I'M NOT THE ONE IN CHARGE.
*HE* IS.

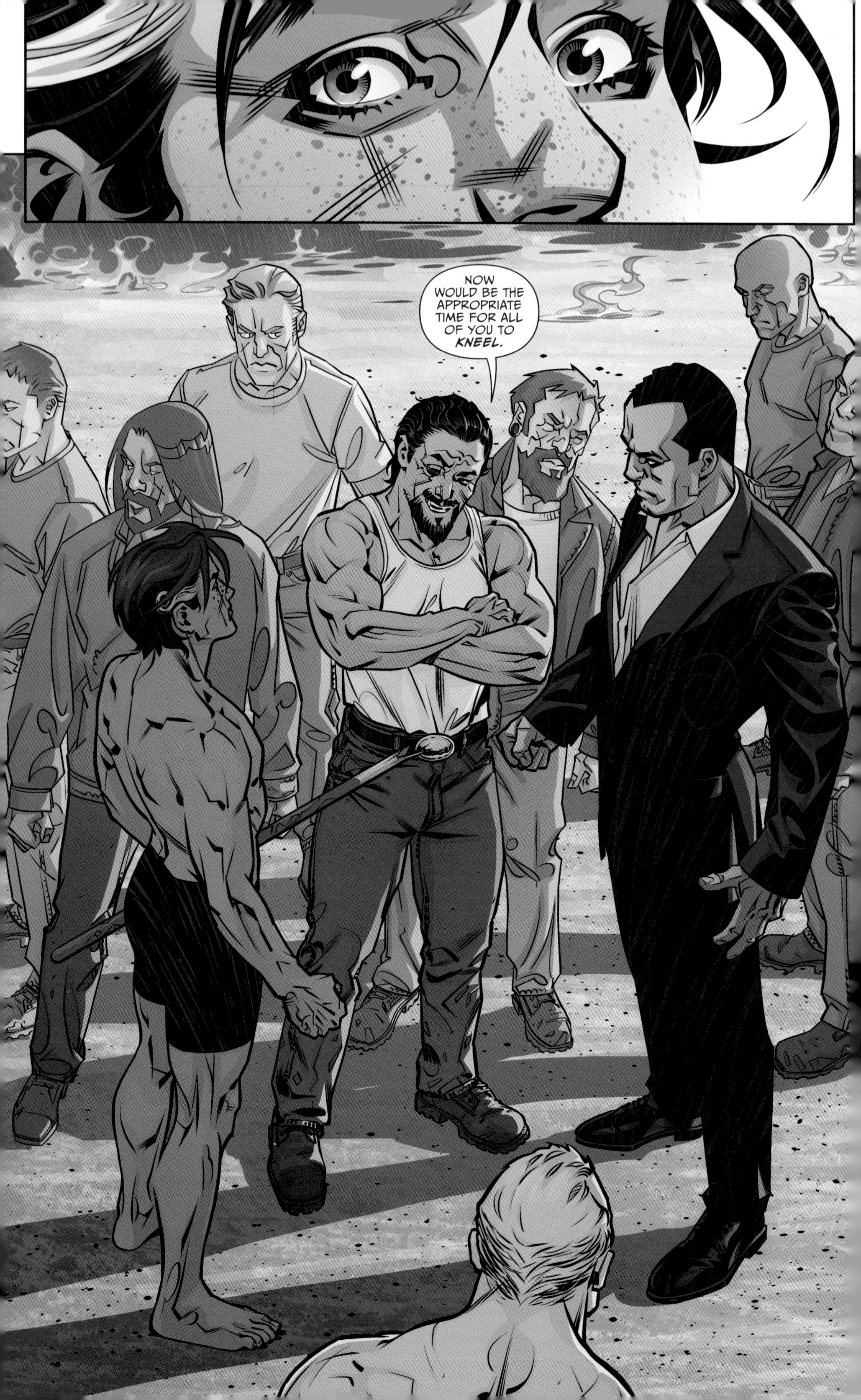
NOW WOULD BE THE APPROPRIATE TIME FOR ALL OF YOU TO KNEEL.

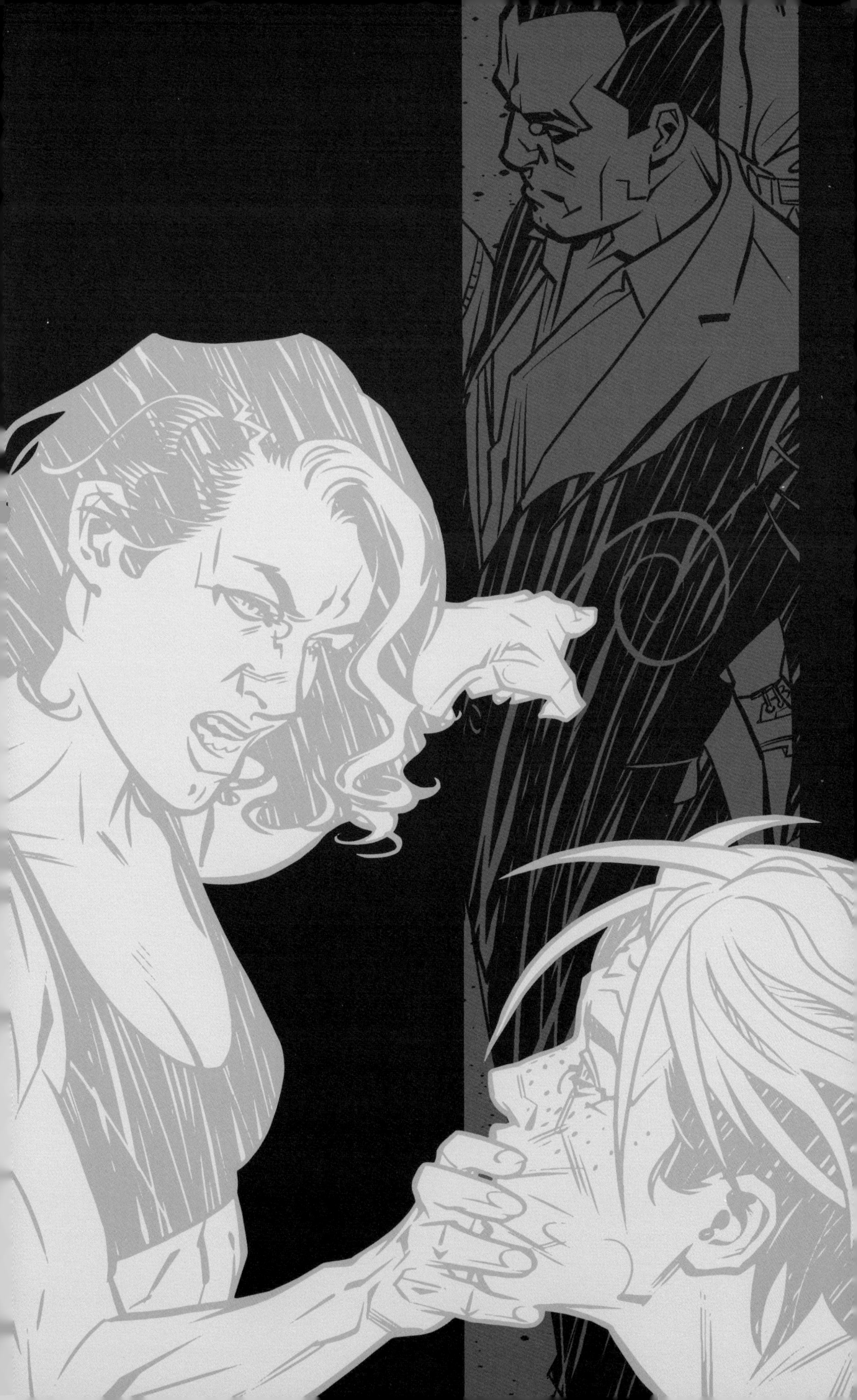

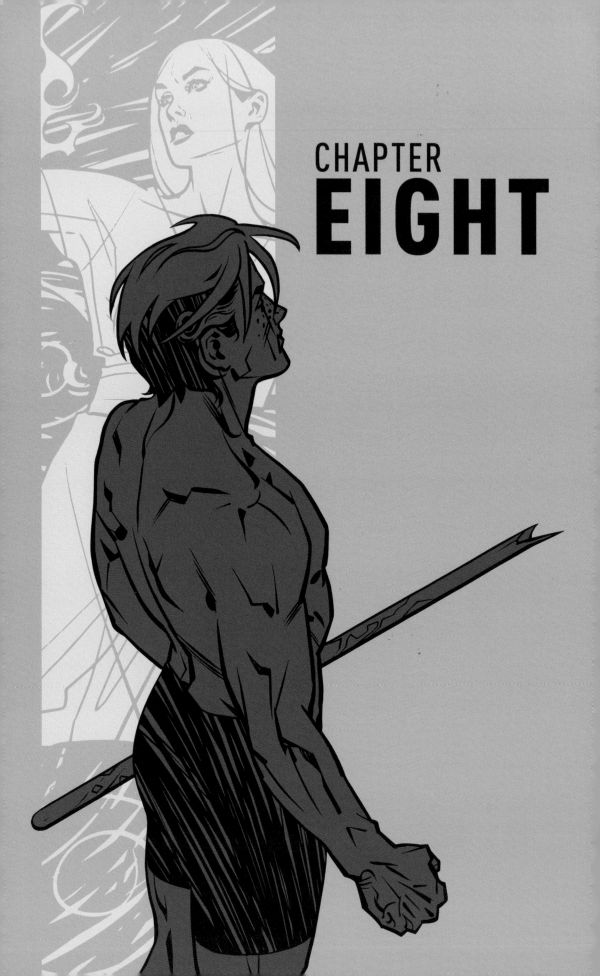

# CHAPTER
# EIGHT

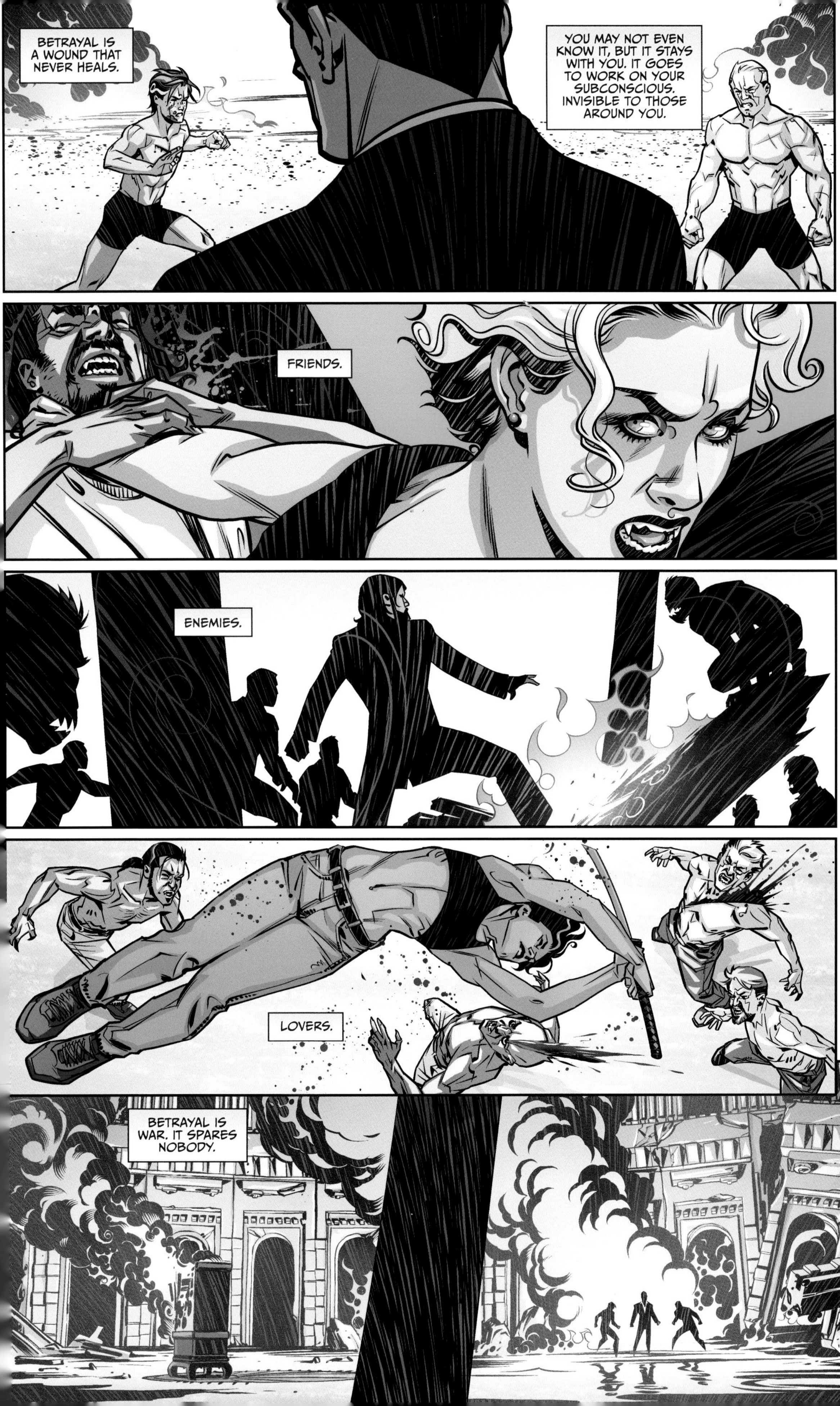
BETRAYAL IS A WOUND THAT NEVER HEALS.
YOU MAY NOT EVEN KNOW IT, BUT IT STAYS WITH YOU. IT GOES TO WORK ON YOUR SUBCONSCIOUS. INVISIBLE TO THOSE AROUND YOU.
FRIENDS.
ENEMIES.
LOVERS.
BETRAYAL IS WAR. IT SPARES NOBODY.

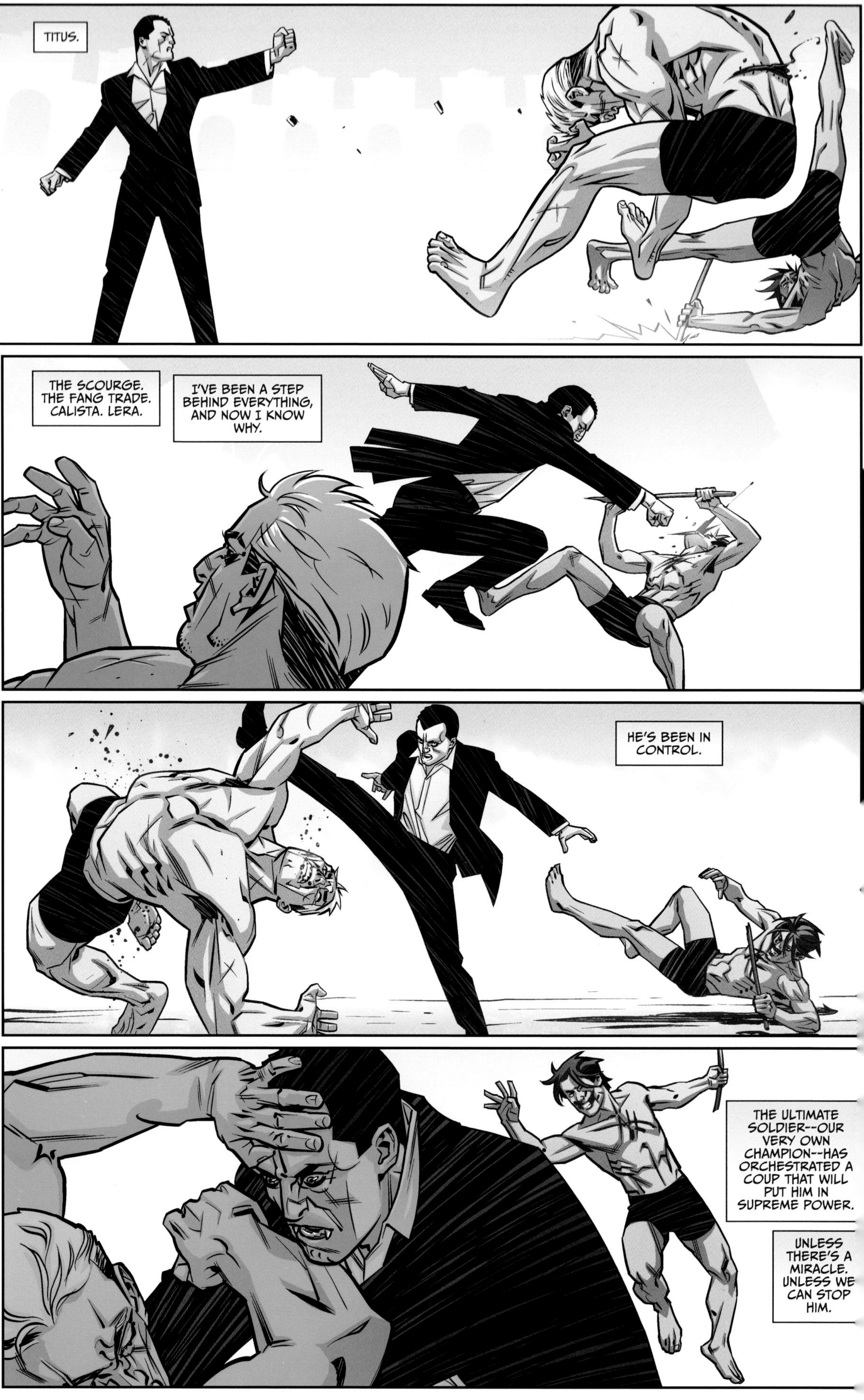
TITUS.
THE SCOURGE. THE FANG TRADE. CALISTA. LERA.
I'VE BEEN A STEP BEHIND EVERYTHING, AND NOW I KNOW WHY.
HE'S BEEN IN CONTROL.
THE ULTIMATE SOLDIER--OUR VERY OWN CHAMPION--HAS ORCHESTRATED A COUP THAT WILL PUT HIM IN SUPREME POWER.
UNLESS THERE'S A MIRACLE. UNLESS WE CAN STOP HIM.

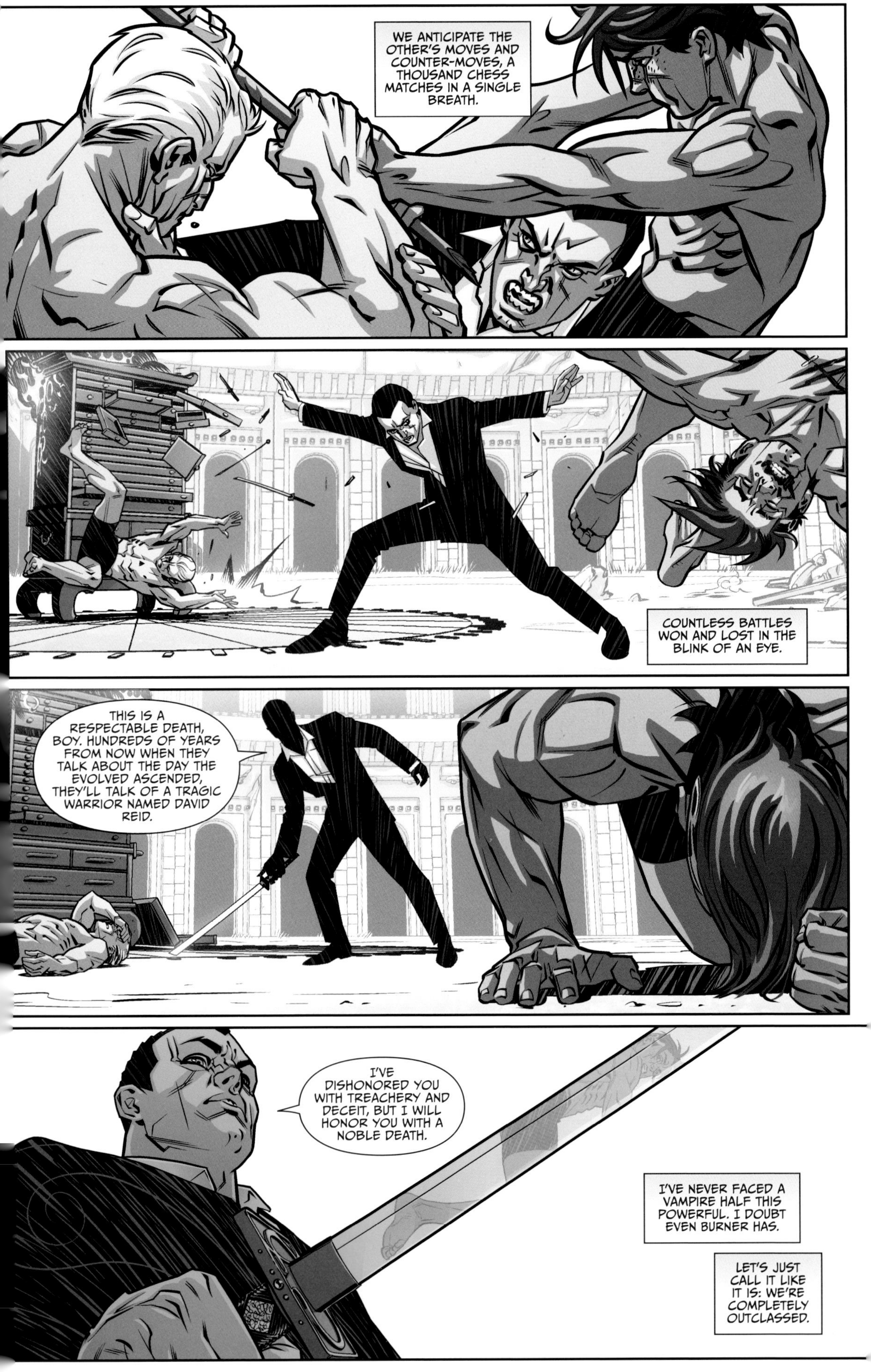
WE ANTICIPATE THE OTHER'S MOVES AND COUNTER-MOVES, A THOUSAND CHESS MATCHES IN A SINGLE BREATH.
COUNTLESS BATTLES WON AND LOST IN THE BLINK OF AN EYE.
THIS IS A RESPECTABLE DEATH, BOY. HUNDREDS OF YEARS FROM NOW WHEN THEY TALK ABOUT THE DAY THE EVOLVED ASCENDED, THEY'LL TALK OF A TRAGIC WARRIOR NAMED DAVID REID.
I'VE DISHONORED YOU WITH TREACHERY AND DECEIT, BUT I WILL HONOR YOU WITH A NOBLE DEATH.
I'VE NEVER FACED A VAMPIRE HALF THIS POWERFUL. I DOUBT EVEN BURNER HAS.
LET'S JUST CALL IT LIKE IT IS: WE'RE COMPLETELY OUTCLASSED.

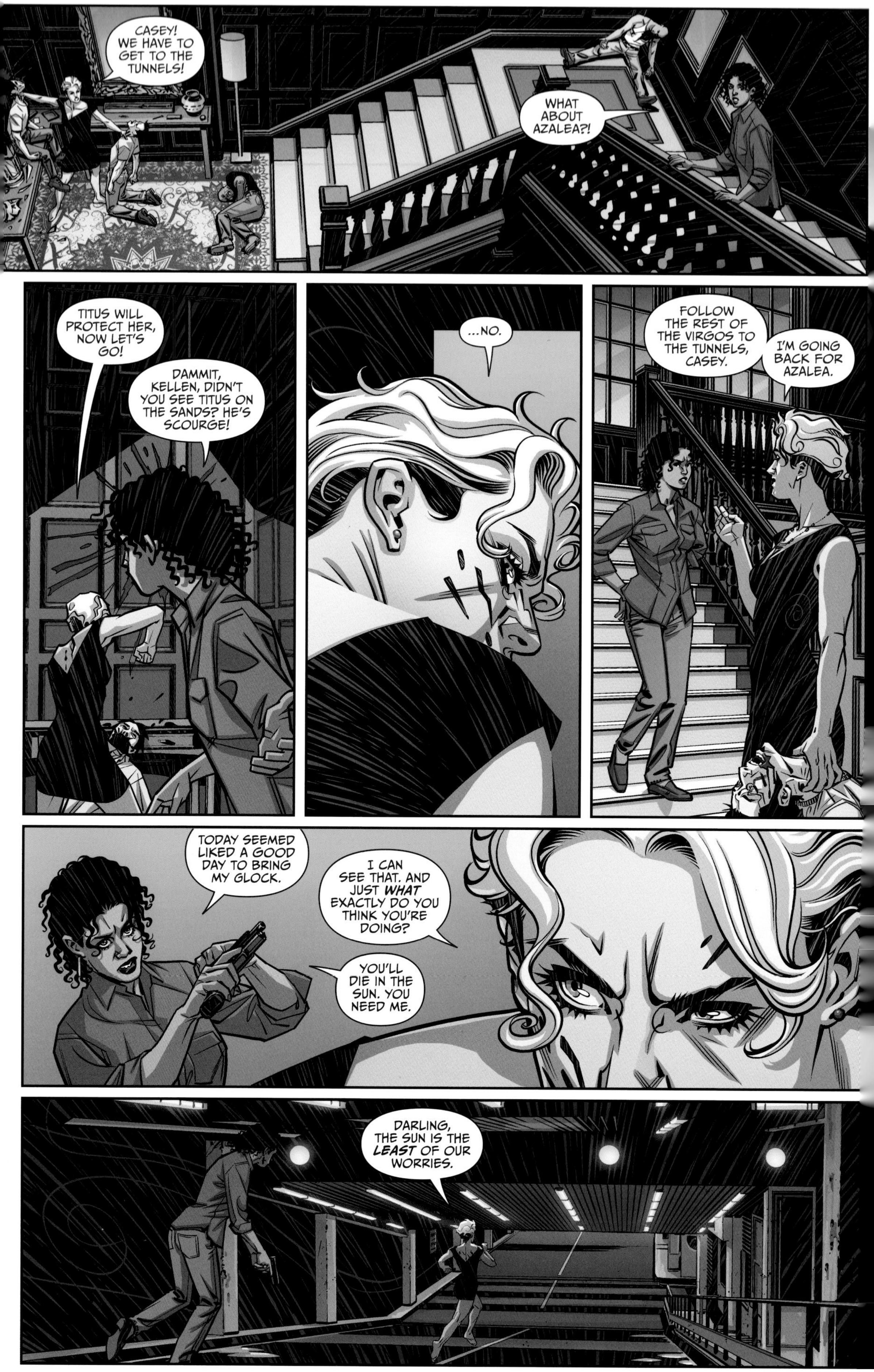
CASEY! WE HAVE TO GET TO THE TUNNELS!
WHAT ABOUT AZALEA?!
TITUS WILL PROTECT HER, NOW LET'S GO!
DAMMIT, KELLEN, DIDN'T YOU SEE TITUS ON THE SANDS? HE'S SCOURGE!
...NO.
FOLLOW THE REST OF THE VIRGOS TO THE TUNNELS, CASEY.
I'M GOING BACK FOR AZALEA.
TODAY SEEMED LIKED A GOOD DAY TO BRING MY GLOCK.
I CAN SEE THAT. AND JUST WHAT EXACTLY DO YOU THINK YOU'RE DOING?
YOU'LL DIE IN THE SUN. YOU NEED ME.
DARLING, THE SUN IS THE LEAST OF OUR WORRIES.

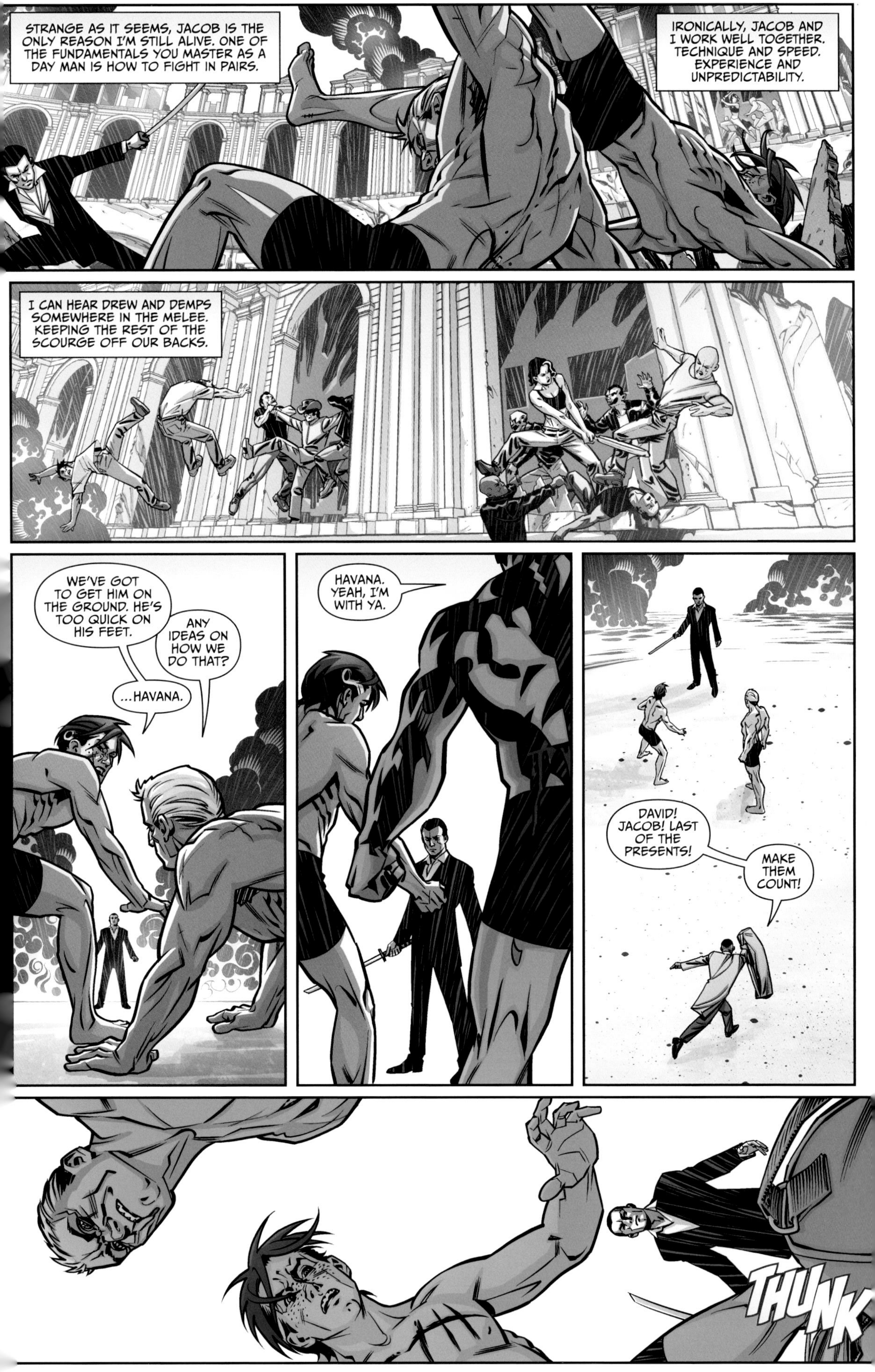

STRANGE AS IT SEEMS, JACOB IS THE ONLY REASON I'M STILL ALIVE. ONE OF THE FUNDAMENTALS YOU MASTER AS A DAY MAN IS HOW TO FIGHT IN PAIRS.
IRONICALLY, JACOB AND I WORK WELL TOGETHER. TECHNIQUE AND SPEED. EXPERIENCE AND UNPREDICTABILITY.
I CAN HEAR DREW AND DEMPS SOMEWHERE IN THE MELEE. KEEPING THE REST OF THE SCOURGE OFF OUR BACKS.
WE'VE GOT TO GET HIM ON THE GROUND. HE'S TOO QUICK ON HIS FEET.
ANY IDEAS ON HOW WE DO THAT?
...HAVANA.
HAVANA. YEAH, I'M WITH YA.
DAVID! JACOB! LAST OF THE PRESENTS!
MAKE THEM COUNT!
THUNK

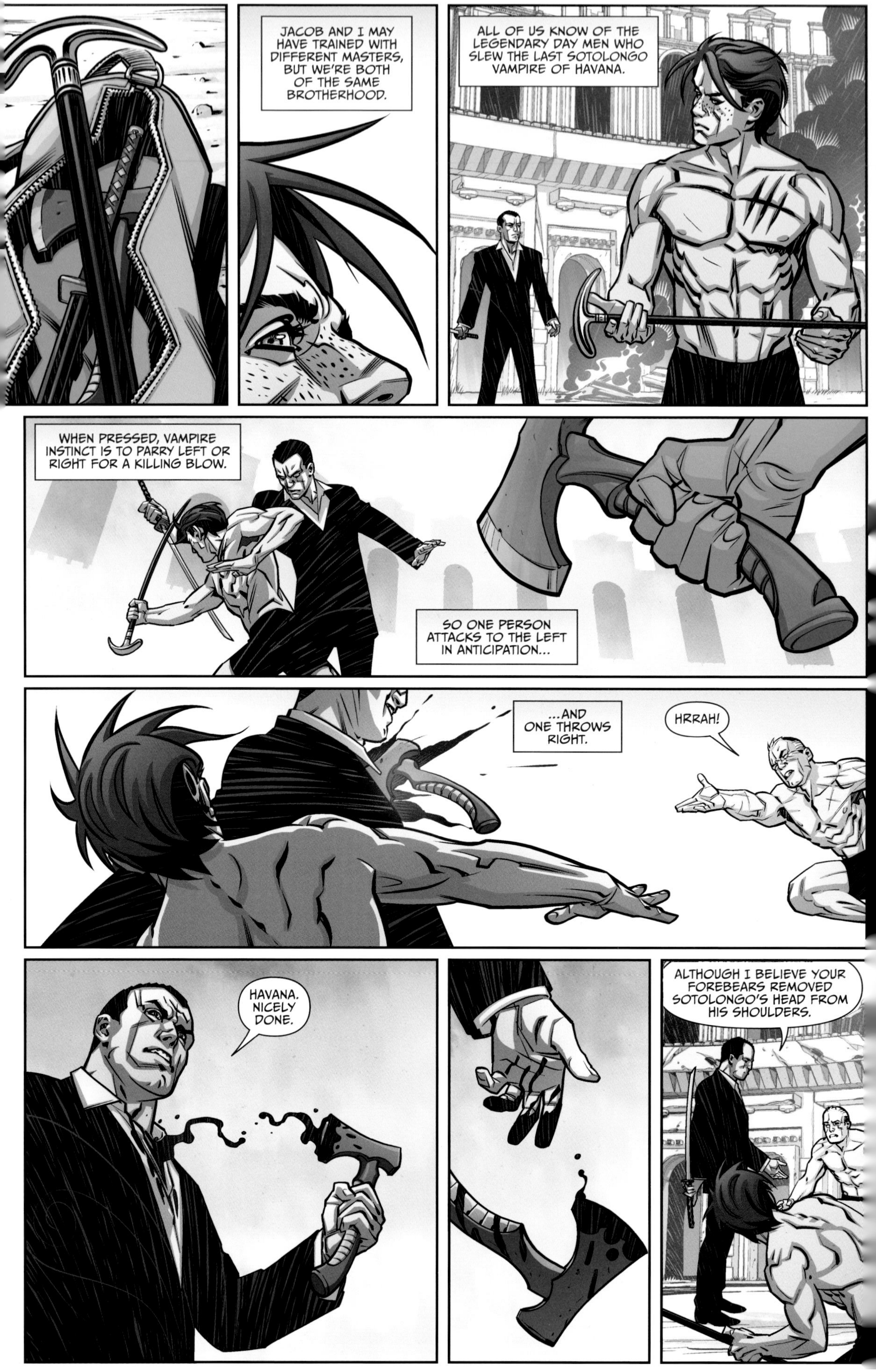
JACOB AND I MAY HAVE TRAINED WITH DIFFERENT MASTERS, BUT WE'RE BOTH OF THE SAME BROTHERHOOD.
ALL OF US KNOW OF THE LEGENDARY DAY MEN WHO SLEW THE LAST SOTOLONGO VAMPIRE OF HAVANA.
WHEN PRESSED, VAMPIRE INSTINCT IS TO PARRY LEFT OR RIGHT FOR A KILLING BLOW.
SO ONE PERSON ATTACKS TO THE LEFT IN ANTICIPATION...
...AND ONE THROWS RIGHT.
HRRAH!
HAVANA. NICELY DONE.
ALTHOUGH I BELIEVE YOUR FOREBEARS REMOVED SOTOLONGO'S HEAD FROM HIS SHOULDERS.

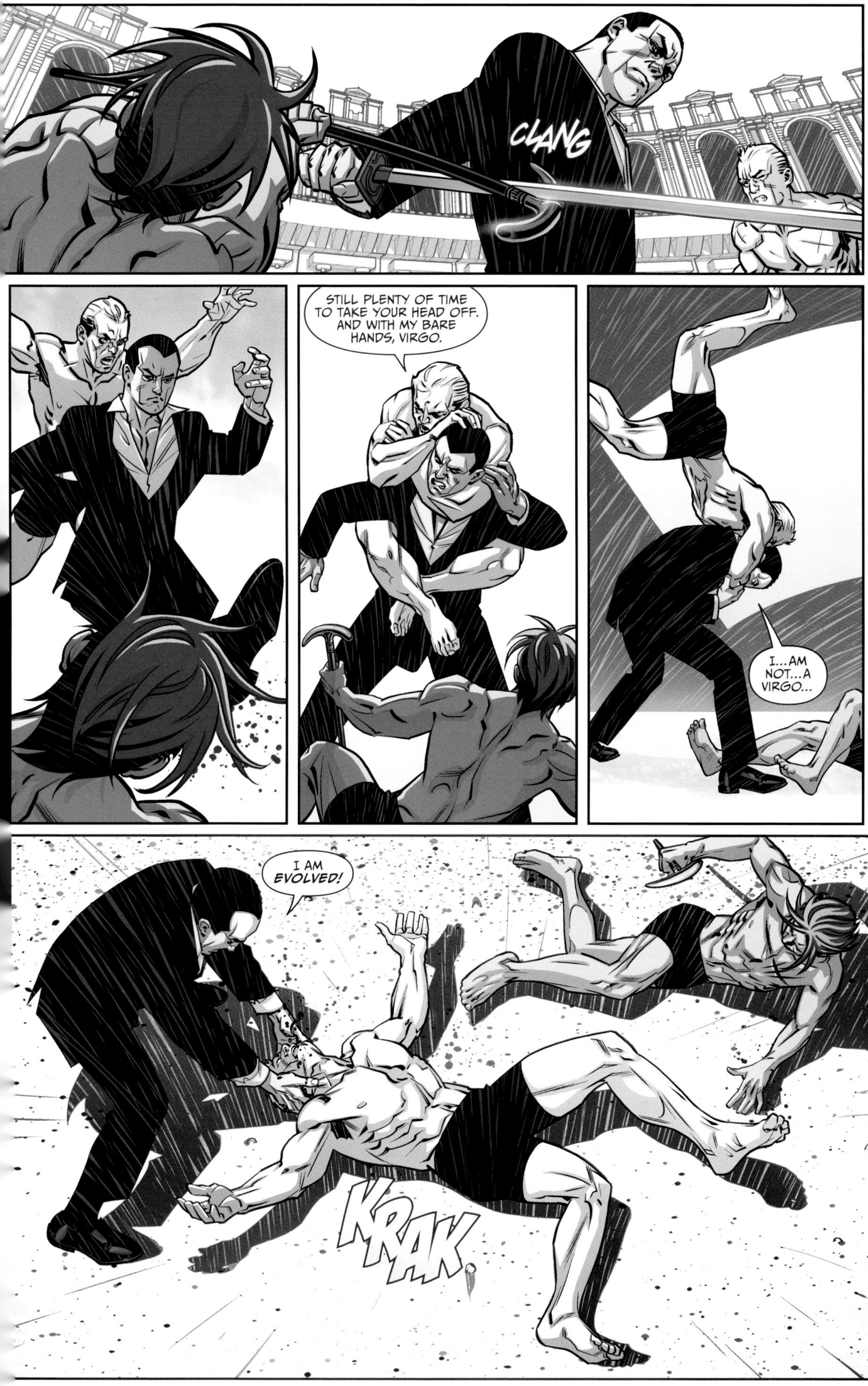
CLANG
STILL PLENTY OF TIME TO TAKE YOUR HEAD OFF. AND WITH MY BARE HANDS, VIRGO.
I...AM NOT...A VIRGO...
I AM EVOLVED!
KRAK

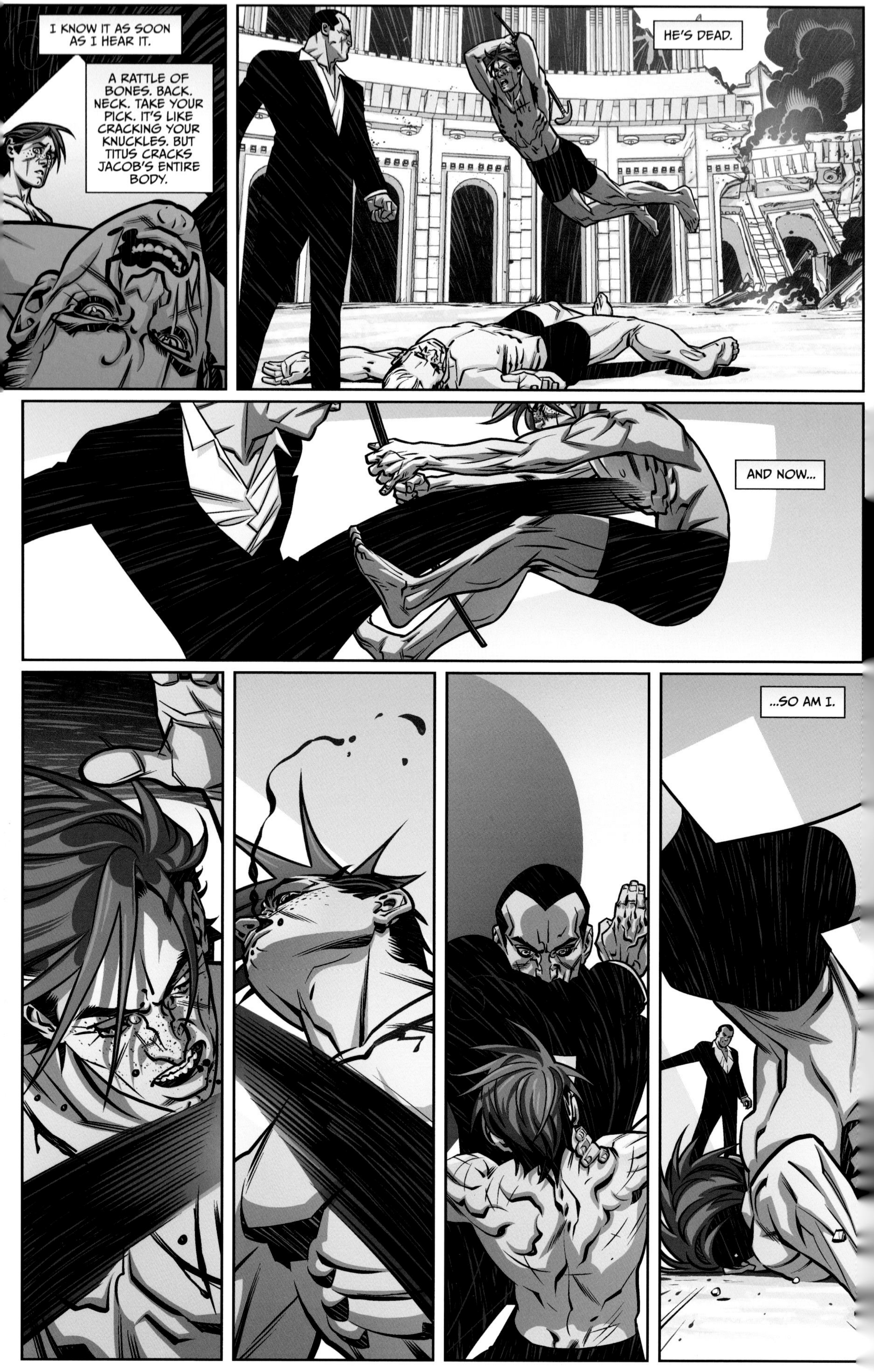
I KNOW IT AS SOON AS I HEAR IT.
A RATTLE OF BONES. BACK. NECK. TAKE YOUR PICK. IT'S LIKE CRACKING YOUR KNUCKLES. BUT TITUS CRACKS JACOB'S ENTIRE BODY.
HE'S DEAD.
AND NOW...
...SO AM I.

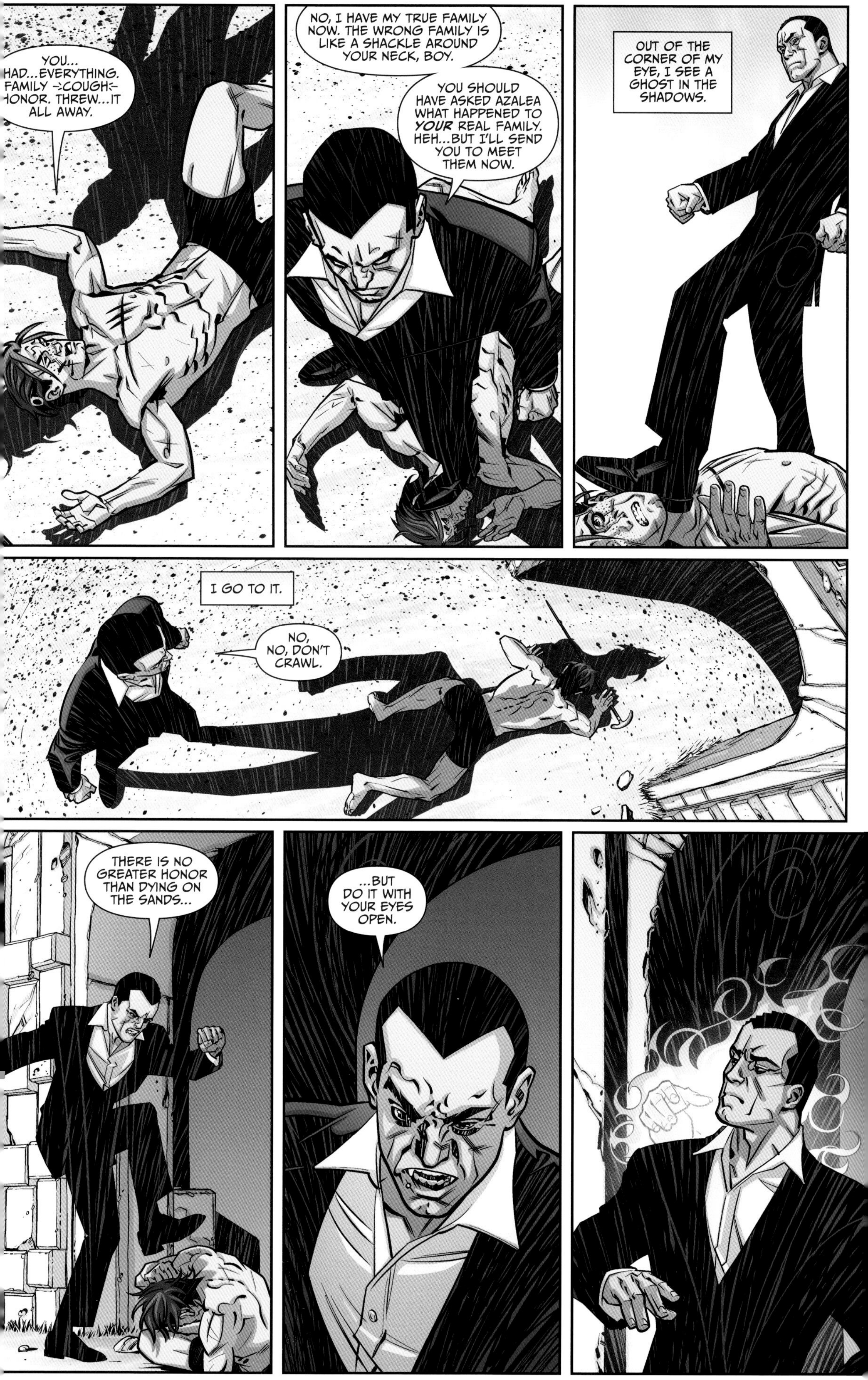
YOU... HAD...EVERYTHING. FAMILY -COUGH- HONOR. THREW...IT ALL AWAY.
NO, I HAVE MY TRUE FAMILY NOW. THE WRONG FAMILY IS LIKE A SHACKLE AROUND YOUR NECK, BOY.
YOU SHOULD HAVE ASKED AZALEA WHAT HAPPENED TO YOUR REAL FAMILY. HEH...BUT I'LL SEND YOU TO MEET THEM NOW.
OUT OF THE CORNER OF MY EYE, I SEE A GHOST IN THE SHADOWS.
I GO TO IT.
NO, NO, DON'T CRAWL.
THERE IS NO GREATER HONOR THAN DYING ON THE SANDS...
...BUT DO IT WITH YOUR EYES OPEN.

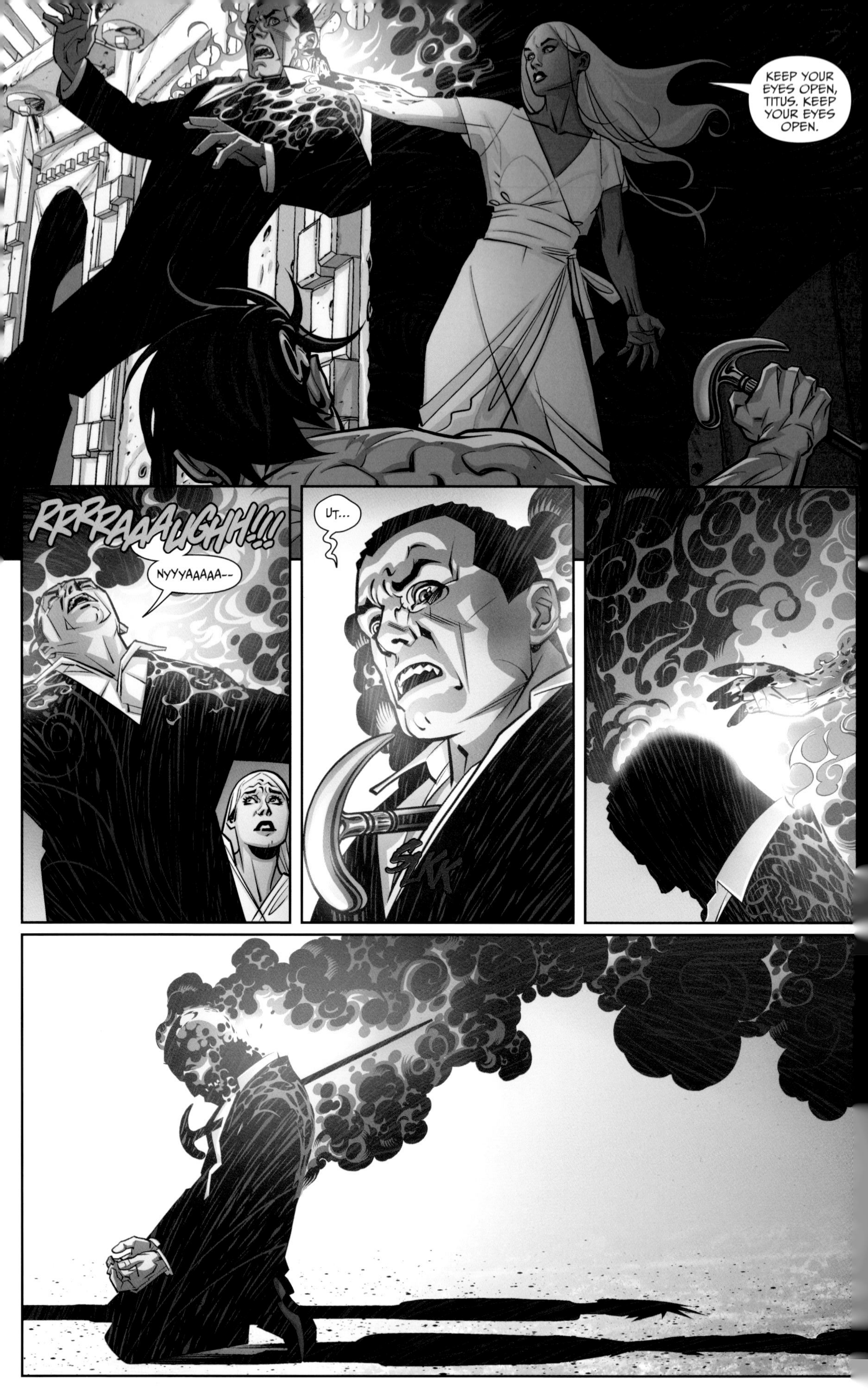
KEEP YOUR EYES OPEN, TITUS. KEEP YOUR EYES OPEN.
RRRRAAAUGHH!!!
NYYYAAAAA--
UT...

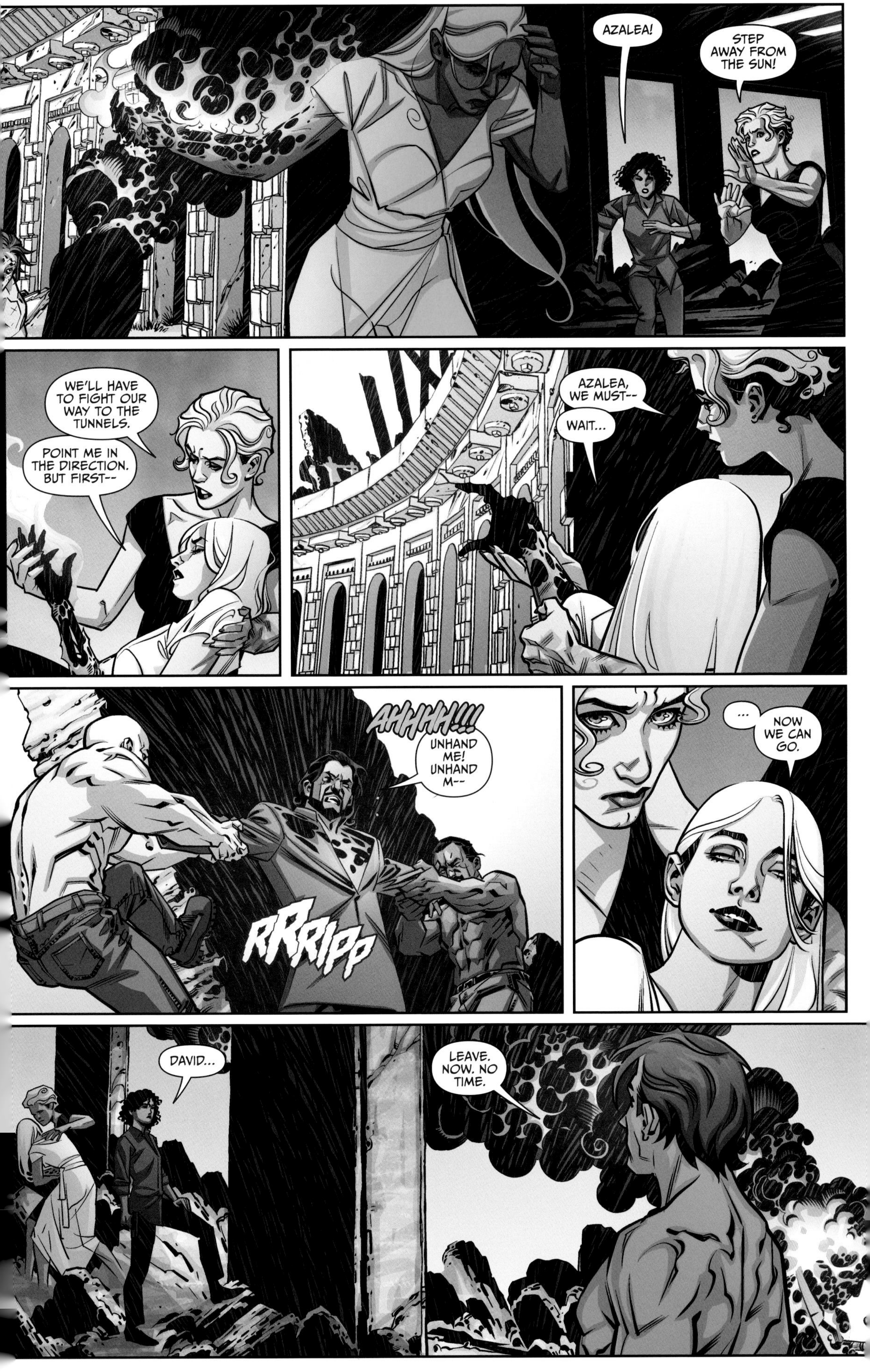
AZALEA!
STEP AWAY FROM THE SUN!
WE'LL HAVE TO FIGHT OUR WAY TO THE TUNNELS.
POINT ME IN THE DIRECTION. BUT FIRST--
AZALEA, WE MUST--
WAIT...
AHHHH!!!
UNHAND ME! UNHAND M--
RRRIPP
... NOW WE CAN GO.
DAVID...
LEAVE. NOW. NO TIME.

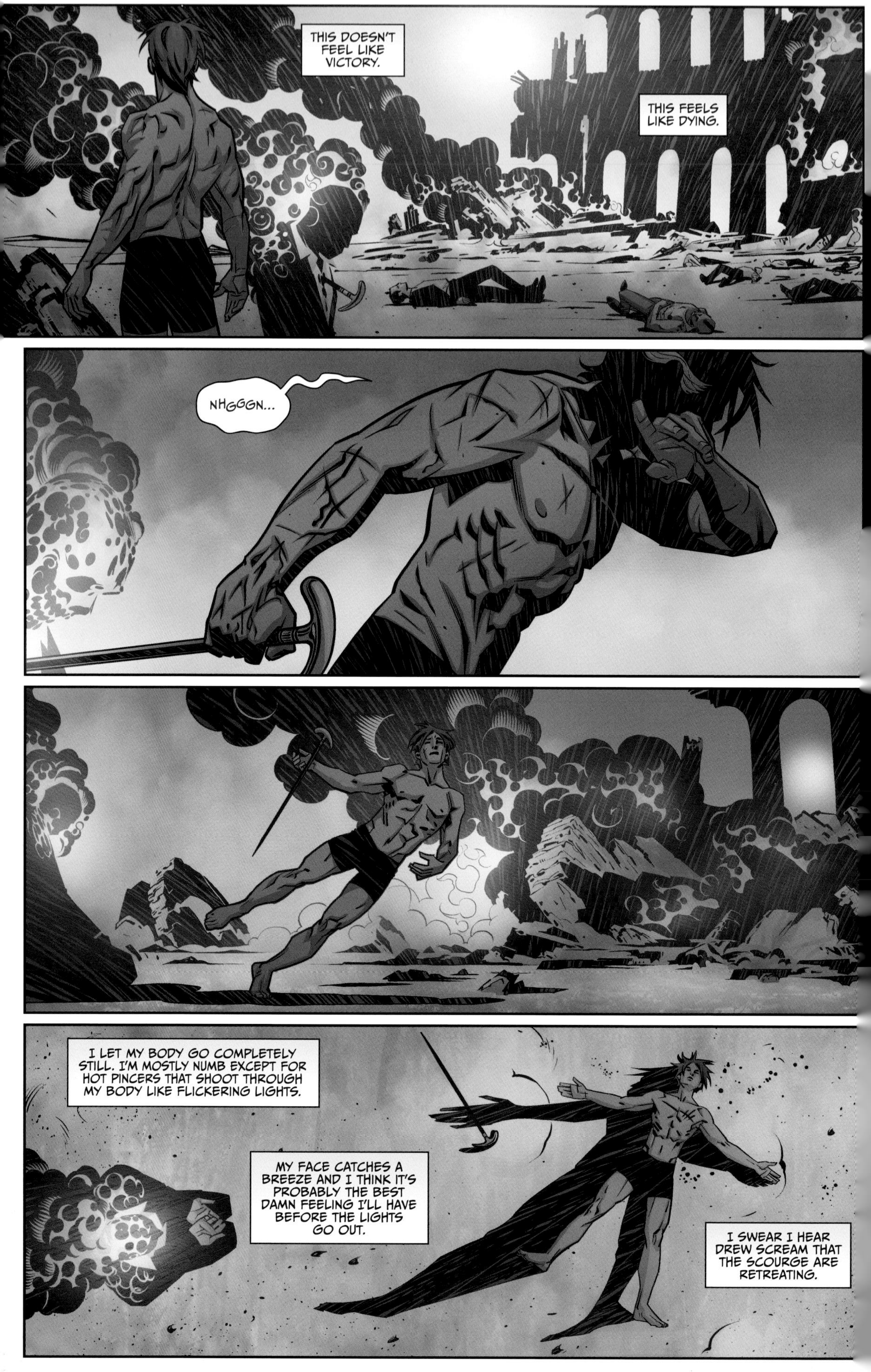
THIS DOESN'T FEEL LIKE VICTORY.
THIS FEELS LIKE DYING.
NHGGGN...
I LET MY BODY GO COMPLETELY STILL. I'M MOSTLY NUMB EXCEPT FOR HOT PINCERS THAT SHOOT THROUGH MY BODY LIKE FLICKERING LIGHTS.
MY FACE CATCHES A BREEZE AND I THINK IT'S PROBABLY THE BEST DAMN FEELING I'LL HAVE BEFORE THE LIGHTS GO OUT.
I SWEAR I HEAR DREW SCREAM THAT THE SCOURGE ARE RETREATING.

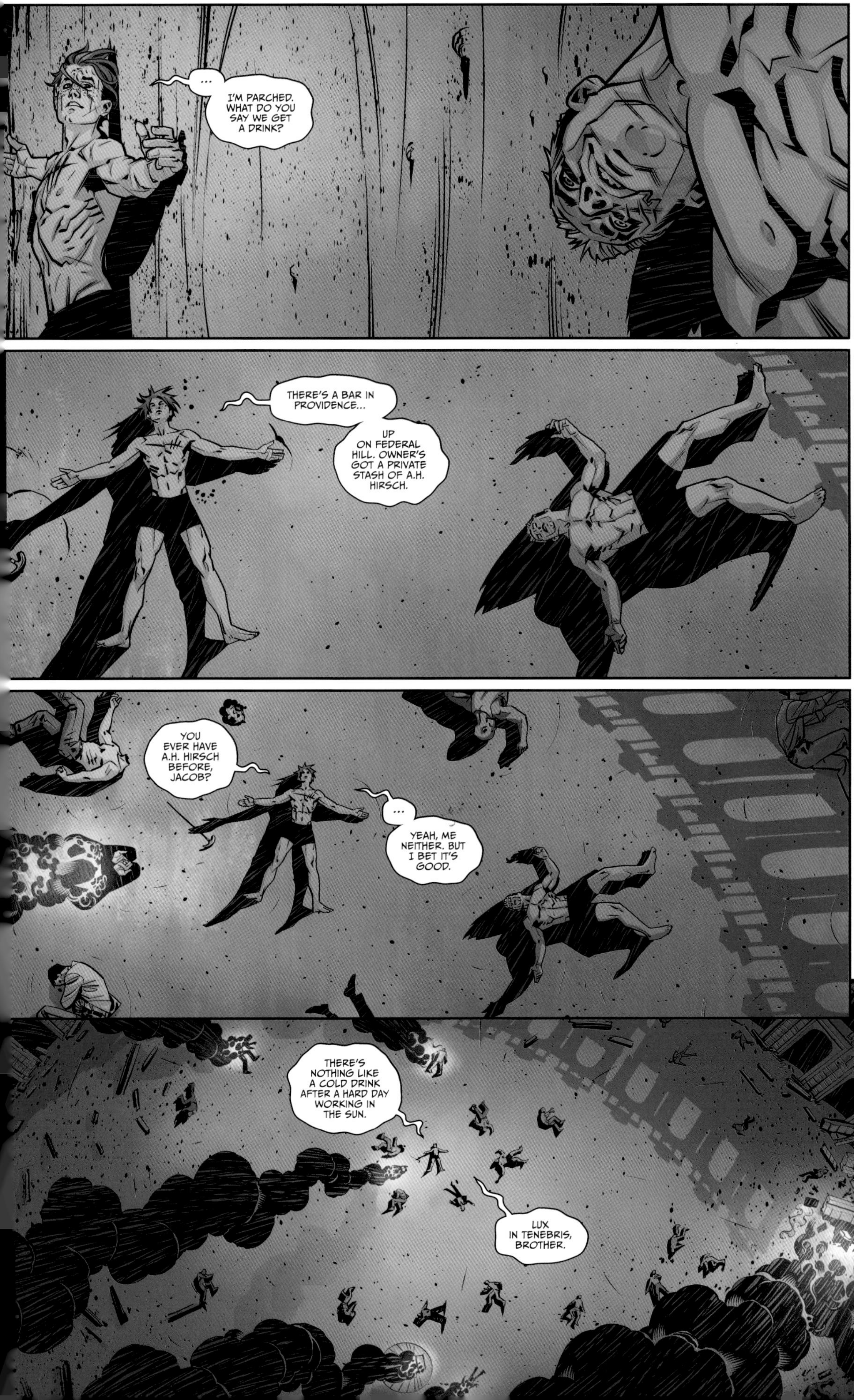
...
I'M PARCHED. WHAT DO YOU SAY WE GET A DRINK?
THERE'S A BAR IN PROVIDENCE...
UP ON FEDERAL HILL. OWNER'S GOT A PRIVATE STASH OF A.H. HIRSCH.
YOU EVER HAVE A.H. HIRSCH BEFORE, JACOB?
...
YEAH, ME NEITHER. BUT I BET IT'S GOOD.
THERE'S NOTHING LIKE A COLD DRINK AFTER A HARD DAY WORKING IN THE SUN.
LUX IN TENEBRIS, BROTHER.

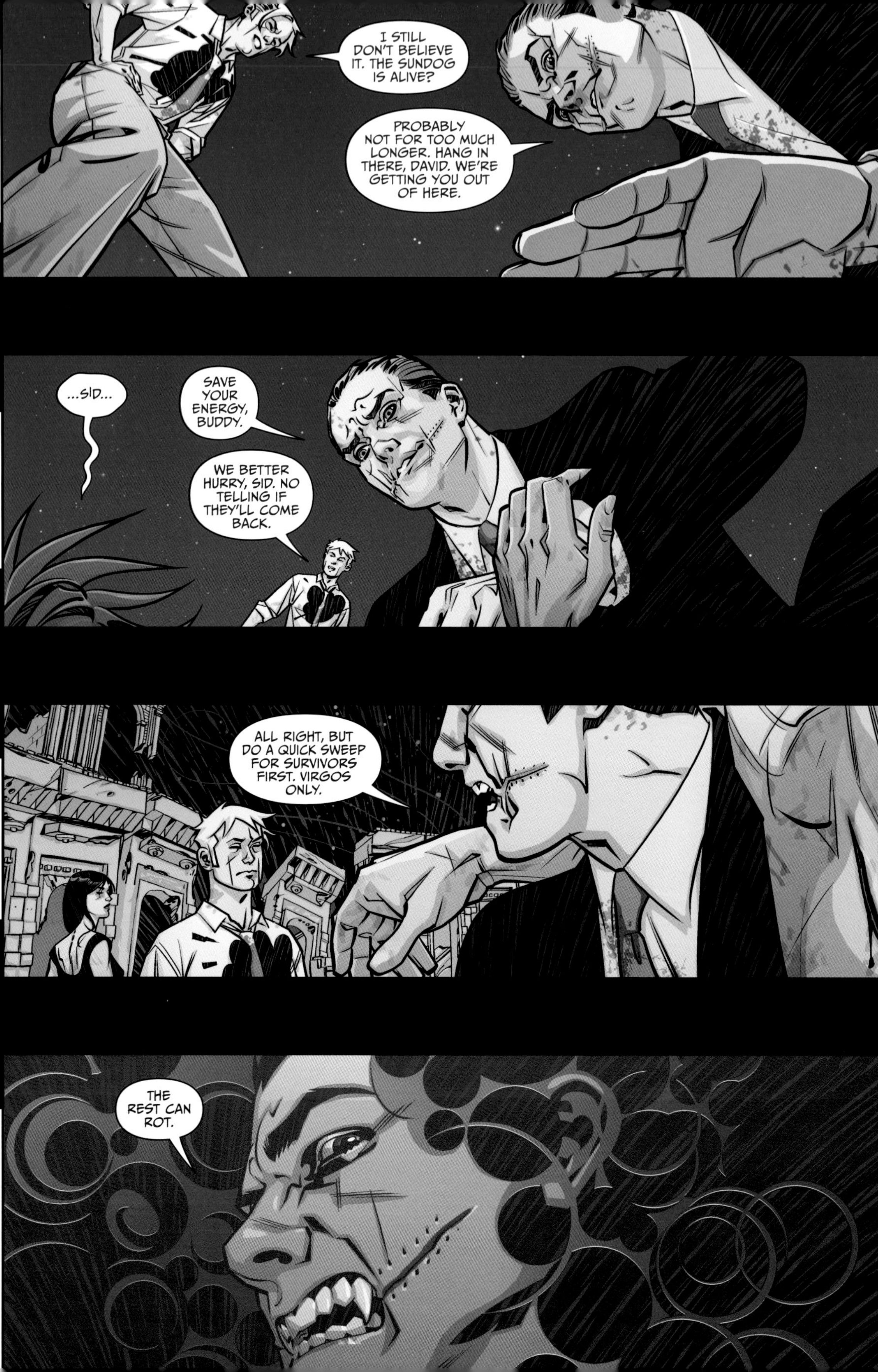
I STILL DON'T BELIEVE IT. THE SUNDOG IS ALIVE?
PROBABLY NOT FOR TOO MUCH LONGER. HANG IN THERE, DAVID. WE'RE GETTING YOU OUT OF HERE.
...SID...
SAVE YOUR ENERGY, BUDDY.
WE BETTER HURRY, SID. NO TELLING IF THEY'LL COME BACK.
ALL RIGHT, BUT DO A QUICK SWEEP FOR SURVIVORS FIRST. VIRGOS ONLY.
THE REST CAN ROT.

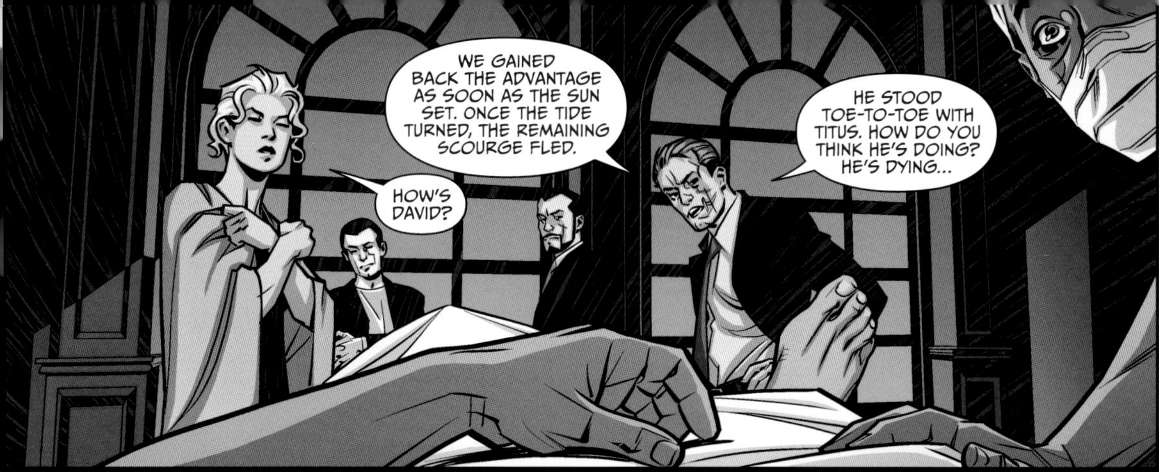
WE GAINED BACK THE ADVANTAGE AS SOON AS THE SUN SET. ONCE THE TIDE TURNED, THE REMAINING SCOURGE FLED.
HOW'S DAVID?
HE STOOD TOE-TO-TOE WITH TITUS. HOW DO YOU THINK HE'S DOING? HE'S DYING...

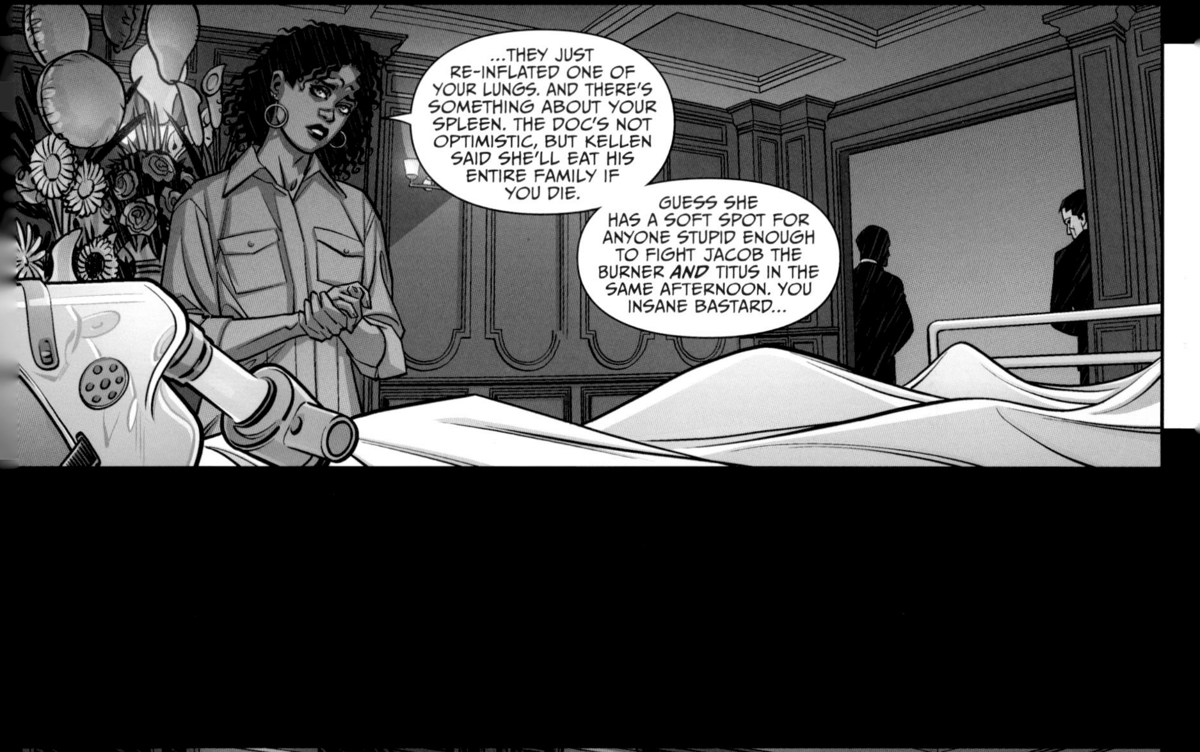
...THEY JUST RE-INFLATED ONE OF YOUR LUNGS. AND THERE'S SOMETHING ABOUT YOUR SPLEEN. THE DOC'S NOT OPTIMISTIC, BUT KELLEN SAID SHE'LL EAT HIS ENTIRE FAMILY IF YOU DIE.
GUESS SHE HAS A SOFT SPOT FOR ANYONE STUPID ENOUGH TO FIGHT JACOB THE BURNER AND TITUS IN THE SAME AFTERNOON. YOU INSANE BASTARD...

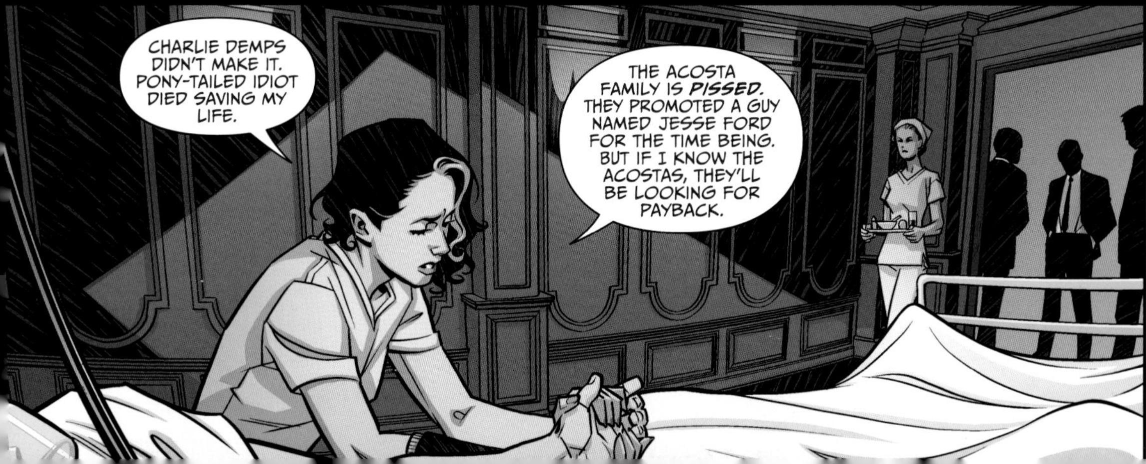
CHARLIE DEMPS DIDN'T MAKE IT. PONY-TAILED IDIOT DIED SAVING MY LIFE.
THE ACOSTA FAMILY IS PISSED. THEY PROMOTED A GUY NAMED JESSE FORD FOR THE TIME BEING. BUT IF I KNOW THE ACOSTAS, THEY'LL BE LOOKING FOR PAYBACK.

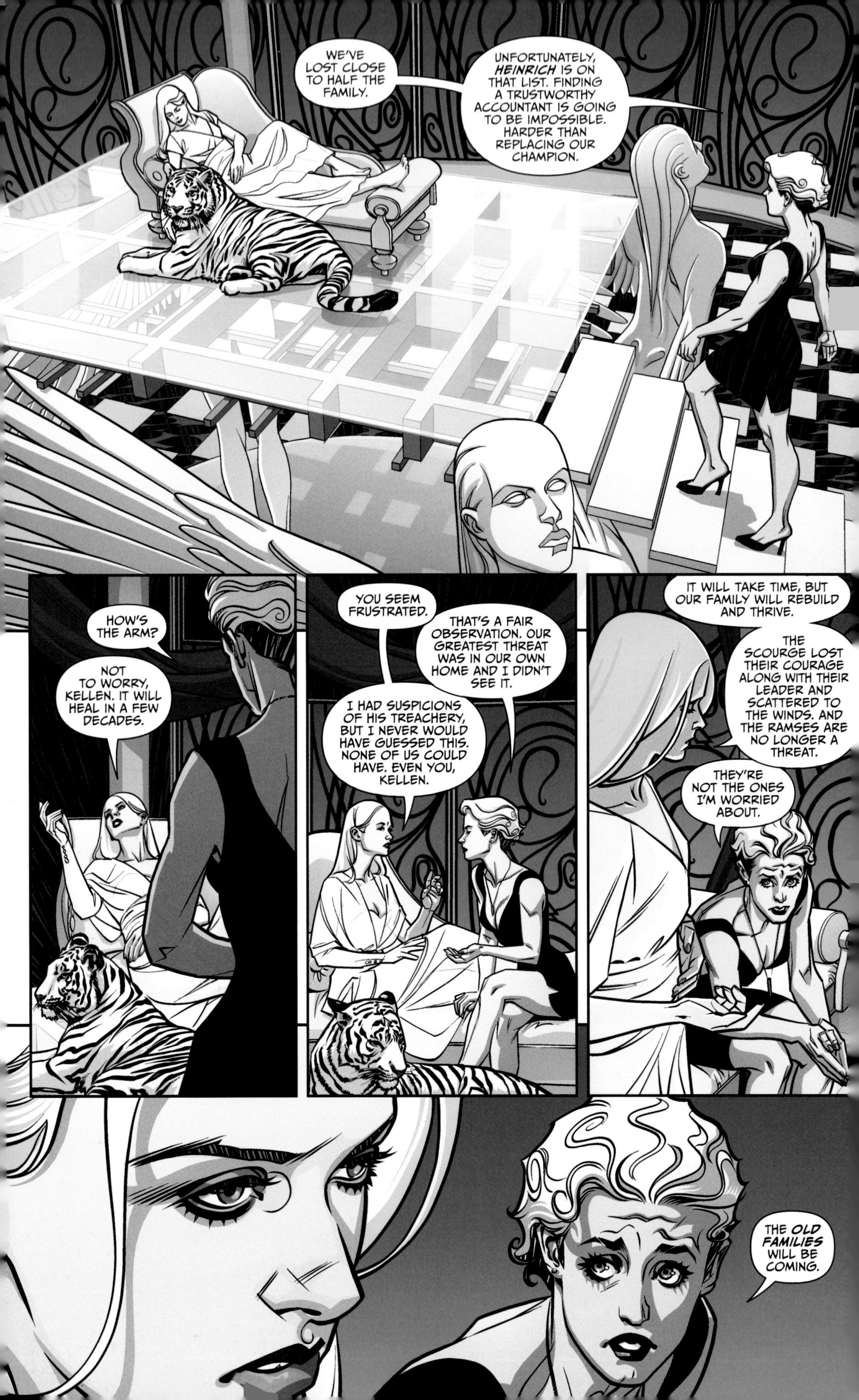
WE'VE LOST CLOSE TO HALF THE FAMILY.
UNFORTUNATELY, HEINRICH IS ON THAT LIST. FINDING A TRUSTWORTHY ACCOUNTANT IS GOING TO BE IMPOSSIBLE. HARDER THAN REPLACING OUR CHAMPION.
HOW'S THE ARM?
NOT TO WORRY, KELLEN. IT WILL HEAL IN A FEW DECADES.
YOU SEEM FRUSTRATED.
THAT'S A FAIR OBSERVATION. OUR GREATEST THREAT WAS IN OUR OWN HOME AND I DIDN'T SEE IT.
I HAD SUSPICIONS OF HIS TREACHERY, BUT I NEVER WOULD HAVE GUESSED THIS. NONE OF US COULD HAVE. EVEN YOU, KELLEN.
IT WILL TAKE TIME, BUT OUR FAMILY WILL REBUILD AND THRIVE.
THE SCOURGE LOST THEIR COURAGE ALONG WITH THEIR LEADER AND SCATTERED TO THE WINDS. AND THE RAMSES ARE NO LONGER A THREAT.
THEY'RE NOT THE ONES I'M WORRIED ABOUT.
THE OLD FAMILIES WILL BE COMING.

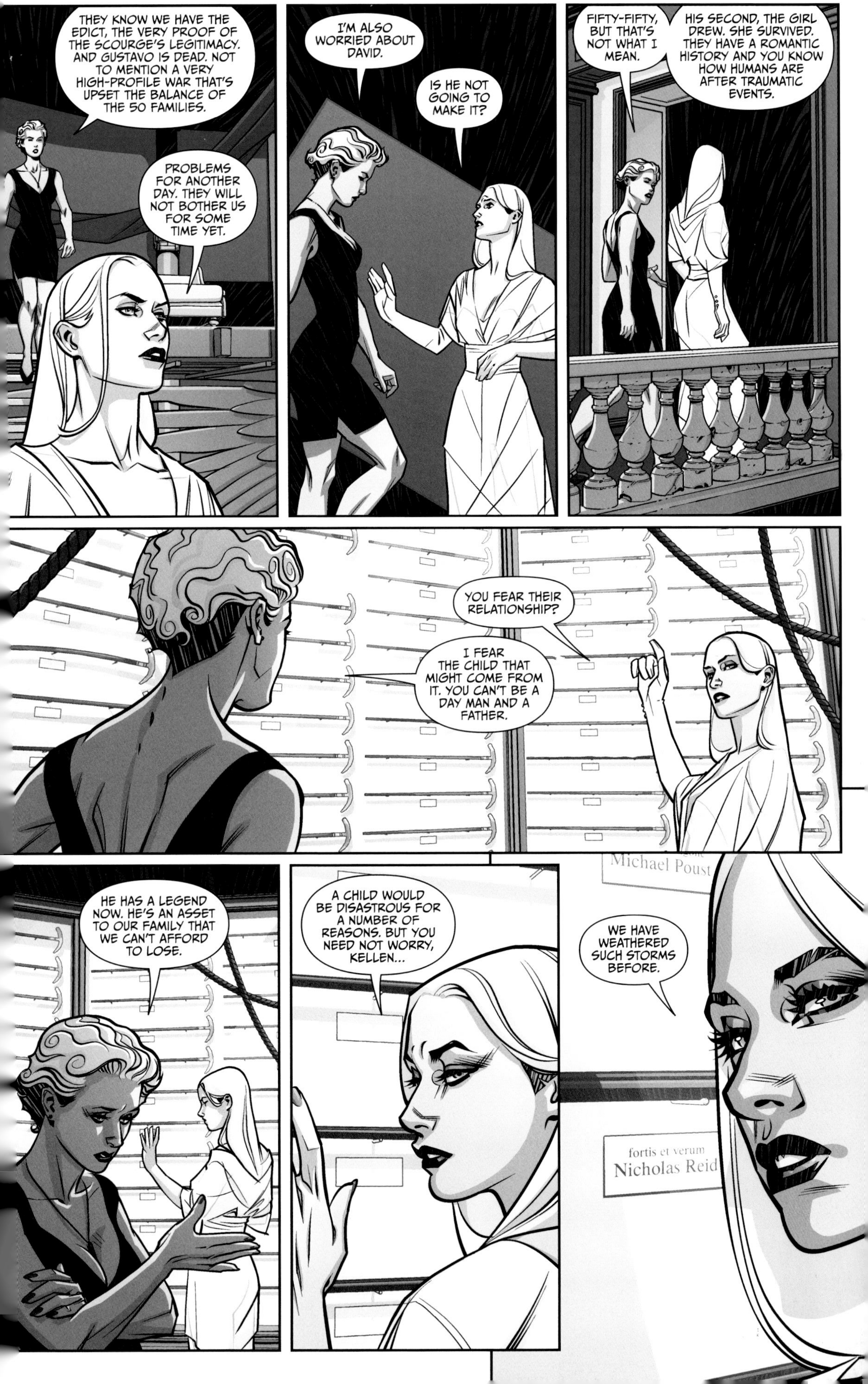
THEY KNOW WE HAVE THE EDICT, THE VERY PROOF OF THE SCOURGE'S LEGITIMACY. AND GUSTAVO IS DEAD. NOT TO MENTION A VERY HIGH-PROFILE WAR THAT'S UPSET THE BALANCE OF THE 50 FAMILIES.
PROBLEMS FOR ANOTHER DAY. THEY WILL NOT BOTHER US FOR SOME TIME YET.
I'M ALSO WORRIED ABOUT DAVID.
IS HE NOT GOING TO MAKE IT?
FIFTY-FIFTY, BUT THAT'S NOT WHAT I MEAN.
HIS SECOND, THE GIRL DREW. SHE SURVIVED. THEY HAVE A ROMANTIC HISTORY AND YOU KNOW HOW HUMANS ARE AFTER TRAUMATIC EVENTS.
YOU FEAR THEIR RELATIONSHIP?
I FEAR THE CHILD THAT MIGHT COME FROM IT. YOU CAN'T BE A DAY MAN AND A FATHER.
HE HAS A LEGEND NOW. HE'S AN ASSET TO OUR FAMILY THAT WE CAN'T AFFORD TO LOSE.
A CHILD WOULD BE DISASTROUS FOR A NUMBER OF REASONS. BUT YOU NEED NOT WORRY, KELLEN...
Michael Poust
WE HAVE WEATHERED SUCH STORMS BEFORE.
fortis et verum
Nicholas Reid

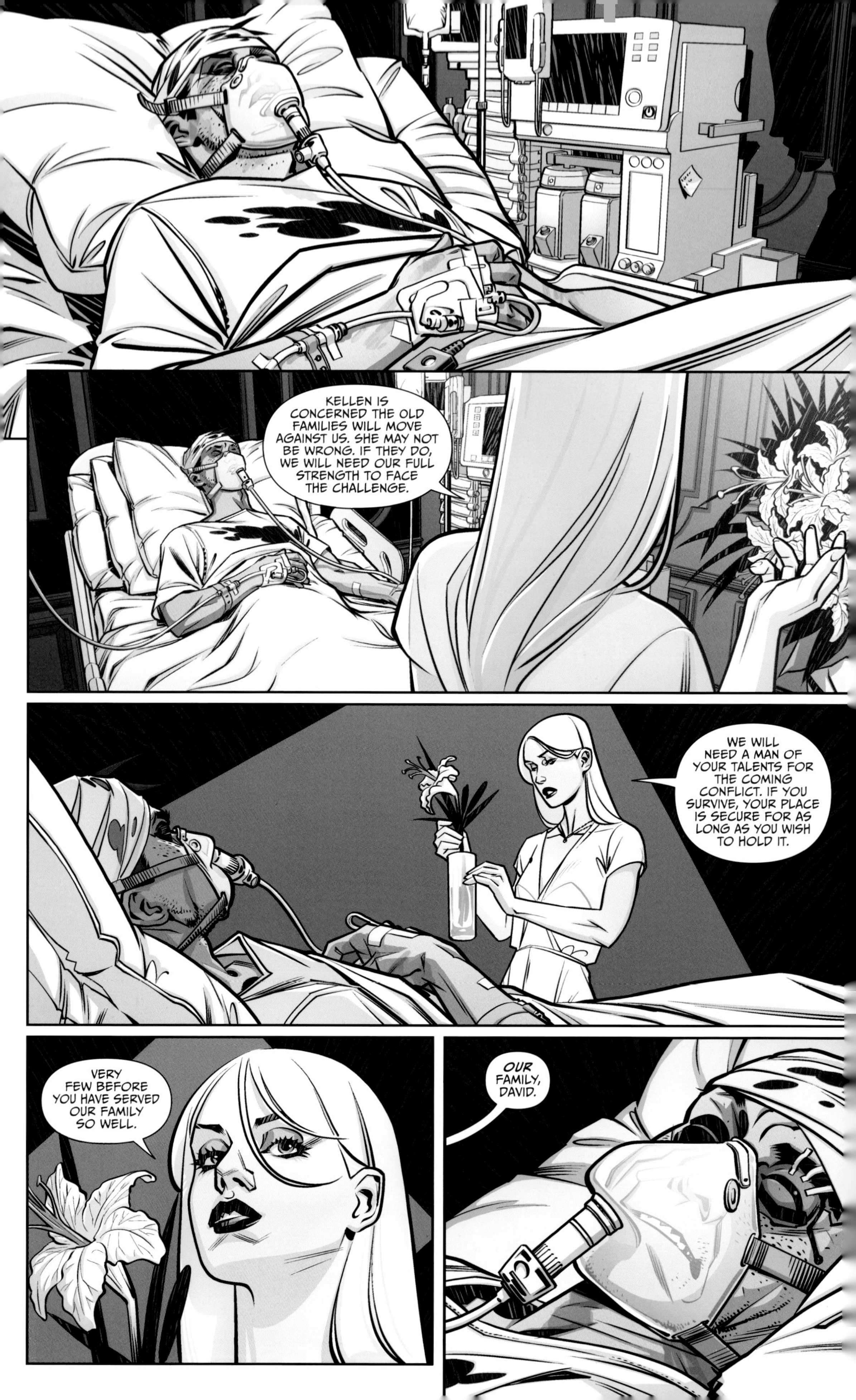
KELLEN IS CONCERNED THE OLD FAMILIES WILL MOVE AGAINST US. SHE MAY NOT BE WRONG. IF THEY DO, WE WILL NEED OUR FULL STRENGTH TO FACE THE CHALLENGE.
WE WILL NEED A MAN OF YOUR TALENTS FOR THE COMING CONFLICT. IF YOU SURVIVE, YOUR PLACE IS SECURE FOR AS LONG AS YOU WISH TO HOLD IT.
VERY FEW BEFORE YOU HAVE SERVED OUR FAMILY SO WELL.
OUR FAMILY, DAVID.

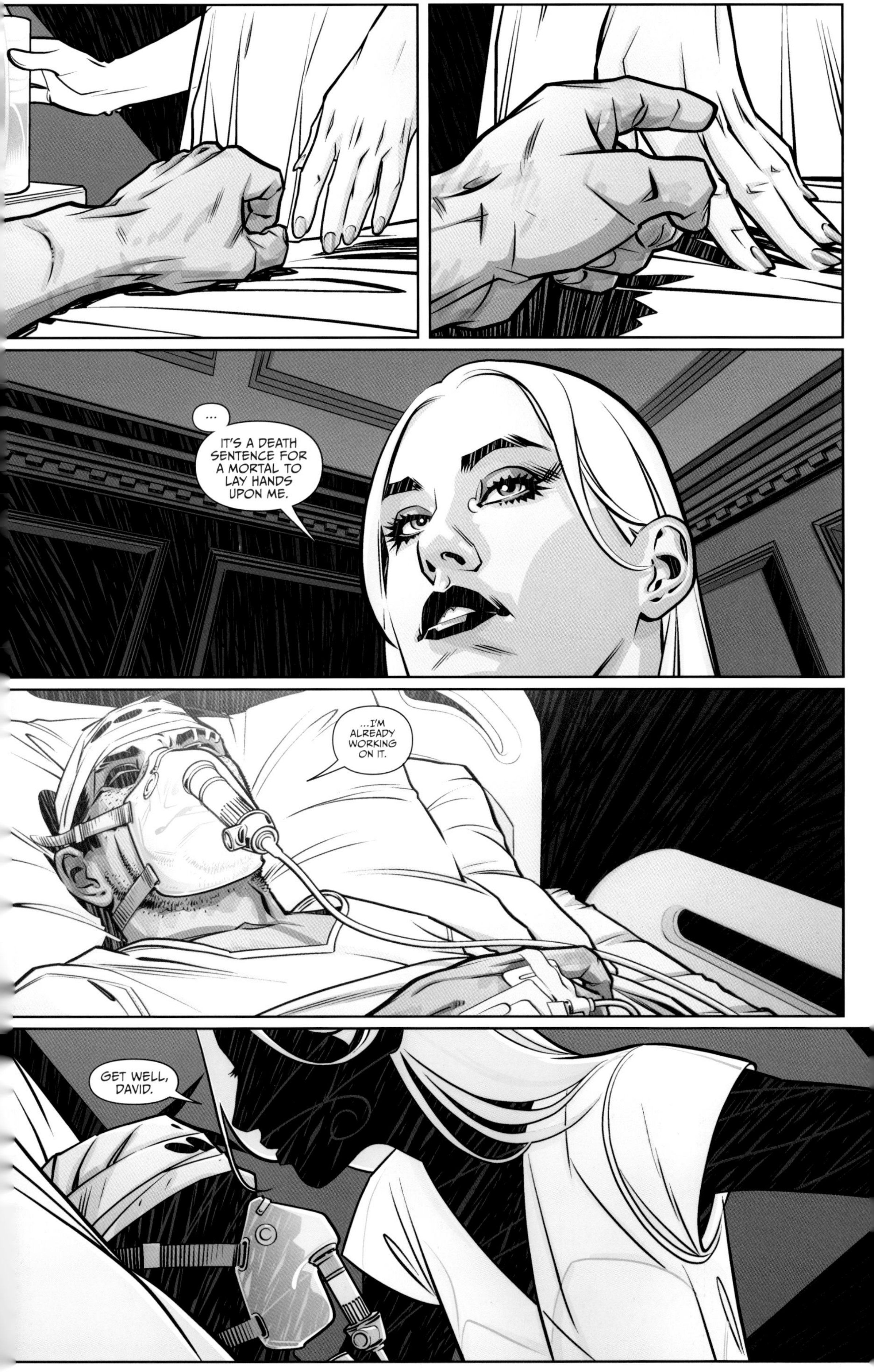
...
IT'S A DEATH SENTENCE FOR A MORTAL TO LAY HANDS UPON ME.
...I'M ALREADY WORKING ON IT.
GET WELL, DAVID.

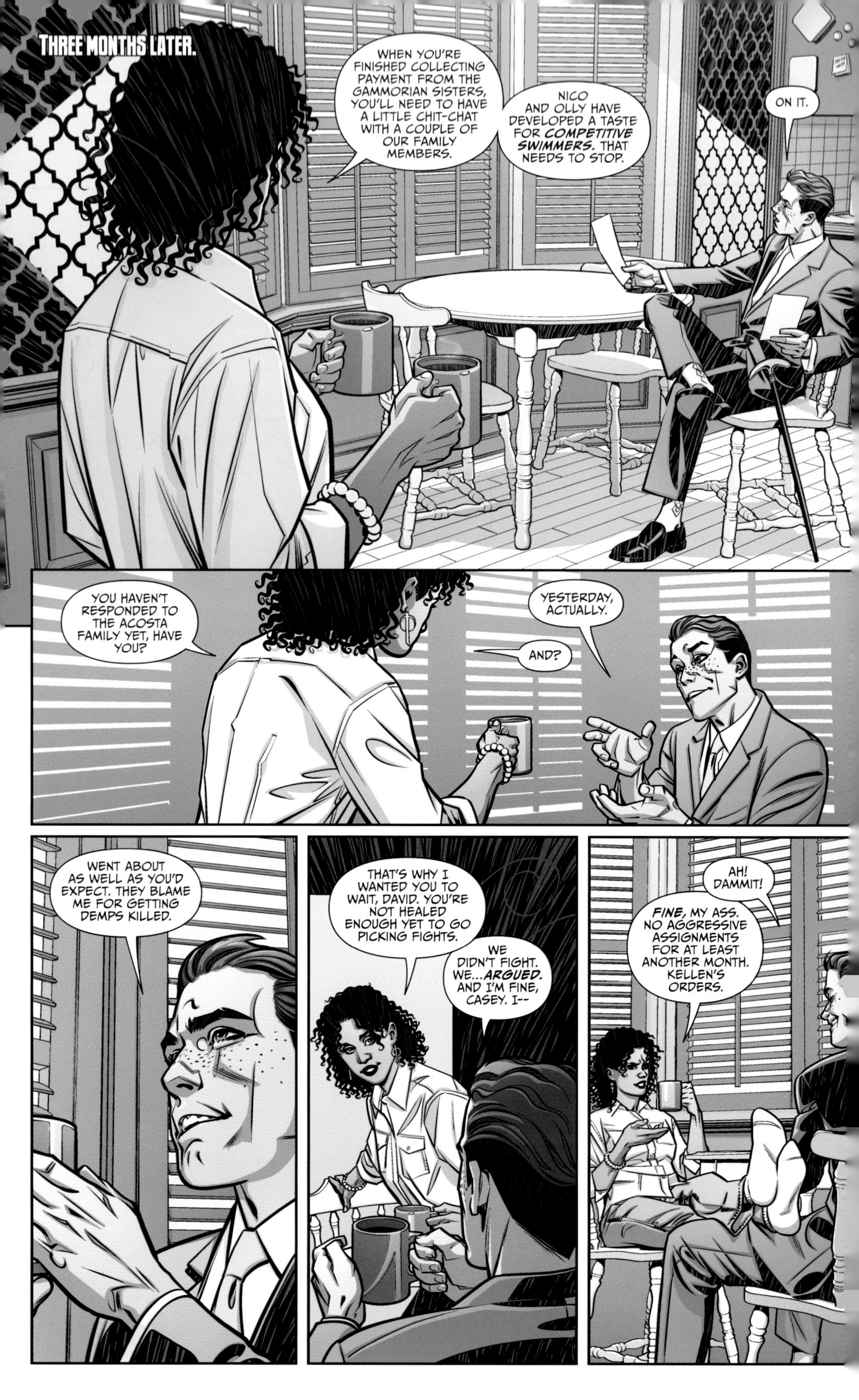
THREE MONTHS LATER.
WHEN YOU'RE FINISHED COLLECTING PAYMENT FROM THE GAMMORIAN SISTERS, YOU'LL NEED TO HAVE A LITTLE CHIT-CHAT WITH A COUPLE OF OUR FAMILY MEMBERS.
NICO AND OLLY HAVE DEVELOPED A TASTE FOR ***COMPETITIVE SWIMMERS.*** THAT NEEDS TO STOP.
ON IT.
YOU HAVEN'T RESPONDED TO THE ACOSTA FAMILY YET, HAVE YOU?
YESTERDAY, ACTUALLY.
AND?
WENT ABOUT AS WELL AS YOU'D EXPECT. THEY BLAME ME FOR GETTING DEMPS KILLED.
THAT'S WHY I WANTED YOU TO WAIT, DAVID. YOU'RE NOT HEALED ENOUGH YET TO GO PICKING FIGHTS.
WE DIDN'T FIGHT. WE...***ARGUED.*** AND I'M FINE, CASEY. I--
AH! DAMMIT!
***FINE,*** MY ASS. NO AGGRESSIVE ASSIGNMENTS FOR AT LEAST ANOTHER MONTH. KELLEN'S ORDERS.

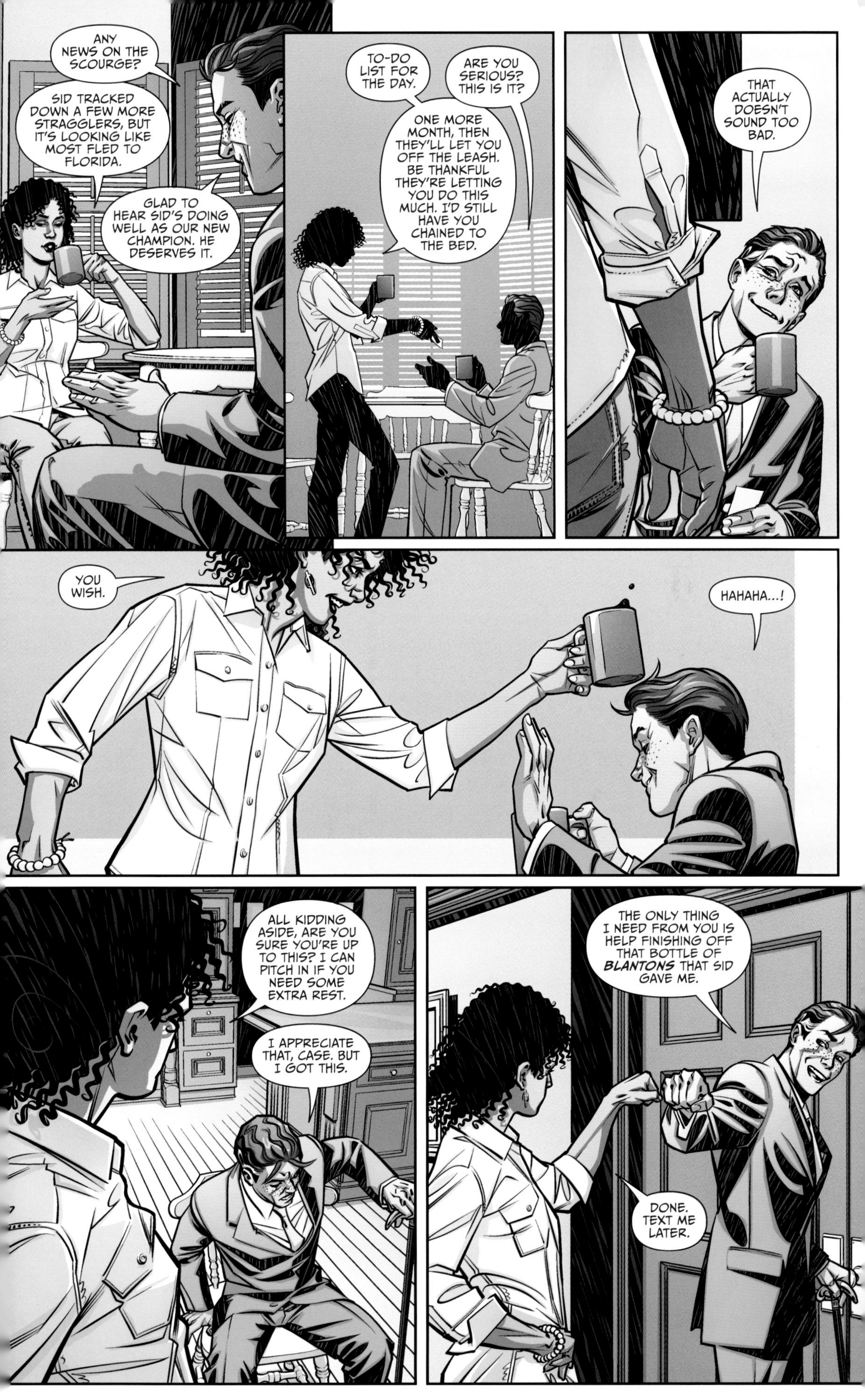
ANY NEWS ON THE SCOURGE?
SID TRACKED DOWN A FEW MORE STRAGGLERS, BUT IT'S LOOKING LIKE MOST FLED TO FLORIDA.
GLAD TO HEAR SID'S DOING WELL AS OUR NEW CHAMPION. HE DESERVES IT.
TO-DO LIST FOR THE DAY.
ARE YOU SERIOUS? THIS IS IT?
ONE MORE MONTH, THEN THEY'LL LET YOU OFF THE LEASH. BE THANKFUL THEY'RE LETTING YOU DO THIS MUCH. I'D STILL HAVE YOU CHAINED TO THE BED.
THAT ACTUALLY DOESN'T SOUND TOO BAD.
YOU WISH.
HAHAHA...!
ALL KIDDING ASIDE, ARE YOU SURE YOU'RE UP TO THIS? I CAN PITCH IN IF YOU NEED SOME EXTRA REST.
I APPRECIATE THAT, CASE. BUT I GOT THIS.
THE ONLY THING I NEED FROM YOU IS HELP FINISHING OFF THAT BOTTLE OF BLANTONS THAT SID GAVE ME.
DONE. TEXT ME LATER.

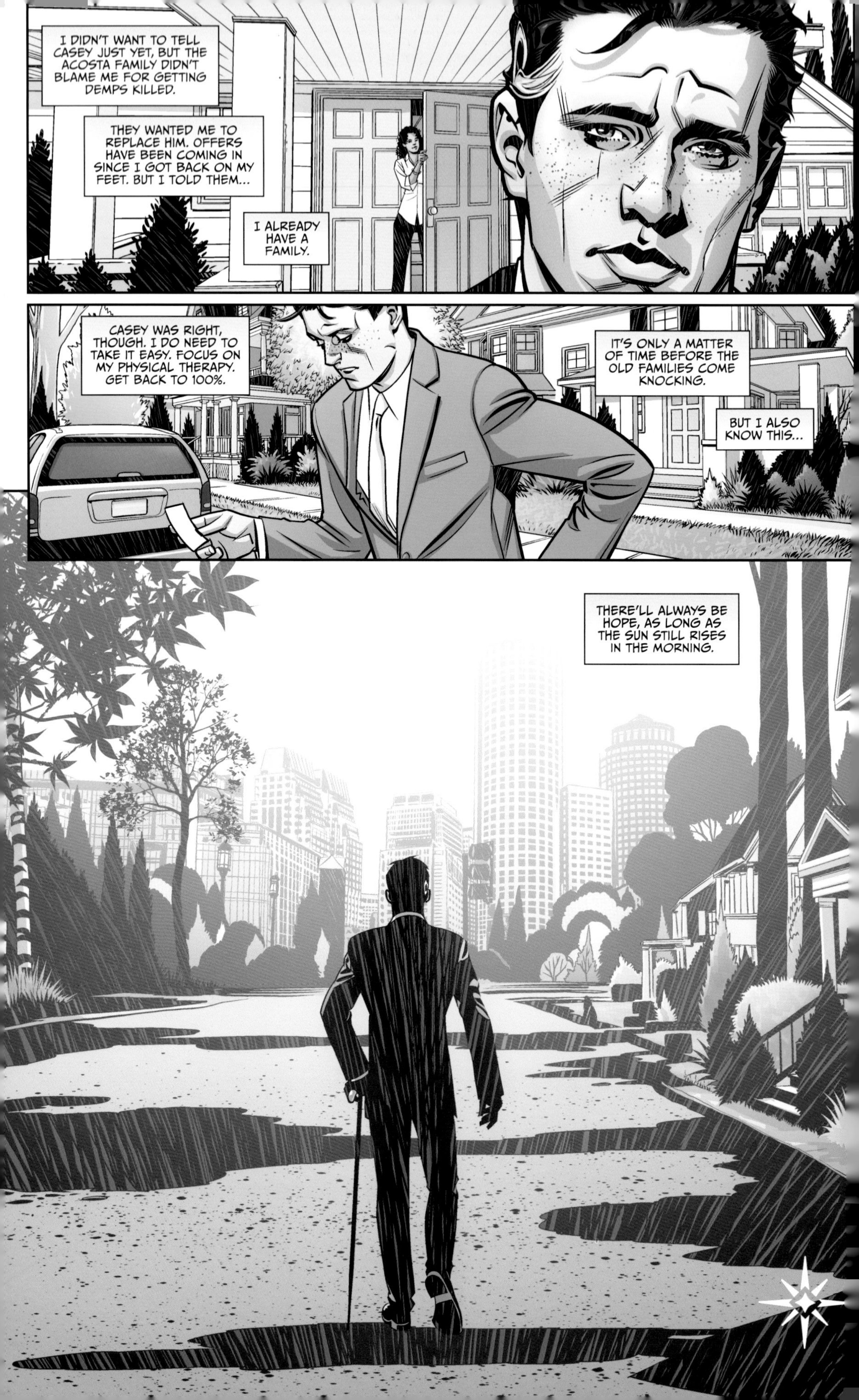
I DIDN'T WANT TO TELL CASEY JUST YET, BUT THE ACOSTA FAMILY DIDN'T BLAME ME FOR GETTING DEMPS KILLED.
THEY WANTED ME TO REPLACE HIM. OFFERS HAVE BEEN COMING IN SINCE I GOT BACK ON MY FEET. BUT I TOLD THEM...
I ALREADY HAVE A FAMILY.
CASEY WAS RIGHT, THOUGH. I DO NEED TO TAKE IT EASY. FOCUS ON MY PHYSICAL THERAPY. GET BACK TO 100%.
IT'S ONLY A MATTER OF TIME BEFORE THE OLD FAMILIES COME KNOCKING.
BUT I ALSO KNOW THIS...
THERE'LL ALWAYS BE HOPE, AS LONG AS THE SUN STILL RISES IN THE MORNING.

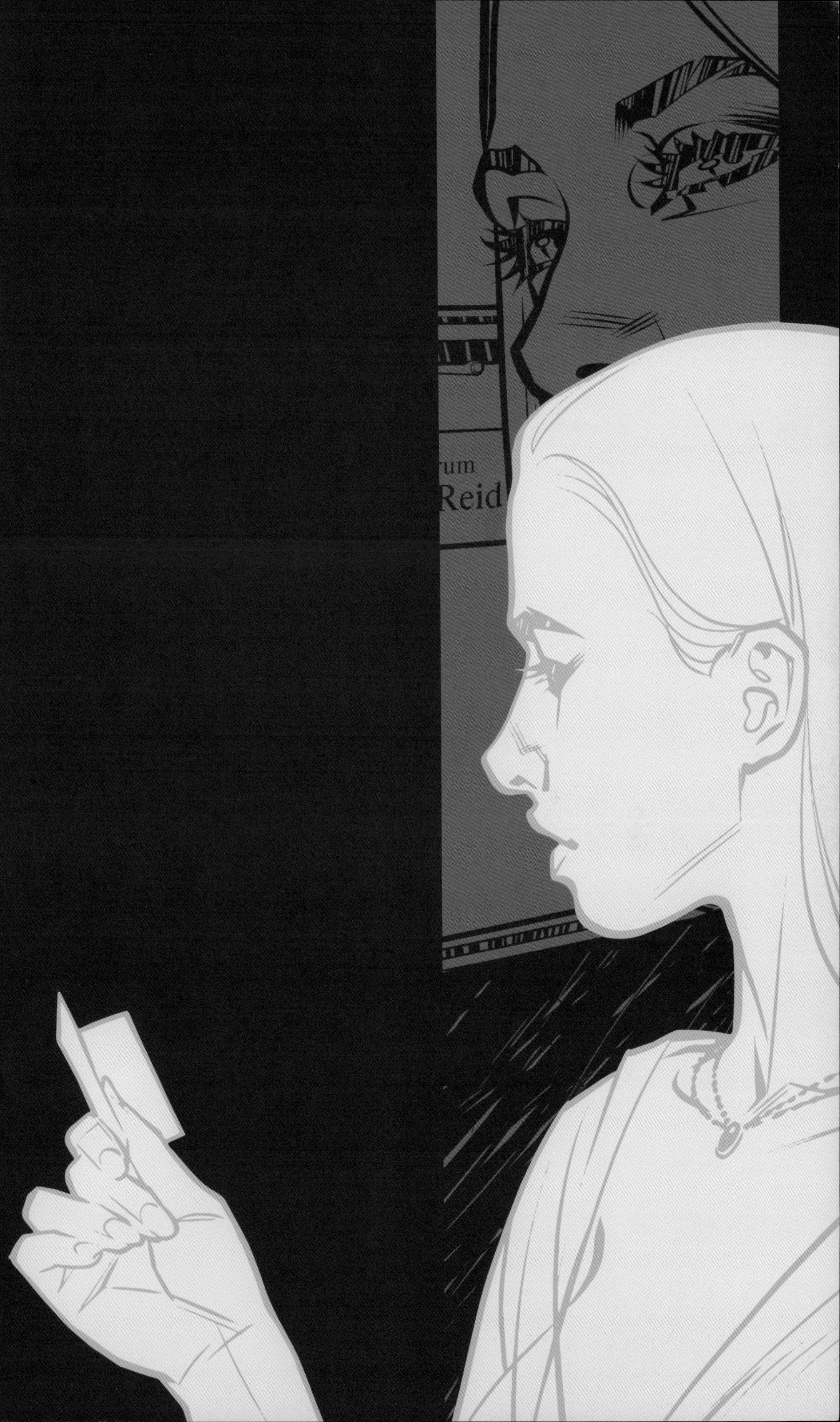
rum
Reid

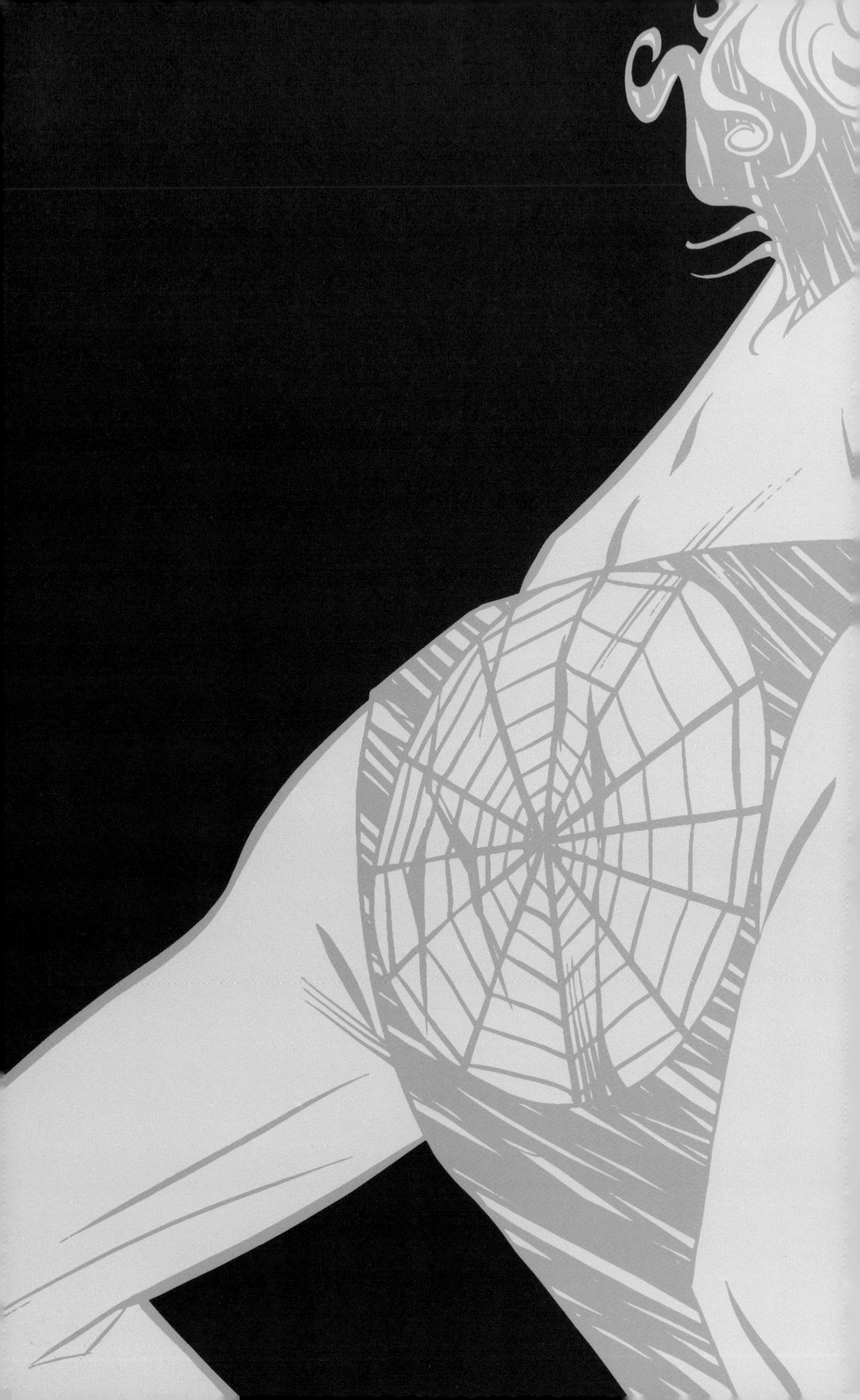

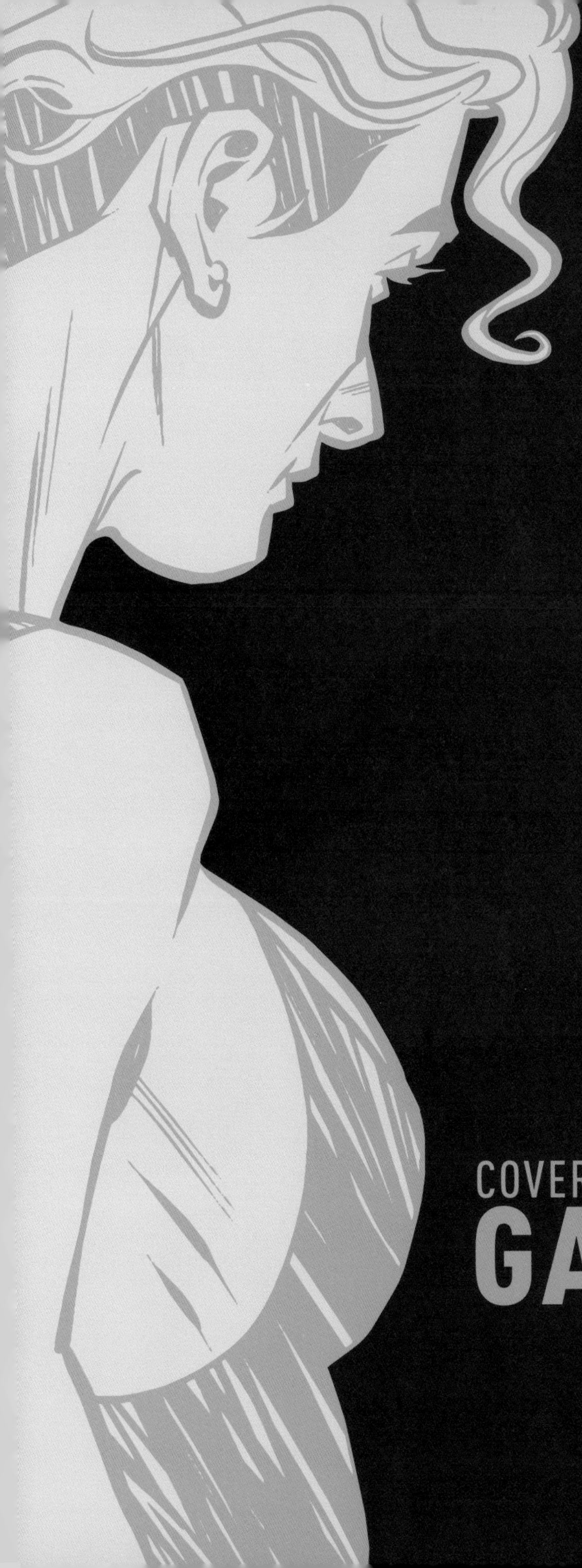

# COVER GALLERY

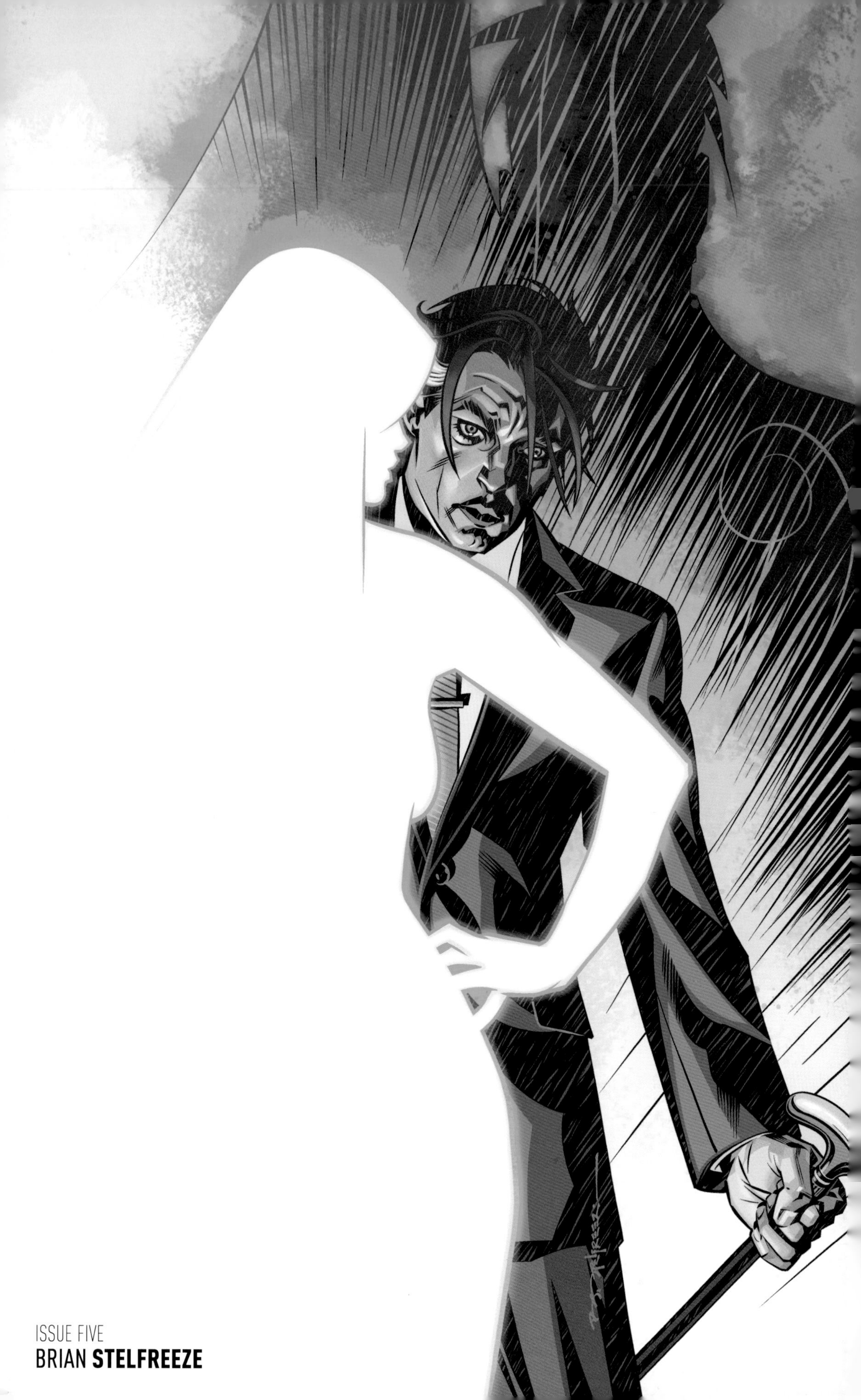

ISSUE FIVE

BRIAN **STELFREEZE**

ISSUE FIVE UNLOCKED RETAILER VARIANT
NICK **ROBLES**

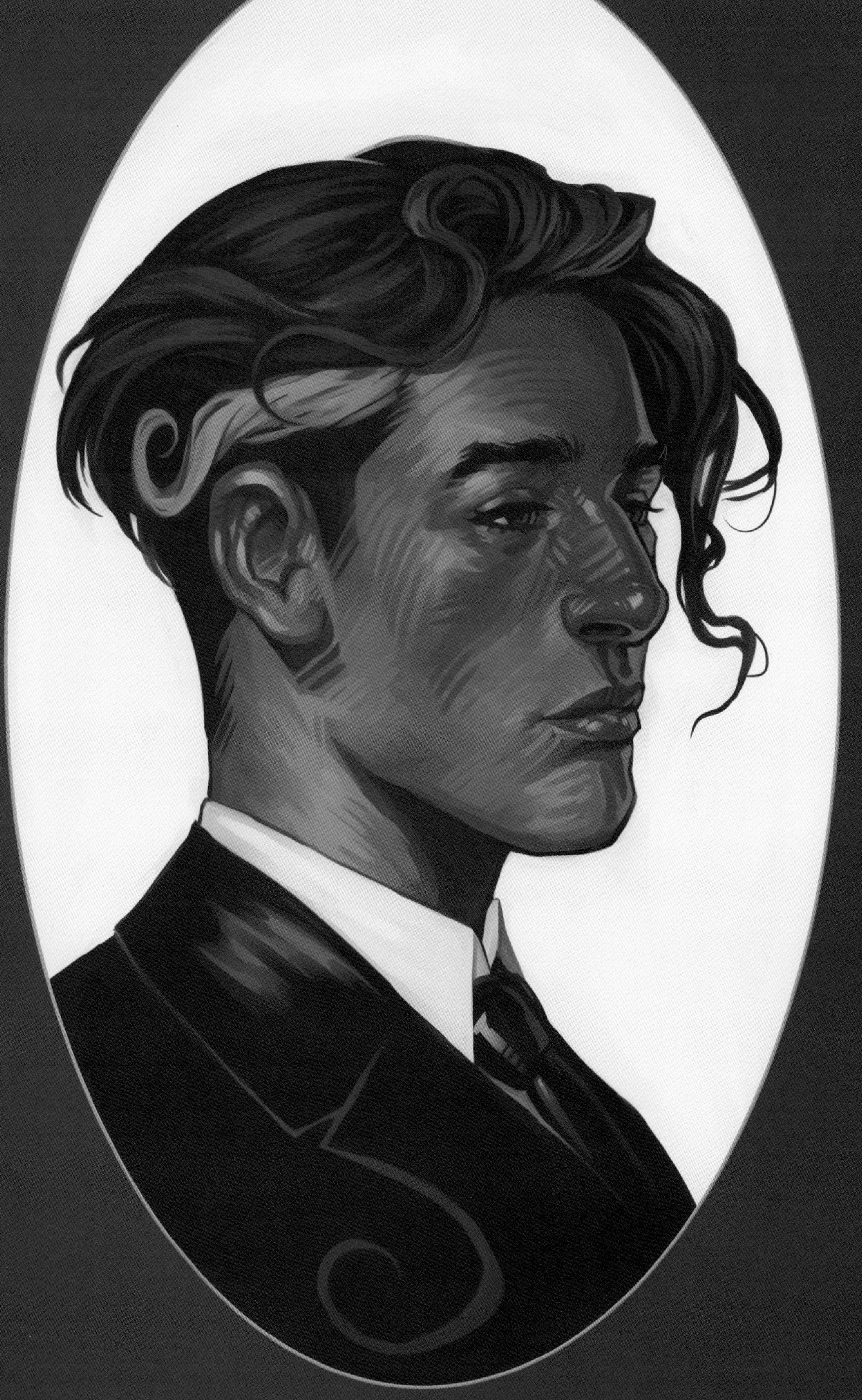

ISSUE FIVE CARDS, COMICS & COLLECTIBLES EXCLUSIVE
**BRIAN STELFREEZE**

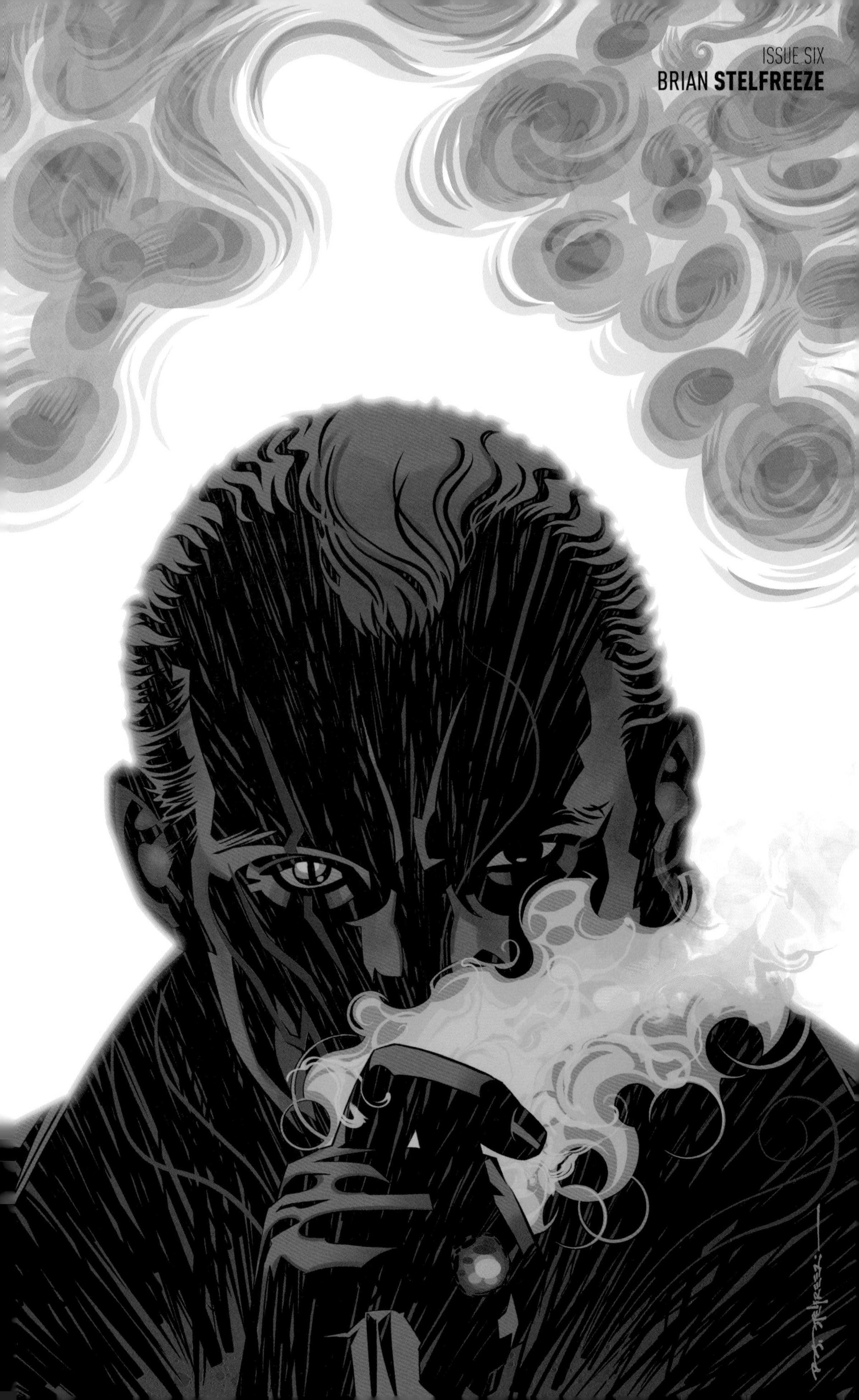

ISSUE SIX
**BRIAN STELFREEZE**

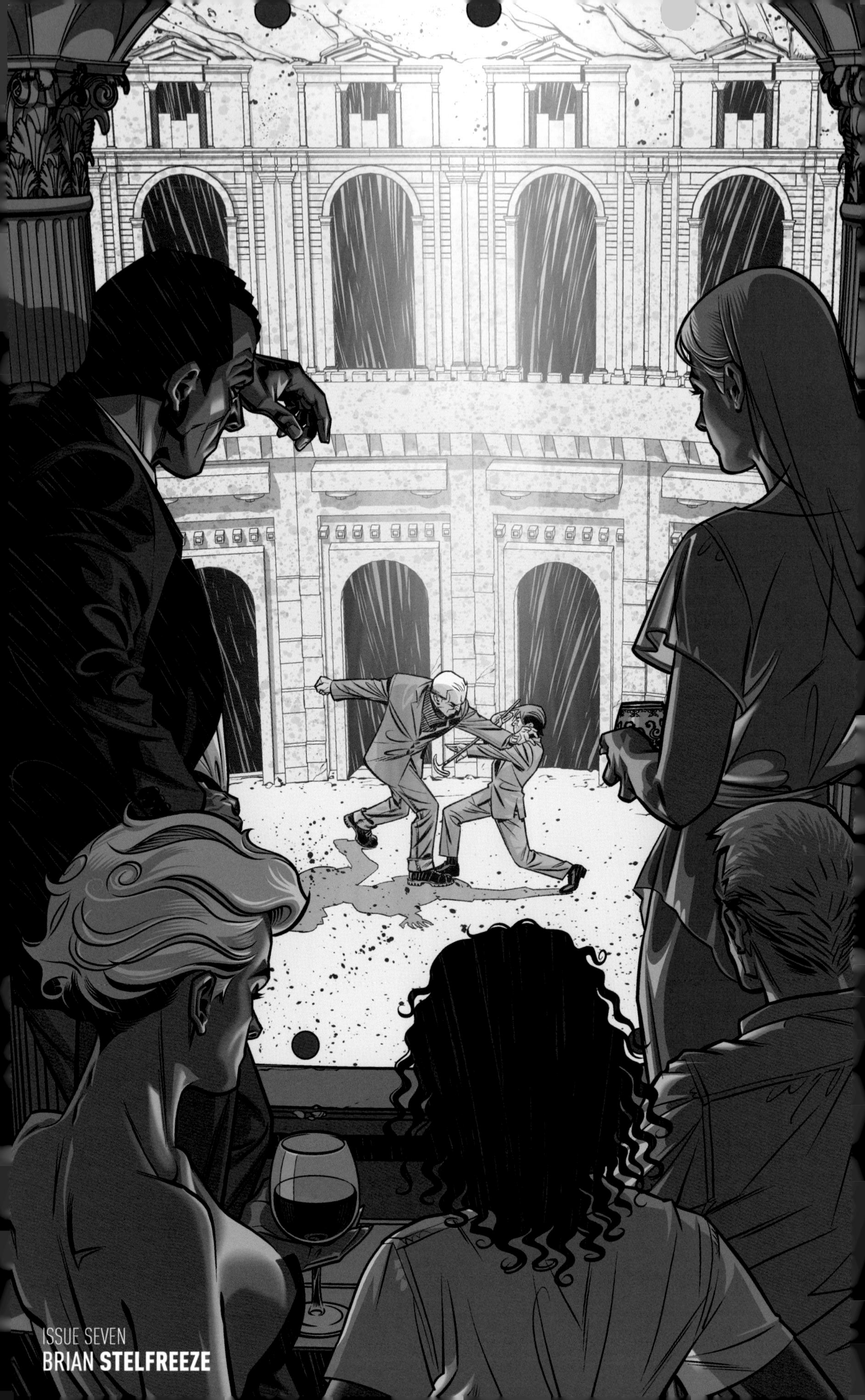

ISSUE SEVEN
**BRIAN STELFREEZE**

ISSUE EIGHT
BRIAN **STELFREEZE**

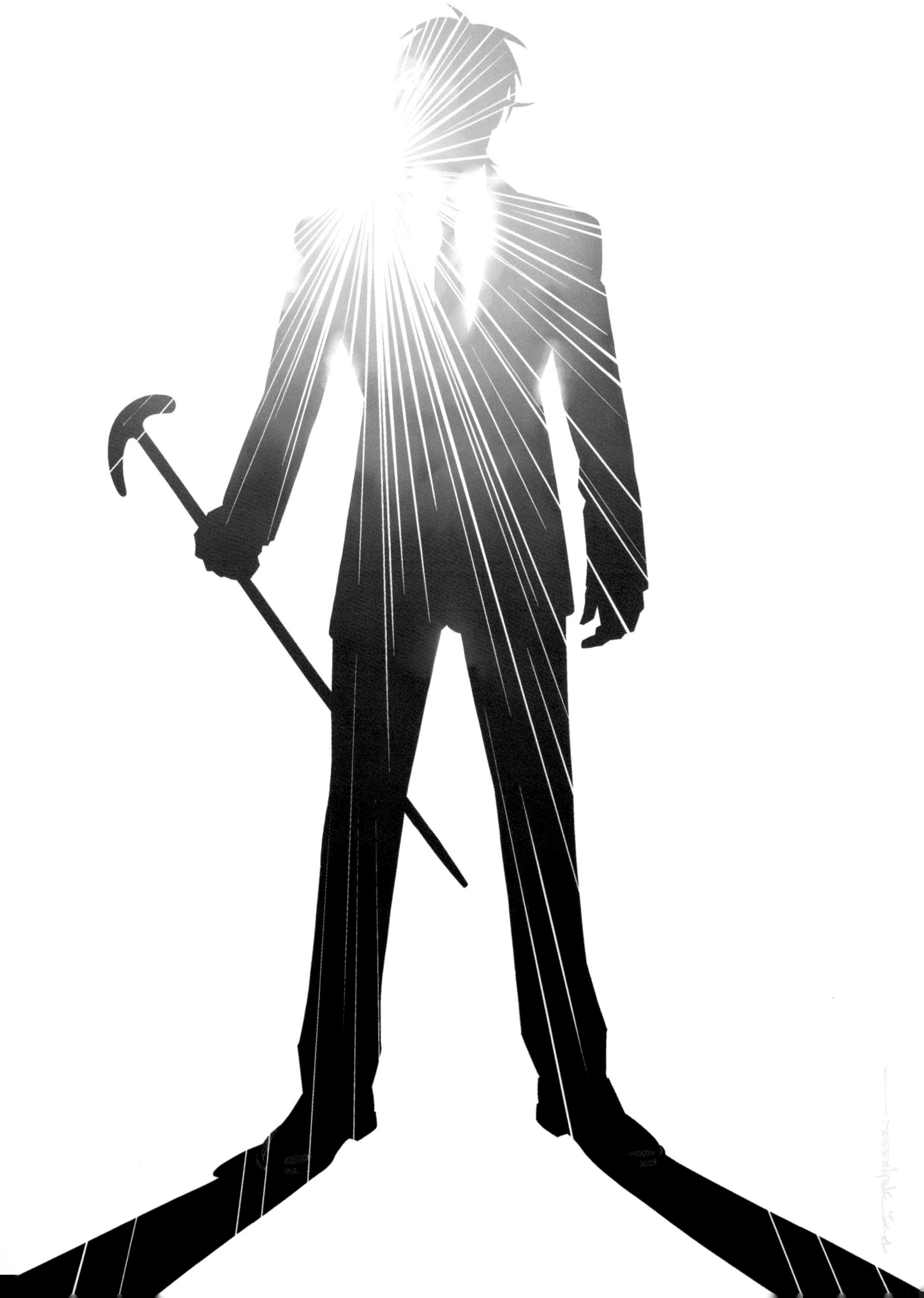

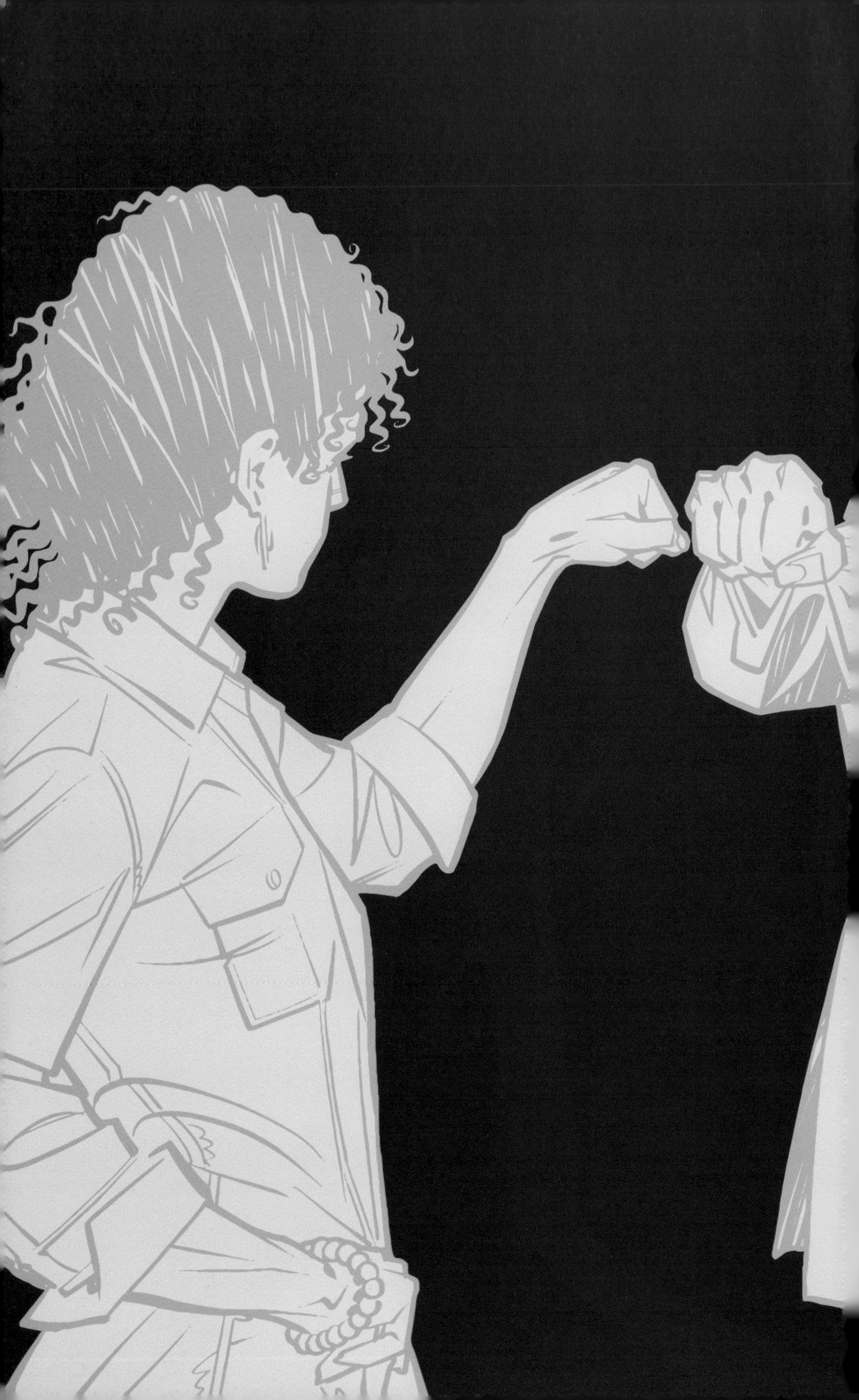

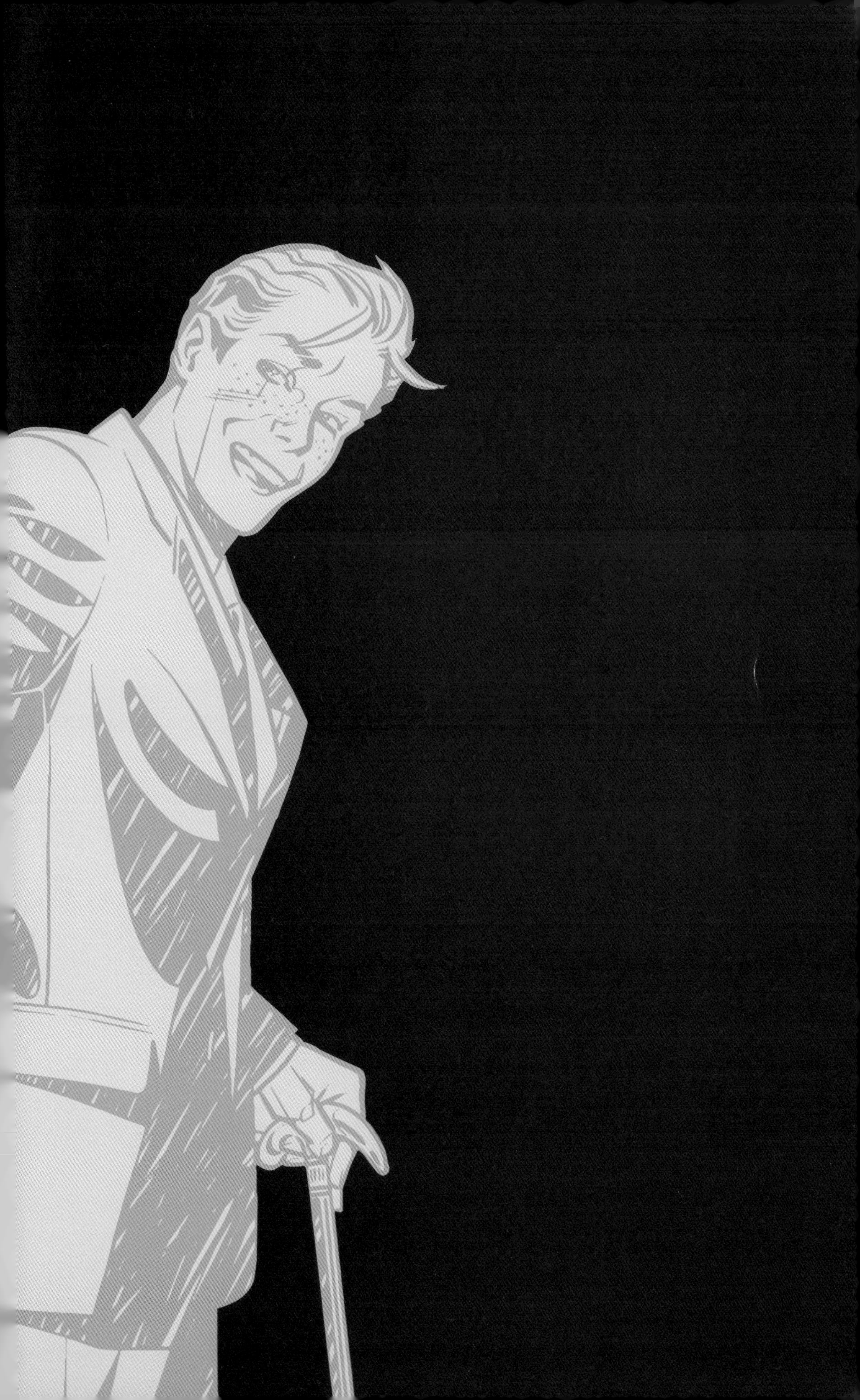

LUX IN TENEBRIS